Reconcilable Differences in Eighteenth-Century English Literature

Author Ipse Invt. & J. M. Delineavit . . . . . — — . .
Herein the Rich, the Honour'd, Famil. and Great,
See the false Scale of Happiness Compleat . . . . . .

Sepia drawing by Pope, probably the original of the frontispiece to the *Essay on Man.* **Courtesy of the Lewis Walpole Library, Yale University Library.**

Reconcilable Differences in Eighteenth-Century English Literature

William Bowman Piper

That each from other differs, first confess . . .

DELAWARE

Newark: University of Delaware Press
London: Associated University Presses

Associated University Presses
440 Forsgate Drive
Cranbury, NJ 08512

Associated University Presses
16 Barter Street
London WC1A 2AH, England

Associated University Presses
P.O. Box 338, Port Credit
Mississauga, Ontario
Canada L5G 4L8

The paper used in this publication meets the requirements
of the American National Standard for Permanence of Paper
for Printed Library Materials Z39.48-1984.

Library of Congress Cataloging-in-Publication Data

Piper, William Bowman, 1927–
    Reconcilable differences in eighteenth-century English literature
/ William Bowman Piper.
        p.   cm.
    Includes bibliographical references (p.   ) and index.
    ISBN 0-87413-683-0 (alk. paper)
    1. English literature—18th century—History and criticism.
    2. Identity (Philosophical concept)—History—18th century.
    3. Resemblance (Philosophy) in literature.   4. Perception
(Philosophy) in literature.   5. Difference (Philosophy) in
literature.   6. Knowledge, Theory of, in literature.
    7. Particularity (Aesthetics)   I. Title.
PR448.P5P56   1999
820.9′005—dc21
                                                                98-54784
                                                                CIP

to the memory of my mother
Anna Zink Piper

Cur dextrae jungere dextram
Non datur ac veras audire et reddere voces?

Contents

Preface

The authors whose works I will examine in this book confronted what might be understood nowadays as a theoretical concern. Swift's *Travels*, Gay's *Trivia*, and Pope's *Essay on Man* are responses—or so I will argue—to the question: What if nature is, as George Berkeley has asserted, strictly perceptual? Radcliffe's *Mysteries of Udolpho* and Austen's *Emma* emerge from an intensification of the same question: What if, not only nature, but the people who inhabit nature are also, as David Hume has asserted, strictly perceptual? Such questions inevitably led to others: If Berkeley and Hume are right, each of these authors asked in turn, what can we know; and what can we do? Can we understand a strictly perceptual world? Can we—or how can we—live here? Swift, Gay, and Pope were chiefly interested, like Berkeley, in problems of knowledge; Radcliffe and Austen were also concerned, as Hume would have suggested, with conduct. They all began, however, with the realm of experience that Berkeley had exposed, that is, with a world altogether unsupported by external matter. And each of them attempted to show how we might endure and enjoy such a place.

The self-consciousness they brought to this concern with what may best be described as "perceptualism" is not altogether determinable. The earlier three of them were personally acquainted with Berkeley; and there is evidence that the later two had some solid knowledge of Hume. But the intellectual atmosphere they all breathed, an atmosphere which had been gathering since Bacon produced his *Magna Instauratio,* is more significant. Locke had augmented this atmosphere with his emphatic advocacy of experience; and the Royal Society, whose principles Thomas Sprat broadcast in his *History,* had also contributed to it. It was so pervasive during the eighteenth century, indeed, that the simple soldier, Captain Tobias Shandy, absorbed one of its basic elements, the succession of ideas, without, as he admitted, even knowing what it meant. Surely Swift and Austen did. Captain Shandy gave a pious rendering to an even more volatile element, that is, Hume's frightening tenet that anything can produce anything,

9

when he assured his brother that there was no other reason for one man's nose being longer than another's but that God would have it so. Berkeley's shocking revision of Locke, to put it crudely, was in the air during the time that Swift and Gay and Pope were creatively active; and Hume's shocking refinement of Berkeley pervaded the atmosphere in which Radcliffe and Austen composed their novels. In this book I will examine major works by Swift, Gay, Pope, Radcliffe, and Austen, therefore, with the same kind of awareness of perceptualism that they must have possessed and describe the connections between their works and this philosophy.

In writing this book I have contracted many debts, chiefly to the tradition of eighteenth-century study, which I hope it enriches. Among the scholars whose work it reflects, I recall Jean Hagstrum, Hoyt Trowbridge, Harold Kelling, Ricardo Quintana, W. K. Wimsatt, Arthur Lovejoy, Samuel Monk, Marvin Mudrick, Aubrey Williams, Queenie Leavis, William Empson, and—more recently—Donald Greene, Frederik Smith, Ruth Yeazell, William Edinger, Christopher Fox, Phillip Harth, Alison Sulloway, Howard Weinbrot, Max Byrd, and William Kupersmith. And there are many more, all of whom I have attempted to recognize in my notes. I owe debts of a more personal kind as well, and first to Professors Julius Weinberg and William Hay, who introduced me to the philosophical ideas that chiefly support my study. I hope they would approve my applications. I am also indebted to such friends as Kristine Wallace, Margaret Wong, Terry Doody, Linda Leavell, Richard Queen, Martin Stevens, John Ambler, Laura Hodges, Patrick Brady, Kris Davis, Wesley Morris, Faye Walker, Olin Joynton, and Vicki Sapp, who have tolerated and encouraged me. And to Christopher Q. Drummond, from whose conversation everything I have written draws benefits. I am grateful to the editors of *PQ*, *The Genres of "Gulliver's Travels,"* and *E-CS*, who printed separate essays that have since been woven into the present composition. I owe a great debt, finally, to Terry Munisteri, who has served as both my typist and my editor.

I am indebted to the curators of the Lewis Walpole Library for permission to reproduce the sepia drawing by Pope for the "Essay on Man."

Reconcilable Differences in Eighteenth-Century English Literature

1

Introduction

It was a principle widely acknowledged throughout the eighteenth century that each thing that exists exists in particular. Although this principle contradicts all assertions of order and retards every creative ambition, it was, according to George Berkeley, universally received.[1] John Locke, who emphasized the differences between particular things, had invoked it in 1690 to enforce his analysis of verbal generality; David Hume, who emphasized the separability of one thing from another, relied on it in 1739 to deconstruct the soul. The commitment Alexander Pope made in 1713 and reaffirmed in 1730 to derive certainty of a cosmological design from observation of a world where all things differ epitomizes the steadiness with which the eighteenth century accepted this reductive, not to say corrosive, principle.

When Henry Fielding described contrast in 1749 as a source of beauty and when Samuel Johnson described variety in 1765 and again in 1779 as a source of pleasure, they were applying it specifically to literature. Johnson thus praised Shakespeare, who had joined tragic and comic incidents to produce pleasing vicissitudes of passion. However, although the principle might be employed to justify literary possessions, it presented to literary composition, because of its severity as well as its universality, a profound and unavoidable challenge. "It is the first act of the mind," Locke admonished all those who would be his followers, "when it has any ideas or sentiments at all, to perceive its ideas, and so far as it perceives them, to know each what it is, and thereby also to perceive their difference, and that one is not another." He urged, further, that all human knowledge depends on the mind's ability "to distinguish one thing from another where there is but the least difference." And between the particular things evident to human awareness there is always, he made clear enough, at least a least difference. This understanding of particularity, to which both Hume and Johnson subscribed, threatened to reduce the literary reconciliation of things, as Locke himself concluded, to a fanciful jumbling of diversities.

The eighteenth century, however, recognized two aspects of nature, as the human mind encounters it, that supported the rational assemblage and organization of different things. In the first place, there were three distinct kinds of things—material atoms or bodies, substantial individuals or objects, and mental percepts or ideas—which allowed each particular thing to be located in one of three general categories. In the second place, there were two apparent relations—resemblance and causation—by reference to which each thing could be accommodated, one way and another, to certain others. Both of these pillars of rational creativity, the categorical and the relational, were subjected by eighteenth-century thinkers to serious criticism, and both endured significant refinements; but they continued throughout the century to sustain exercises of reconciliation in literature as well as philosophy.

Things

The first kind of things, material atoms or bodies, was steadily espoused by Locke, although, as Berkeley would explain, this compromised his grasp of the third kind, mental percepts or ideas, to which he professed his primary allegiance. The atoms, which were individually too small to be perceived, were described by Leucippus, Democritus, and Epicurus in the ancient world and transferred to modern times in Lucretius's *De Rerum Natura*. They had been extensively considered in the seventeenth century by the British scientist, Robert Boyle, and the French sage, Pierre Gassendi. The physical universe, these thinkers agreed, consisted entirely of insensible particles of matter, as Locke himself called them, and of the space—the void—through which they flowed chaos-like, together crushed and bruised. Everything humankind could experience—and thus explain—was a compound, both accidental and transient, created from collisions and collections of such particles. Jonathan Swift parodied this teaching when he described the chaotic room from which the recently arrayed Celia had issued as a "void," the "material litter" of which he would list; and later in the same poem when, in a phrase Milton had used to describe a Lucretian chaos, he likened Celia's close stool to "the hoary deep." The real force of atomic materialism is evident, however, in his earlier *Tale of a Tub:* not only in the frequent allusions to Lucretius, but in the doctrine that words have weight, in the explanation of human eccentricity as the press of particulate vapors on the brain, and in the gastrointestinal account of inspiration. The great advances in physics made by Locke's and Swift's countrymen, advances that seemed both to be founded on a belief in Lucretius's insensible particles and to confirm their existence, ensured their persistent presence in British imagination.

The second kind of things, the particularity of which the eighteenth century observed, are the substantial objects of sensual experience: individual stones, horses, people, cherries. These are the different things human beings live among as members of what Hume called "the vulgar" and on the persistent integrities of which we base our hopes and our conduct. William Empson has detected this normal human dependency in John Gay's *Beggar's Opera*, describing as its central teaching that "only the individual [person] can be admired."[2] Swift also emphasized individual personality when he declared in a famous letter to his beloved friend, Alexander, that he hated humankind in general and loved only particular people, "John, Peter, Thomas, and so forth." Johnson confirmed it when he attacked the institution of slavery, arguing that, although "an individual may . . . forfeit his [own] liberty by a crime . . . he cannot . . . forfeit the liberty of his children"—this despite the Christian doctrine of original sin. For Johnson, as for Swift and Gay, each person exists in particular. This tenet also underlies the American *Declaration of Independence* although Johnson, who once asked, "How is it that we hear the loudest *yelps* for liberty among the drivers of negroes?" would have bridled at the imputed agreement. In kicking the stone to oppose Berkeley's privileging of the third category of things, that is, perceptions, Johnson asserted, likewise, his confidence in the substantial integrity of natural objects, a tendency of mind Berkeley himself, who liked to talk about "this glove," "this cherry," and "this stone," often demonstrated.

The third kind of things, which Shakespeare once acknowledged with the phrase, "tender feeling to base touches prone," are the separate perceptions, the sense data, of personal awareness. Every percept, as Berkeley and Hume insisted, was particular, different and thus separable from every other. Each touch and sight and sound, no matter how base, was a thing;[3] and each of the particular substances, the individual people and stones that Johnson attended, for instance, was a compound of these things congruent in time and place (by the grace of God, perhaps, or by sheer accident), which one found integrated (in so far as they were indeed integrated) by similarity and contiguity. Here is Berkeley's account, from *Three Dialogues between Hylas and Philonous,* of one such substance or "congeries," as he calls it:

> I see this *cherry,* I feel it, I taste it: and I am sure *nothing* cannot be seen, or felt, or tasted: it is therefore *real.* Take away the sensations of softness, moisture, redness, tartness, and you take away the *cherry.* Since it is not a being distinct from sensations; a *cherry,* I say, is nothing but a congeries of sensible impressions, or ideas perceived by various senses: which ideas are united into one thing (or have one name given them) by the mind; because they are observed to attend each other. Thus, when the palate is affected with such a particular taste, the sight is affected with a red colour, the touch with roundness, softness, &c. Hence, when I see, and feel, and taste, in sundry certain manners, I am sure the *cherry* exists, or is real; its reality being in my opinion nothing abstracted from those sensations.

The actually existing things are the sensations, a certain taste, a red color, the immediate impressions of roundness, softness, moisture, and tartness, which Berkeley "observed to attend each other" in the common course of his experience. The term *cherry* simply stands as a convenient sign for the many similar occurrences of these customarily contiguous things.

The three kinds of things, bodies, substances, and perceptions, were often yoked together, usually two and not all three of them at once, in eighteenth-century discourse. In defining "the same man" as "a participation in the same continued life by constantly fleeting particles of matter," Locke had connected the first two; and in describing "the same person" as an "extended consciousness" that maintained at once present and remembered perceptions he had connected the second and the third. Such pairing is sometimes less a meeting ground, admittedly, than a battle ground: when, for example, Locke notes that "Words . . . stand for nothing but the ideas in the mind of him that uses them" and mocks those that "suppose" their words "stand also for the reality of things." When Johnson kicked the stone, again, he was opposing the second kind (no doubt reinforced in his mind by the first) to the third. When, on the other hand, Johnson employed the expression, "the atoms of probability," he was using the things of Lucretian materialism as a metaphor for the immaterial things of the mind, likening the third kind, that is, to the first.[4] In choosing the term "impression" to represent an individual sensation Hume also yoked the first things and the third together although he might have been chagrined to have it brought to his attention. He and Berkeley held the belief in material things—although practically necessary to most people—to be a superstition; both of them, however, described the uniting of percepts to compose substances as a primary intellectual task. This task Berkeley assigned very pointedly: each person must study "to know what [percepts] are connected together [he asserted]; and the more a person knows of the connexion of [his percepts], the more he is said to know of the nature of things." One's gathering of his percepts of a particular taste, a red color, and certain customarily accompanying impressions of roundness, softness, moisture, and tartness, for example, would amount in time to one's knowing the nature of a cherry. The procedure for knowing the nature of a struldbrugg or a yahoo presents the same intellectual demands. And so does the desire to know the nature of Atossa or Valancourt or Frank Churchill.[5]

The literary exercise required of eighteenth-century English authors, no matter what position they took on the true or primary meaning of *thing*, was in general the same: how, that is, and to what extent might particular things all strictly different and strictly separate—whether conceived as bodies, substances, or perceptions—be reconciled to one another to form discursive tissues; and how might different tissues be reconciled to one another to form more—and more—inclusive ones? Isaac Newton acknowledged this kind of exercise in the preface of his *Optics* (1704), describing it as a continuous resolution of "analysis" and "composition." Thomas Sprat, following Bacon, had recognized it in the *History of the Royal Society* (1667) as a purposive traverse between the examination of particular perceptions and the proposal of general rules; and had accordingly advocated an energetic movement "from experimenting to demonstrating and from demonstrating to experimenting again." The problems of such an exercise varied, of course, as one attempted to demonstrate institutions in a storm of corporeal collisions or to compose personalities from a season of social engagements. Putting the mirror up to the flux of nature and thus drawing support from mere truth to material reality is quite a different business from organizing one's own ideas either for polite solicitation or for private purposes. There is, nevertheless, a strong family connection between discursive works as diverse as Swift's *Tale* and Austen's *Emma*, a connection deriving from their authors' shared determination to reconcile differences among things.

Resemblance

Joseph Addison made a significant contribution to this exercise in 1711 in his famous *Spectator* No. 62. He wished, he said modestly, to add a refinement to an "admirable" suggestion Locke had made about the relation of resemblance in his *Essay concerning Human Understanding*, the suggestion that judgment, the primary attribute of philosophy, was concerned with the difference between things and that wit, the genius of poetry, was concerned with their resemblance. Addison asserted at first that a resemblance must be surprising to be classified as wit. This narrows the definition, of course, limiting wit to a certain kind of resemblance. The great heroic poets who (as Pope was saying at almost the same time) strictly followed nature and, consequently, produced altogether unsurprising resemblances—likening Ajax to a donkey, for instance—"have seldom anything," Addison said, "that can be called wit." He then illustrated this understanding of wit as a surprising resemblance: "When a Poet tells us, the Bosom of his Mistress is as white as Snow, there is no Wit in the Comparison; but when he adds, with a Sigh, that it is as cold too, it then grows into Wit." The two ways in which, according to the poet, a bosom resembles snow, it may be noticed already, are different in themselves and in their effect: the naturally snow-white bosom inspires love; the conventionally snow-cold bosom quells it.

This illustration and the whole refinement of Locke's definition are compromised, moreover, by a further refinement, Addison's distinction between true wit, false wit, and mixed wit. True wit, he suggests, presents natural resemblances, thus bringing Homer and Vergil back into the realm of wit; false wit, exemplified by Ovid and Martial, presents verbal resemblances; mixed wit weaves natural and verbal resemblances together. Addison has failed to acknowledge that true wit could hardly be surprising, although such a conclusion seems inescapable. He has also failed to acknowledge that the description of the bosom by which he has just shown how a resemblance could "grow into Wit" is, at best, what he now calls mixed wit. One's mistress may have a bosom really like snow in color, but its coldness is just a form of speech and altogether false to nature. This instance is congruent, indeed, with the collection of cases Addison has displayed to illustrate mixed wit, all of them based on the metaphor of love as a flame, which he derived from the poems of Cowley. "Cowley observing the cold Regard of his Mistress's Eyes, and at the same Time their Power of producing Love in him, considers them as Burning-Glasses made of Ice." If icy cold eyes are false to nature, so is a snowy cold bosom. Thus wit in Addison's first refinement, that is, resemblance plus surprise, is reduced to mixed wit in the second.

Addison seems himself to have noticed this discrepancy in his understanding, although he has neglected to admit it, because immediately after giving several instances of mixed wit, he modifies his definition again, withdrawing the element of surprise from it—and the mixture of word play—and asserting that "the Basis of all Wit is Truth." This virtually cancels surprise, but it does not bring Addison back to Locke for whom—"all things . . . being particulars"—every imputed resemblance is tainted with falsehood: Ajax is not really like a donkey even at his most mulish. Only judgment, Locke would insist, which discriminates between all things, is capable of truth to nature. "True Wit" he would have declared a contradiction in terms. Addison, who did not confront this point of stress between himself and his authority, has developed the notion that for wit to be true it must reflect what Johnson would call general nature. And this new dedication to truth and nature eventually leads him still further from Locke to the point that he has mentioned, if in a rather off-hand way, in this the last paragraph of his remarkably lively and challenging little essay:

> I must not dismiss this Subject without observing, that as Mr. *Locke* in the Passage above-mentioned has discovered the most fruitful Source of Wit, so there is another of a quite contrary Nature to it, which does likewise branch it self out into several Kinds. For not only the *Resemblance*, but the *Opposition* of Ideas does very often produce Wit; as I could shew in several little Points, Turns, and Antitheses, that I may possibly enlarge upon in some future Speculation.

Addison did not in fact enlarge upon this discovery. But even so, it constitutes an understanding of literary activity that is of major importance.

To state Addison's final position: wit is the exposition of naturally true resemblances and naturally true differences. This means, since every element of experience, however closely it may resemble any other, is different from every other, that wit is intellectually dynamic, involving judgment at every point. And Locke's condescension toward poetic discourse or, as he calls it, "the gaiety of fancy," the formulations of which it would be "a kind of affront . . . to examine by the severe rules of truth and good reason," must be rejected. As Sterne argued in the next generation and as Pope suggested in this one: "*Wit* and *Judgment* often are at strife, / Tho' meant each others Aid, like *Man* and *Wife.*"

In reading such an exercise of "fancy" as this from Pope's *Rape of the Lock* about how Queen Anne at Hampton Court "[does] sometimes *Counsel* take—and sometimes *Tea*," one must engage in altogether good rational examination.[6] Counsel and tea are similar in that they can both be "taken" and "taken," moreover, in a social setting—in the same social setting, indeed. They may also be similar in importance, depending on her sense of her office (a question this line illuminates) to the Queen. But although the common verb enforces resemblance, the different terms and their placing in different half-lines declare a difference—a difference that splits the verb into two different meanings, as well. Thus either the reader shares with the Queen a sense of the difference between the two actions she engages in at Hampton Court or notes a difference of which she is insufficiently aware and endures in himself a difference from her. Consider, again, this couplet, also from the *Rape*, which describes certain things on Belinda's dressing table:

> The Tortoise here and Elephant unite,
> Transform'd to *Combs*, the speckled and the white.

The suspension of the verb in the first line has a special effect, allowing one to feel the apparently irreconcilable diversity of tortoise and elephant before (bawdily?) denying it. The caesura, moreover, enforces the difference that the verb finally cancels, requiring a reader to recognize that it is only "here" that such natural diversities can be reconciled. The next line analyzes the announced reconciliation: giving, in the first half-line, the plural substantive, "*Combs*," to which one kind of thing these properly diverse things have been transformed to serve Belinda's vanity; and then, in the last half-line, the recalcitrant trace of difference. In both these cases poetic pleasure has a decidedly rational and, indeed, judgmental cast.

Addison's acknowledging "*Opposition*" in the last paragraph of his essay strongly indicates his understanding that such accommodations of difference as these made by Pope represent, not simply a second "Source of Wit," but one aspect of a single reconciliation between what Addison himself has described as "contrary" impulses.[7] This reconciliation, this dynamic teasing and testing of the diverse elements of experience for their full likenesses and differences, is also implicit in Addison's recognition of "Antitheses." The self-conscious, rhetorical organization by which comparable things are shown to be different and different things comparable had been, in fact, a central aspect of English poetic intelligence and practice for more than a century before Addison took notice of it. It is chiefly evident in the compellingly antithetical promptings of heroic-couplet poetry, to the development of which Addison himself contributed. Donne exposed a certain plagiarist sometime before 1600, for instance, describing him under the figure of a glutton who had fed on his poetry and insisting, "The meate was mine, th'excrement is his own." Marlowe, earlier still, distinguished between two aspects of a certain minor poet in his translation of Ovid's *Amores* "[whose] Arte excelld, although his witte was weake."

Or consider at more length this passage from Lord Falkland's commendatory verses on the appearance of George Sandys's *Paraphrase upon the Psalms* (1636), in which the poet defends against Puritan reproof such a literary embellishment of scripture as Sandys had attempted. After invoking the authority of Paul, who "would be at least content," Falkland asserts, that "Some for the Curious should be Eloquent," the poem advances this argument:

> For since the Way to Heaven is Rugged, who
> Would have the Way to that Way be so too?
> Or thinks it fit, we should not leave obtaine,
> To learne with Pleasure, what we act with Paine?

The repeated term "Way" in line two acknowledges a possible resemblance in ruggedness between the learning and the living of a Christian life; but the caesural division of the two ways and their syntactic difference, the second being the object of a prepositional phrase modifying the first, strongly recommend a discrimination between the two. (Here Falkland, before Locke's sixth birthday but after his own heart, strongly wishes to observe even the least difference between two different things.) Although sequentially contiguous to one another, one "Way" leading to the next, and no doubt causally connected as well, they may be differentiated at least with respect to ruggedness. In line four, diction, syntax and meter unite to underscore this allowable difference. The term "what," meaning "that which," preserves the resemblance between learning and living and, indeed, their possible identity; so does the alliteration uniting "Pleasure" that modifies the one way with "Paine" that modifies the other: the Puritan determination to make religious instruction and religious conduct equivalent in ruggedness is thus honored even while being opposed. The statement otherwise discriminates between the two concerns of learning and living, the antithesis between pain and pleasure making the opposition, which syntactic difference and caesural definition confirm, overwhelmingly sensible; and it attributes this discrimination, moreover, to the tactfully recognized will of God. The various usages of wit thus accommodate both a difference of opinion and a difference of subject, maintaining the complexity of human experience while bringing it within the compass of judgment.

Addison himself had recently contributed—in *The Campaign* of 1704—to this dynamic exercise of wit and judgment or, rather, of rational wit. This quotation, for example, develops a resemblance between John Churchill, the leader of the British forces, and his ally, Prince Eugene of Savoy:

> At length the fame of England's hero drew
> Eugenio to the glorious interview.
> Great souls by instinct to each other turn,
> Demand alliance, and in friendship burn;
> A sudden friendship, while with stretch'd-out rays   5
> They meet each other, mingling blaze with blaze.
> Polish'd in courts, and harden'd in the field,
> Renown'd for conquest, and in council skill'd,
> Their courage dwells not in a troubled flood
> Of mounting spirits, and fermenting blood;   10
> Lodg'd in the soul, with virtue overrul'd,
> Inflam'd by reason, and by reason cool'd,
> In hours of peace content to be unknown,
> And only in the field of battle shown:
> To souls like these, in mutual friendship join'd,   15
> Heav'n dares entrust the cause of human-kind.

The two heroes perfectly resemble one another these lines insist; they are so similar, indeed, "mingling blaze with blaze," that they can be discussed as if they were one. It may be noted in passing that such a formula justifies Locke's skepticism of poetic fancy, which forces resemblance where there is surely a little bit of difference. Addison does, however, analyze the heroes' joint attributes, representing the resembling pair in different situations, "courts . . . and . . . field," "conquest . . . and . . . council." In courts they both appear like "polish'd" jewels, in the field, like "harden'd" steel; that is, at the appropriately different times, like the bejewelled medals they wear at court and like the bright swords they wield in battle. Even here there is a similarity which becomes apparent if this difference is carried just one degree into abstraction: the two men are (equally) bright and hard in both situations. The two are also equal to one another in "conquest" and in "council," as their joint inclusion in line eight indicates, although there is a specific difference between their eminence in the different situations, their conduct in battle being marked by fame unlike the necessarily unpublicized skill they practice in the secrecy of consultation. The poem also analyzes their "courage," finally, into diverse aspects: although it is always governed in the same way, that is, by reason, on some occasions reason inflames and on others it cools. These patterns of resemblance and differ-ence lack the seriousness of Falkland's, in part because of the obviously inaccurate equation between the two heroes on which they are based. The whole passage constitutes little more, indeed, than social puffery. But even so, it exemplifies the dynamic recon-ciliation of resemblances and differences recognized at the end of *Spectator* No. 62 to which other poets gave more serious attention.

Causation

To explain the full importance of resemblance in accommodat-ing nature's particularities, I turn to the second kind of relation between and among things: causation. If Locke was excessively skeptical of resemblance, he was excessively confident of this rela-tion, which he called *"cause* and *effect"* and advocated as "the most comprehensive relation." Although the understanding of it changed enormously during the eighteenth century—from a power in external bodies (Locke's belief) to a habit within the individual mind (Hume's)—the age always relied upon it. If dif-ferent things could not be reconciled with one another in fabrics of resemblance, they might still be reconciled as chains of causality.

Locke seems in the *First Letter* to Stillingfleet to see causation as a certainty of reason—the idea of beginning being necessarily connected with the idea of "something operating, which we call a cause." But throughout the *Essay* he bases the awareness of this relation firmly on experience:

> In the notice that our senses take of the constant vicissitude of things, we cannot but observe that several particular both qualities and substances begin to exist, and that they receive their existence from the due application and operation of some other being. From this observation we get our ideas of *cause* and *effect*.

Before pointing out the irremovable grain of resemblance in this accumulative process, the advocacy of which Locke shares with Hume, I must notice the apparent advantages causation has over resemblance as a means of connecting together the different things of nature. We see a difference, as Locke has insisted, between any two things no matter how resembling; and to calculate what resemblance there may be, moreover, we willfully force the two things together. On the other hand, to arrive at the idea of causation, we simply observe two things occurring naturally together and see, no matter how alike or different they may be, that the first (the cause) is always followed by the second (the effect) and that the second never occurs without the first. Since resemblance is thus dependent on human tampering (on a poet's yoking tea and counsel together) and productive necessarily of at least a little falsehood (even the smoothest tortoise shell being somewhat unlike ivory), causation is a philosophically superior relation in two obvious ways: it is simply a recurrent observation of what precisely occurs in nature. Thus Locke quite rationally, or so it may seem, finds this relation "a true principle of reason."

That resemblance underlies the process by which this true principle is established, however, becomes apparent in another passage from the *Essay*, in which Locke considers the causative power thus observable in nature:

> The mind being every day informed by the senses, of the alteration of those simple ideas it observes in things without; and taking notice how one comes to an end and ceases to be, and another begins to exist which was not before; reflecting also on what passes within itself and observing a constant change of its ideas, sometimes by the impression of outward objects on the senses, and sometimes by the determination of its own choice; and concluding from what it has so constantly observed to have been, that the like changes will for the future be made in the same things by like agents, and by the like ways, considers in one thing the possibility of having any of its simple ideas changed [that is, as an effect], and in another the possibility of

making that change [that is, as a cause]; and so comes by that idea which we call *power.*

In this passage, as elsewhere in the *Essay,*[8] Locke's ingratiating style disguises serious intellectual problems. The mind discovers causation, he insists, "every day," finding it in what it has "constantly observed to have been." Each person sees that changes are made "in the same things by like agents . . . and so comes by" the idea of causal power. The process thus seems inarguably commonplace. But in fact, as "constantly" and "like" should reveal, what one actually sees is a number of resembling cases, never in fact seeing "things [that are] the same," but only things that are roughly similar. And the awareness of causation, which Locke has thus raised in a nest of resemblances, reveals the same deficiencies as that awareness which underlies the fancies of metaphor and allusion:[9] it requires the willful collection of widely scattered resemblances in one's experience and the determined tolerance of at least a little bit of difference among them.

Hume, although he confined the things of human attention to so many items of mental furniture, described the process by which each person acquires what he called "the habit" of causal inference just as Locke had done, that is, by considering experience and observation. He enforces the role of resemblance, however, that Locke tucked away in equivocal and unemphatic diction. "'Tis not . . . from any one instance," Hume insists in his *Treatise of Human Nature,* "that we arrive at the idea of cause and effect, of a necessary connexion, of power, of force, of energy and of efficacy," piling up the synonyms to mock his predecessors—among them Locke, of course—who begged the question of causation with mere words:

> Did we never see any but particular conjunctions of objects, entirely different from each other, we should never be able to form any such ideas.
> But . . . suppose we observe several instances, in which the same objects are always conjoin'd together, we immediately conceive a connexion betwixt them, and begin to draw an inference from one to another. This multiplicity of resembling instances, therefore, constitutes the very essence of power or connexion, and is the source, from which the idea of it arises.

"This multiplicity of resembling instances" inspires in each of us, Hume explains, "the presumption of a resemblance betwixt those objects of which we have had experience and those of which we have had none." Here I may commend Locke's poisoned chalice to his own lips: two instances of contiguity, no matter how similar, are the least bit different, each of them being individual, particular, as judgment must recognize. Only by tampering with the multiplicity of resembling cases, moreover, gathering the widely scattered instances and considering them together, can one determine a necessary connection between all such resembling cases and rationally infer a like effect whenever one sees a like cause. "One who concludes somebody to be near him when he hears an articulate voice in the dark [to give one of Hume's cases] reasons justly and naturally; tho' that conclusion be derived from nothing but custom [that is, a multiplicity of resembling instances], which infixes and inlivens the idea of a human creature, on account of his usual conjunction with the present impression." And thus is Ann Radcliffe's romantic practice readied and rationalized for *The Mysteries of Udolpho.*

I have illustrated the dynamics of resemblance, showing how it spans from an almost complete difference between things ("Damnation and a Mistres") or a difference between them in every way but one (*"Counsel* [and] *Tea"*) to a virtual identity (Churchill and Savoy).[10] Causation presents a span that is equally dynamic. It invests every kind and degree of contiguity between different things from things seen together only once or only a few times to things seen together every day; from things seen sometimes, but not always, in sequential contiguity to things seen connected with one another in every resembling instance. Thus adding the dynamic range of this relation to that of resemblance supplies all three of the relations—resemblance, contiguity, and causation—with which eighteenth-century English authors attempted to explain the order of nature and to compose orders of their own. Hume sums up their understanding in his *Enquiries:* " . . . there appear to be only three principles of connexion among ideas, namely, *Resemblance, Contiguity* in time or place, and *Cause* or *Effect."* (Hobbes in *Leviathan* had actually lumped contiguity and causation together under the term "Purpose" and thus described two principles of connection, "Purpose" and "Resemblance.") Resemblance, as I have tried to show, represents a scale on which different things are tested for kinds and degrees of similitude; causation represents a scale on which pluralities of different things are tested for the degree to which they are necessarily in contiguity. From contiguity in even one instance the mind embarks on a process, sifting its experience for multiplicities of resembling contiguities; once assured of enough—and we are a very impatient race—it proposes a necessary connection, causation, power, and so forth, as Hume explained.

In *Tristram Shandy*, the narrator presents contiguities of the strangest kind, for example, as patterns of causality, the vividness of his retrospection giving him a confidence that we normally derive only from a multiplicity of resembling cases. The book begins:

> I wish my father or my mother . . . had duly consider'd how much depended upon what they were doing . . . when they begot me.

Throughout the account of his life Tristram reaches backward to explain such things as this, that is, what caused his parents to neglect "what they were doing," and forward to deduce its enormous train of consequences. Even the way Tristram set up his top at the age of five, or so his father believed, could be causally reconciled with the inadvertent conception: "My Tristram's misfortunes [he complained to his brother Toby] began nine months before ever he came into the world." And the aging Tristram has taken it upon himself to explain how such things as this came to pass, that is, to describe the connection between his bungled conception and the hiring of Dr. Slop as the attendant obstetrician at his birth; the connection between that and his bungled delivery; the connection between that and his father's plan to name him Trismegistus; the connection between that and his actually being christened Tristram. Tristram gives causal dignity to all the odd contiguities of his life, explaining with great precision how such widely different things as an odd legal agreement, a cut thumb, the loose hinge on a forceps, a sash window, a devotion to England's wars, one servant's loyalty, another's carelessness, and the fact that nothing was well-hung in the Shandy family could become interconnected to blight all his hopes as a man.

Such an interplay of contiguous objects and events can also be traced, with just a little more interpretive effort, in the novels of Jane Austen. Because Charlotte Lucas married Mr. Collins in *Pride and Prejudice*, for instance, she moved into the vicinity of Mr. Collins's patroness, Lady Catherine de Bourgh; because Elizabeth Bennet was Charlotte's best friend, she and she alone of the Bennets paid Charlotte a visit there; because Darcy was Lady Catherine's nephew, he also entered this environment; because this reacquaintance with Elizabeth was unhampered by the presence of her embarrassing family—as it must have been if Mary Bennet had married Mr. Collins—Darcy's love of her grew; and because of this love, he proposed. Underlying each of these connections is a foundation of customary connectedness supporting the present case. Young women do often—although not always—have best friends; often chosen on the basis of intellectual compatibility (as in this case); and best friends often visit one another; if they live at a distance, moreover, the visit may last for several days or weeks. This foundation of customary contiguities, an awareness of which all readers share, allows them to accept this new instance. Like almost all novelists, Austen constructed her patterns of causality with the reliable if largely unadmitted connivance of her readership.

Although Austen does not, in part because of this connivance, underscore the connections between the different events of her novels as I have just done and as Tristram does in telling his highly peculiar story, she is vividly aware of them. When a shocking event emerges, she is always careful to go back, imaginatively, and account for it. When Fanny Price learns the terrible news that Henry Crawford and Maria Rushworth have eloped, she considers: "*His* unsettled affections, wavering with his vanity, *Maria's* decided attachment, and no sufficient principle on either side, gave it possibility." And thus the recent course of events, none of which Fanny has seen, is firmly if generally indicated, not as a necessary, but as a credible concatenation. Anne Elliot, similarly, tries to find the connections to explain the shocking news of an engagement between Captain Benwick and Louisa Musgrove.

> The high-spirited, joyous-talking Louisa Musgrove, and the dejected, thinking, feeling, reading Captain Benwick, seemed each of them everything that would not suit the other. Their minds most dissimilar! Where could have been the attraction? The answer soon presented itself. It had been in situation. They had been thrown together several weeks; they had been living in the same small family party . . . they must have been depending almost entirely on each other, and Louisa, just recovering from illness, had been in an interesting state, and Captain Benwick was not inconsolable.

And so, with this and a little more imaginative detail of the same kind—"of course they had fallen in love over poetry"—Anne is able to reconcile the diversities of personality and explain the union of even so odd a pair of lovers.

One may be inclined to pause and recollect that novels are primarily developments of the relation of contiguity[11] whereas poems are primarily developments of the relation of resemblance. It may seem, furthermore, that the English novel's development and eventual ascendancy are owing to the privilege accorded—as a result perhaps of Locke's influence—first to differences as discerned by judgment and second to causation, by the power of which differences could best be both preserved and reconciled at once. Novels, indeed, being composed of different things in sequences, do move within the span of causation, that is, between mere contiguity (or coincidence) and necessary connection (or inevitability); whereas poems, which are usually composed in non-narrative patterns, dwell normally in the span of resemblance. As the dependency of causation on resemblance should suggest, however, the two relations are and must both be employed in compositions of any scope.

A couple of instances will underscore their interconnectedness in eighteenth-century sensibilities. In his *Treatise,* Hume accounted for the vulgar belief in an external world of matter, the existence of which was both vain to question and impossible to establish, by invoking these two interwoven aspects of experience, its *constancy* and its *coherence.* Constancy, as Hume describes this, is based squarely on the apprehension of resemblance; and coherence, as he puts it, on "a kind of reasoning from causation." It is, as he shows, from the many cases of resemblance and from the multiplicity of resembling cases of contiguity, the two of which are richly supportive of one another in natural experience, that we maintain our sense of natural externality, that is, of nature as external to awareness.[12] Or consider a somewhat more famous example, Locke's exposition in the *Essay* of primary and secondary qualities. This explanation of the connectedness between the external world and human experience, in which, once again, the relations of resemblance and causation are amalgamated, Locke derived from the tradition of atomic materialism; it was confirmed without question by Immanuel Kant and still stirs philosophers to this day.[13]

All the elements of sensation are produced, Locke has confidently asserted, by the impulses of atomic particles on different senses. They produce (much as Lucretius taught in the ancient world and as Gassendi taught in modern times) two kinds of impressions or ideas, as Locke calls them, real and imputed; and the powers by which they do so he labels, respectively, primary qualities and secondary qualities.

> . . . The power to produce any idea in our mind, I call *quality* of the subject wherein that power is. . . . Qualities thus considered in bodies are, First, such as are utterly inseparable from the [atomically

composed] body in what estate soever it be and such as sense constantly finds in every particle of matter which has bulk enough to be perceived and the mind finds inseparable from every particle of matter [down to the atomic particles], though less than to make itself singly perceived by our senses. . . . These I call *original* or *primary qualities* of body.

The qualities that qualify as primary vary somewhat in Locke's lists of them, solidity, extension, figure, and mobility being sometimes augmented by texture and weight; but the inseparability of primary qualities from material reality is firm. Not so with secondary qualities: these, he explains,

which in truth are nothing in [material] objects themselves, but powers to produce various sensations in us by their primary qualities [beget in us such sensations as] colours, sounds, tastes etc.; these I call *secondary qualities.*

Both kinds of sensation, the real and the imputed, are causally produced in each person individually in the same way, "by the operation of insensible particles on our senses." "The impulse of . . . insensible particles of matter of peculiar figure and bulk," Locke explains more fully, "and in different degrees and modifications of their motions causes [both kinds of sensations in our minds]." "The ideas of primary qualities [however] are resemblances of them, and their patterns do really exist in the bodies themselves; but the ideas produced in us by these secondary qualities [of bodies] have no resemblance of them at all." Once again, then, there is a connection between resemblance and causation: for, although the secondary qualities merely cause certain sensations, the primary qualities both cause and resemble certain other sensations.

This teaching was so well-known, so popular, indeed, that Mr. Spectator could represent it as the property of the nieces of an old fellow, Abraham Thrifty, and describe them trying to make him understand it:

When I desired . . . one of them to put my Blue Cloak on my Knees [one day], she answered, Sir, I will reach the Cloak [an object with extension, figure, and so forth]; but, take notice, I do not do it as allowing your Description, for it might as well be called Yellow as Blue; for Colour is nothing but the various Infractions of the Rays of the Sun. Miss *Molly* told me one Day [Abraham continues], That to say Snow is white, is allowing a vulgar Error; for as it contains a great

Quantity of Nitrous Particles, it may more reasonably be supposed to be Black.[14]

According to "the young Husseys," as Abraham calls them, "to believe one's Eyes is a sure way to be deceived." On the other hand, the husseys, who want black atoms to produce a black sensation, are no doubt excessively (unphilosophically, indeed) concerned with visual resemblance. And yet, Locke too is strongly moved by this concern contrary to what might have been expected from his dismissal of wit. He obviously privileges the resembling, that is, the primary, qualities over the secondary, the non-resembling, ones. His labeling the primary qualities "real," describing the secondary as "imputed," suggests as much; so does his argument that the secondary would quite disappear if we "had senses acute enough to discover the minute particles of bodies." With good enough eyes or a good enough microscope, Locke consoles himself, we would see only "an admirable texture of parts of a certain size and figure." This obviously confirms resemblance as a relation of the first importance since it is the resemblance of ideas to external nature—that is, of the ideas that *are* resembling—that allows us rationally to bridge over to material reality. Locke, however, might truly find in cause and effect the most comprehensive relation since both the primary and the secondary sensations, as he understood things, are causally produced by bodies in human minds.

Perceptions

These two relations, resemblance and causation, justified exercises in literary reconciliation throughout the eighteenth century. No matter what kinds or what combinations of things concerned an author, these relations reconciled the parts and cemented the composition. There was, however, a major development in eighteenth-century literature as the understanding of things underwent a change. The nature of this change, which philosophers emphatically promoted, may already have begun to emerge, especially in my sketch of the things in question, that is, bodies, substances, and perceptions. To describe it adequately, however, I must directly confront the "paradigms" or "constellations of belief," as Thomas Kuhn might call them,[15] in which these things are embedded. The eighteenth century's grasp of paradigms, as should become evident, was firmly connected with its sense of things; as one changed, the other changed as well.

The eighteenth century conventionally embraced the broad constellations of belief, first, that nature entire was a restless congregation of material bodies existing altogether external to consciousness and, second, that each person, each individual consciousness, was an immaterial substance or soul. Although these two paradigms are apparently incongruous, the one with the other, they shared the central principle, to which I have already referred, that each thing that exists exists in particular. This meant, in the first case, that every material body was essentially different from every other body, essentially different by virtue of its difference in atomic or corpuscular constitution. It meant, in the second case, that each person was essentially different from every other person, essentially different by virtue of his own soul.

Berkeley proposed an alternative to the first of these paradigms in the *Principles* of 1710, arguing that nature was not entirely material, as had always been believed, but that it was entirely perceptual. Hume, picking up a suggestion from Locke, proposed an alternative to the second in the *Treatise* of 1739, arguing that the individual consciousness was not a substance, a soul, as had always been believed, but a train of perceptions. Berkeley and Hume embraced the principle of particularity, that is, that each thing is particular, as strongly as their contemporaries; but the term *thing* as it figures in this principle they redefined and, significantly, both in the same way. *Thing* did not stand for either a *material body* or an *immaterial substance* in the teaching of these philosophers: it stood, rather, for a *sense impression* or *idea* or, more broadly speaking, for a *perception*. This redefinition of *thing* represented a change in the paradigm of physical nature, as Berkeley explained, from a turbulent chaos of great-and-small bodies to an inexhaustible fountain of sensations; and a change in psychological paradigm, as Hume explained, that was still more extreme.

The tenet that all things were perceptions did not merely change the soul; it dissolved it. Individual mental substance, which had persisted in Berkeley's teaching as the necessary support for one train and another of perceptual experience, Hume rejected. He argued that perceptual things, each of them being different and separable from everything else, were, indeed, different and separable from everything else: thus they required no connection with a supportive mind either as a whole or as they emerged here and there in human awareness. Individual mental support was simply unnecessary in a world of perceptions. And the sentient self dwindled from a substance to mere consciousness. "When I enter most intimately into what I call *myself*," Hume asserted, "I always stumble on some particular perception or other. . . . I never can catch *myself* at any time without a perception, and never can observe anything but the perception." "The identity [of the self is therefore] only a fictitious one." The alternative paradigms of Berkeley and of Hume thus resolved the incongruity between matter and mind that had driven Berkeley to what he himself called "the obvious but amazing truth," reducing all things, that is, to perceptions. But this resolution was achieved at a serious cost to individual human identity, a cost the eighteenth century was reluctant to pay.

The incongruity between the two conventional paradigms, as Berkeley described and responded to this, the incongruity, that is, between corporeal nature and incorporeal souls, did not for the most part seriously trouble eighteenth-century culture. Its members embraced both matter and mind with apparently unshakable confidence—partly, perhaps, because they disliked the alternatives. This dual allegiance, which is obtrusively evident in Defoe and Addison and Fielding and Richardson, can also be accounted for, at least in part, by the intellectually diverse origins of these two paradigms, by the great antiquity of each one as a cultural property, and by the special reinforcement each one had received separately in the preceding century.

The reliance on matter as a necessary support of the physical universe—a reliance still shared, no doubt, by most people—can be traced back through the middle ages to Lucretius, and on to Epicurus, and on before that; it can be traced forward to Francis Bacon, Thomas Hobbes, and the Royal Society. *Ex nihilo nihil fit.* This reliance on matter, which troubled Christian theology throughout its history, Newton accommodated to religious teaching or, at least, to religious sensibilities with his universal law of gravity. His famous doctrine that each atom of matter possessed an innate power equally to attract every other atom apparently infused corporeal nature, the compositions and the movements of which Lucretius had attributed to sheer accident, with divine energy and orderliness, filling the universe of bodies with God's omnipresent control. The materialistic paradigm was thus, if anything, more comfortably established in the early eighteenth century than ever before. The Christian assurance of a unique psychological substance or soul—unique, that is, not only to human beings, but to each one separately—can also be traced back to antiquity, but to an altogether different teacher, not Epicurus but Plato. St. Augustine derived his famous definition of the individual person as "a soul that uses a body," both from Scripture and, as Gilson has explained, from Platonism.[16] Although this Augustinian definition was extensively tested and refined by the Schoolmen, it survived even the corrosive nominalism of Occam[17] and continued—as it still continues—to be conferred throughout Christendom on each and every one of God's children. This sense of personal being or substance was strengthened by the Reformation and, especially in English understandings, by the recently resolved violence to which that had led. English people of the eighteenth century had suffered too much too recently in the struggle over the extent to which each person, each soul, might attain its own salvation to sacrifice this immortal part.

Each of the conventional paradigms, the physical and the psychological, being different in its history and in the quality of its appeal, was held with a certain difference. Robert Boyle before the beginning of the century and Samuel Johnson near its close felt some discomfort in maintaining both at once. But Boyle and Johnson embraced both after all; and both were otherwise almost unquestionably entrenched in eighteenth-century culture as a whole. To drive this point home, we may recall the neglect which greeted Berkeley's *Principles* and the fact that, as Hume himself acknowledged, his *Treatise* fell dead-born from the press. Although the conventional constellations of belief in a material universe and in immaterial souls were firmly held by English society throughout the eighteenth century, however, they came under powerful attack, not only from philosophy but, as I will argue, from literature as well. Despite the firmness with which society held these good old paradigms and despite the fear inspired by Berkeley's and Hume's revolutionary alternatives, this attack, especially in its literary forms, was extensive and protracted.

It is important, however, before we turn our attention toward the attack, to recognize that the alternatives, especially when apprehended in abstract form, were—and still are—indeed frightening. Berkeley's argument that the physical universe was created—was continually being created, actually—not from matter but from experience, although less scary than the psychology of Hume, is plenty scary enough. In the world it represents where, as Berkeley put it, "*esse* is *percipi*," not-to-be-perceived is not-to-exist. And the dearest objects of human interest, our homes, our books, and (as Johnson warned his friends) our friends keep fading away: out of mind, out of existence. They keep fading away, that is, unless, as Berkeley slyly indicated, they continue to be supported by an omniscient mind. Each particular thing, that is, each item of awareness, is assured a natural persistence only if it is maintained by the eternal awareness of God. The devout Berkeley, who saw matter as a source of atheism, believed that his immaterialist paradigm, by thus making all physical nature immediately dependent on divine support, had provided assurance of God's existence, omnipotence, and benevolence. Nevertheless, most of Berkeley's contemporaries, religious and skeptical alike, agreed with the devout Johnson strenuously to resist it. The second revolutionary paradigm, that suggested by Locke and clinched by Hume, reduced the psychological realm altogether, as I have indicated, to so many trains of consciousness. Each person, each self, Hume asserted in an infamous passage, was/is "nothing but a bundle or collection of different perceptions, which succeed each other with inconceivable rapidity, and are in a perpetual flux and movement." Thus Hume has reduced both the physical universe and the consciousness that beholds it to a number of perceptual streams.

It was this frightening reduction of both nature and human kind to a flickering show and, indeed, to the same flickering show that satirists, poets, and novelists recognized as the eighteenth century progressed.

2

Swift's Satires

Samuel Johnson's doubt that Jonathan Swift wrote *A Tale of a Tub*, like many of his apparent errors, is very illuminating. The *Tale*, Johnson remarked, "has so much more thinking, more knowledge, more power, more colour, than any of the works which are indisputably his." Formally affirming, if not his doubt, his sense of the difference between the *Tale* and Swift's later work, Johnson wrote in *Lives of the Poets*, "His *Tale of a Tub* has little resemblance to his other pieces." He told Boswell that these other pieces, the chief among which is *Gulliver's Travels*, are "clear but shallow"; and the *Travels* itself amounted to almost nothing, he once said, beyond the conception of big men and little men. If we free these comments of their pejorative tone, Swift himself would agree. The *Travels* is as shallow and as clear as he could make it although, as he understood only too well, this might not be clear or shallow enough. All its contents are immediately available, at any rate, for understanding; all are totally present in the easy, circumstantial English of Lemuel Gulliver. The *Tale* is a different matter: it presents "thinking," "knowledge," "power," and "colour," as Johnson recognized, and is thus, in a word, referential, persistently pointing outside itself to a restless mass of obtrusive bodies, attitudes, and institutions in the material world.

The "remote" images of the *Travels*, all of them surrounded by the halo of mendacity, require immediate response and immediate understanding. A reader must consider strictly in themselves the sense in Gulliver's description of a "convenient sledge," the appropriateness of his adult complacency toward Glumdalclitch—"a Child of towardly Parts for her Age"—and his judgment that the height of the Emperor of Lilliput was "enough to strike an Awe into the Beholders." Even the most suggestive references are so vividly individuated that they are, like the rest of the *Travels*, immediately significant.[1] The Irish rejection of Wood's half-pence, which scholars have identified in the Lindalinian rebellion against the Flying Island, need not be invoked for a modern reader to find in Swift's fable a telling presentation of oligarchic tyranny and popular resistance. Every one recognizes that the struldbruggs are strictly fictional, existing only within the *Travels*, and that they constitute, nevertheless, a powerful case against dreams of earthly immortality. The political gymnastics of courtiers in Lilliput are, likewise, meaningful in themselves. They illuminate modern political experiences—the debates between American presidential candidates, say—as well as any activities at the court of George. The very fact of explicit reference to England made by Gulliver in the second and fourth voyages, his telling the King and the Master about society, law, warfare, and religion in his own distant land, enforces the prevailing lack of referentiality in the *Travels* at large.

The *Travels* refers by name to hardly any living person and only in brief incidents to historical figures. The *Tale*, on the other hand, bristles with real people. "There is now actually in being, a certain poet called *John Dryden*," the Author reminds us, "whose translation of *Virgil* was lately printed in a large Folio, well bound, and if diligent search were made, for ought I know, is yet to be seen." The Author recalls another work of "our famous *Dryden*," *The Hind and the Panther*, speculatively attributes to him still another, *Tommy Potts*, and praises him for his clever practice of dedicating separate sections of his individual works to "a multiplicity of *Godfathers*." He gives even more attention to "my worthy and ingenious Friend Mr. W-tt-on, Batchelor of Divinity," although courteously disguising his name with the omission of a letter or two; and he attaches quite a few atoms of Wotton's scholarship to the fifth edition of his own work. Other contemporary literary men, among them Bentley, Tate, Dunton, and Durfey, are also honored by the Author's notice; and many personages from recent history including Hobbes, Descartes, Calvin, James I, Charles II, Cromwell, Louis XIV, John Knox, and the Lord Mayor of London are drawn into his discourse. The *Tale* is also rich in the sights and sounds—not to speak of the smells—of the Author's London and its environs. Place names are common: Bedlam, Leicester Fields, Will's, Moorfields, Gresham, White Hall, the Inns of Court, the Houses of Parliament, Newgate. The court, churches, book sellers' shops, pubs, theaters, and coffee houses all radiate from "the very Garret I am now writing in" and fill the Author's London with characteristic noise and activity. Almost every station of life from whore, bailiff, bully, and beau to lords, ladies, merchants, and courtiers is discovered in typical exercises. And this is as true of the allegorical sections of the *Tale* as of the others. When the unadorned brothers, who have just come up to town, step "to the *Rose* to take a Bottle, the Drawer would cry, *Friend we sell no Ale*." And once, after they have determined to follow fashion, a London mercer brings a new fad to their notice: "*An please your Worships* (said he) *My Lord C—, and Sir J.W. had linings out of this very piece last Night; it takes wonderfully, and I shall not have a Remnant left, enough to make my Wife a Pin-cushion by to morrow Morning at ten a Clock*." The *Tale* in short projects around itself the noisy, bustling world of London from which it arose.

This emphatic externality of reference makes the *Tale* cry out for judgment—for approval, of course, if we accept the professions and arguments of the Author.[2] A "devoted servant of all Modern Forms," who has "just come from having the Honor conferred upon me, to be adopted a Member of [the] illustrious Fraternity" of Grub Street, he espouses all modern institutions. His chief objects of approval—and our chief objects of judgment—are the different religious institutions and the less formal intellectual organizations developed by the English people. These institutions, formal and informal, are a response, as Swift strongly indicates, to the recently absorbed social turbulence represented by the Reformation—that "famous Rupture," as the Author calls it—and the English Civil War which grew out of it.[3] Traces of this recently moderated turbulence, each of them threatening a return of it, have continued to surge to the surface of English society throughout the life of the Author as he reveals in acknowledging his own involvement "in *Pro's* and *Con's* upon *Popish Plots*, and *Meal-Tubs*, and *Exclusion Bills*, and *Passive Obedience*, and *Addresses of Lives and Fortunes;* and *Prerogative*, and *Property*, and *Liberty of Conscience*," political conflicts and crises that were aggravated by "Malignants of the opposite Factions."

Throughout the *Tale*, Swift looks back apprehensively upon a chaotic time, a time to which John Donne in *The First Anniversary* of 1612 looked apprehensively forward. The human world, as Donne described things, was suffering an earthquake; it had fits and a consumption that was becoming feverish; its whole frame was disintegrating.

> The sun is lost, and the earth, and no man's wit
> Can well direct him where to look for it.
> And freely men confess that this world's spent,
> When in the planets and the firmament
> They seek so many new; they see that this   5

Is crumbled out again to his atomies.
'Tis all in pieces, all coherence gone;
All just supply, and all relation:
Prince, subject; father, son, are things forgot,
For every man alone thinks he hath got   10
To be a phoenix, and that there can be
None of that kind of which he is, but he.

Here Donne at the beginning of the seventeenth century uses atomic materialism, with its teaching of the accidental order and inevitable dissolution of the physical universe, to describe the encroaching chaos in human society. Like individual atoms in corporeal compositions, every person, determined to be his own phoenix, that is, to search for happiness and salvation strictly on his own, breaks away from all human institutions; and the institutions thus disintegrate. Swift has developed the same analogy at the end of the century, seeing the same resemblance between the human and the natural worlds that Donne saw and likewise representing in terms of material organization and dissolution the shifting orders and the threatening confusion in human society. What Donne and Swift imagined from opposite points of vantage Thomas Hobbes, who lived through the English Civil War, described in a famous statement in *Leviathan*. Positing the extreme case that Donne had feared, that is, the politically atomistic "war . . . of every man against every man," he discovered human life strictly devoid of human institutions:

In such a condition there is no place for industry, because the fruit therof is uncertain, and consequently no culture of the earth; no navigation nor the use of the commodities that may be imported by sea; no commodious building; no instruments of moving and removing, such things as require much force; no knowledge of the face of the earth; no account of time; no arts; no letters; no society; and, which is worst of all, continual fear, and danger of violent death; and the life of man, solitary, poor, nasty, brutish, and short.

The traces of such a time, in which human singularity led to the brink of such a situation, and the signs of such conditions' surging up again to overwhelm the human community Swift has infused into the *Tale*. The Author refers emphatically to *Leviathan* in the Preface while presenting "horrible Apprehensions," shared by "the Grandees of Church and State," that ruinous new holes may be started in the commonwealth. Attributing the source of the danger to *Leviathan* itself, which tosses and plays with "schemes of Religion and Government," he presents his book, his *Tale of a Tub*, as a temporary measure in support of those "schemes" that are presently in place.

This concern for the institutional order of England Swift enforces with recurrent allusions to Lucretian atomism, developing as a pervasive presence in the discourse an analogy, first, between certain individual human beings and the material universe that Lucretius described and, second, between this universe and larger orders of human society. The Author's account of genius (or "madness," as he labels it) as a rising of vapors from the lower regions recalls, first, Lucretius's account of vaporous exhalations from the earth (especially of sour, sulphurous exhalations) and, second, the Roman poet's repeated insistence that it is not the atoms themselves—since these are essentially alike—but the ways they fall, strike, fasten, and hook together that determine the nature of all things physical and intellectual. Here is Swift:

> The *upper Region* of Man, is furnished like the *middle Region* of the Air; The Materials are formed from causes of the widest differences, yet produce at last the same Substance and Effect. Mists arise from the Earth, Steams from Dunghils, Exhalations from the Sea, and Smoak from Fire; yet all Clouds are the same in Composition, as well as Consequences: and the Fumes issuing from a Jakes, will furnish as comely and useful a Vapor, as Incense from an Altar. . . . Now, the former Postulatum being held, that it is of no Import from what Originals this *Vapour* proceeds, but either in what *Angles* it strikes and spreads over the Understanding, or upon what *Species* of Brain it ascends; It will be a very delicate Point, to cut the Feather, and divide the several Reasons to a Nice and Curious Reader, how this numerical Difference in the Brain, can produce Effects of so vast a Difference from the same *Vapour,* as to be the sole point of individuation between *Alexander the Great, Jack of Leyden,* and *Monsieur Des Cartes.*

This is atomic materialism with a vengeance as "Materials," "Composition," "Strikes," and "numerical Difference" declare. The attribution of intellectual "Disturbance" to strictly material agency, that is, to the striking of certain particulate bodies on a certain coporeal ground producing a "Transposition of the Brain" (not "the mind"), recalls Lucretius's extended demonstration that mind and spirit are composed, like everything else, "of minute particles of matter"; and that developments in mind and spirit, like all natural events, are merely shifts and changes in these bodily compositions.[4]

Swift's circumstantial representation of an Aeolist's inspiration is very similar to Lucretius's representation of an epileptic fit. Lucretius reminds us:

> We have often seen someone constrained on a sudden by the violence of disease, who, as if struck by a thunderbolt, falls to the ground, foams at the mouth, groans and shudders, raves, grows rigid, twists, pants irregularly, outwearies himself with contortions; assuredly because the spirit, torn asunder by the violence of the disease throughout the frame, is in turmoil and foams, just as in the salt sea the waves boil under the mighty strength of the winds. Further, groans are forced out because the limbs are afflicted with pain, and in general because the seeds of the voice are ejected and rush forth from the mouth in a mass.[5]

We may note here the easy analogy between man and nature—easy because both are material compositions—and the description of the vocal sounds, accompanied with foam, which are ejected as a mass of particles. Now here is Swift, describing, not a fit of epilepsy, but a fit of religious enthusiasm:

> The Great Characteristick by which the [Aeolists'] chief Sages were best distinguished, was a certain Position of the Countenance, which gave undoubted Intelligence to what Degree or Proportion, the Spirit agitated the inward Mass. For, after certain Grippings, the *Wind* and *Vapours* issuing forth; having first by their Turbulence and Convulsions within, caused an Earthquake in Man's little World; distorted the Mouth, bloated the Cheeks, and gave the Eyes a terrible kind of *Relievo*. At which Junctures, all their Belches were received for Sacred, the Sourer the better. . . .

Just before this description Swift reduced the outpourings of these sages by arguing, *"Words are but wind; and Learning is nothing but Words; Ergo, Learning is nothing but Wind."* This degradation of articulate human intelligence to a puff of air Swift here intensifies, reducing the teachings of evangelists to belches and to belches the composition of which is strengthened by hooked or rough atoms, as Lucretius would explain it, that fill the "meager Devotees" with sensations of sourness. Notice also the easy commerce between the natural world and the "little World" of man; and the persistent corporeal implications of the passage as a whole, its representation of masses in motion and of bodies under pressure. Like Lucretius, Swift often refers to the human body as a vessel, describing the spirit as wind or vapor which inflates and distorts it. Locke defined individual man as "nothing but a participation of the same continued life by constantly fleeting particles of matter, in succession vitally united to the same organized body." Swift here has similarly reduced—if not every man—at least the single, inspired evangelist to a composition of atoms accidentally created and accidentally inflated, a composition that will swell and contract as particles first gather and then disperse.

In the *Travels*, the things Swift describes are perceptual: first, particular impressions and ideas once endured and now recollected by Gulliver; second, general opinions and attitudes widely, variously, and often thoughtlessly held, to which these particulars are related as either illustrations or exceptions. The things Swift presents in the *Tale*, however—not only brains and people, but books and institutions—all emerge from the Author's exposition and advocacy as external collocations of Lucretius's corporeal atoms. The individual literary compositions produced by the Author's colleagues in modernity, for example, run "parallel to those of Dyet in our Nation, which among Men of judicious Taste, are drest up in various Compounds, consisting in *Soups* and *Ollio's, Fricassées*, and *Ragousts*," composed—both the stews and the books—"by jumbling fifty things together."[6] The modern Author's common-place book, another jumble of things, is a preliminary accumulation of this kind. And so are both the individual members of the "Grub Street Fraternity"—when conceived as creative intellects—and their fraternity as a whole: they "strike all things out of themselves, or at least, by Collision, from each other." Their separate pieces of wit, the books composed of these pieces, and the collections of these books are represented, similarly, as chance collocations of matter; and they all suffer the fate Lucretius prophesied. There is nothing so "tender," the Author complains, "as a *Modern* piece of Wit." Almost any "Carriage" will lead to its dissolution: inflict "the smallest Transposal or Misapplication," and it will become "utterly annihilate."

Swift pointedly submits words and the books composed of words to atomic reduction and to the consequent annihilation. The Author gives these directions, for instance, to anyone who wishes to enjoy the full weight of his own "wonderful discourse": "I have couched a very profound Mystery in the Number of 0's mutiply'd by *Seven* and divided by *Nine*." This will recall Peter's similar reduction of the words of the Will "totidem literis" in his determination to spell out the allowance he needs to adorn his coat: for both Peter and the Author, letters, not words, are the atoms of signification.[7] The Author prescribes a more radical application of atomic materialism in coping with all the intellectual exercises he most admires:

> You take fair correct Copies, well bound in Calfs Skin, and Lettered at the Back, of all Modern Bodies of Arts and Sciences whatsoever, and in what Language you please. These you distil in balneo Mariae, infusing Quintessence of Poppy Q.S. together with three Pints of Lethe, to be had from the Apothecaries. You cleanse away carefully the Sordes and Caput mortuum, letting all that is volatile evaporate. You preserve only the first Running, which is again to be distilled seventeen times, till what remains will amount to about two Drams. This you keep in a Glass Viol Hermetically sealed, for one and twenty Days. Then you begin your Catholick Treatise, taking every Morning fasting, (first shaking the Viol) three Drops of this Elixir, snuffing it strongly up your Nose. It will dilate it self about the Brain (where there is any) in fourteen Minutes, and you immediately preceive in your Head an infinite Number of Abstracts, Summaries, Compendiums, Extracts, Collections, Medulla's, Excerpta quaedam's, Florilegia's and the like, all disposed into great Order, and reducible upon Paper.[8]

This reduction "of all Modern Bodies of Arts and Sciences whatsoever" to their corporeal minima, it should be noticed, will produce new compounds, first in the brain of a scholar-disciple and then in the issuance of new verbal "Collections." The world of learning thus waxes and wanes, presenting an analogy to the external universe described by Lucretius.

The Author often represents words as having material weight and falling downward to inflate the human vessels waiting with their jaws open below. Lucretius represented the same phenomenon—if in a different spirit:

> One word often awakens the ears of a whole crowd when uttered by a crier's lips. Therefore one voice is dispersed suddenly into many voices, since it distributes itself amongst separate ears, stamping on the words a shape and clear sound. But those of the voices which do not fall quite into the ears are carried past and lost, being scattered abroad without effect into the air—

or dashed and mangled upon the ground. Swift's Author, who replaces the crier with an evangelist and substitutes mouths for ears as the recipient organs, describes a happier situation. After explicitly quoting Lucretius on the materiality of sound, he comments:

> I am the readier to favor this conjecture, from a common Observation, that in the several Assemblies of these Orators [evangelists, con-

demned criminals, and mountebanks], Nature itself hath instructed the Hearers, to stand with their Mouths open, and erected parallel to the Horizon, so as they may be intersected by a perpendicular Line from the Zenith to the Center of the Earth. In which Position, if the Audience be well compact, every one carries home a Share, and little or nothing is lost.

Not only words but the books composed of them the Author chiefly values, in exaggerated accordance with the teachings of atomic materialism, for their weight, their bulk, and their number. It is by a comparison of these qualities that the habitués of Will's and Gresham hope to determine the relative preeminence between their productions and those claimed by the Grub Street fraternity. Their challenge to compare all the books that can be jumbled together as belonging to one or the other of these three societies "both as to *Weight* and *Number*" the Author considers with great solemnity. Elsewhere he has praised the Grub Street productions for their lightness: "Are they sunk [he asks Prince Posterity] in the Abyss of Things? 'Tis certain that in their own nature they were *light* enough to swim upon the Surface for all Eternity." And, indeed, as his exposition of theatrical discourse shows, literary materials can be variously light or heavy, soaring to the twelve-penny gallery or falling "plum into the jaws of certain *Criticks.*" But they are always material compositions, chance collocations of verbal or literal atoms that exist for a brief spell until time or chance or human meddling reduces them to their constituent particles.

This recurrent Lucretian strain, which is underscored by the Author's many avowed quotations from *De Rerum Natura*, has two important but largely contrary values in the *Tale*. In the first place, it emphasizes the externality of the Author's subject matter, enforcing his concern with the intellectual and religious life of London and its environs and requiring the reader either to approve things in London or to condemn them. In the second place, it seriously tempers the apparently correct judgment, that is, the radical rejection of the "modern" institutions, works, and attitudes the Author advocates and, indeed, embodies.[9] The pervasive Lucretian strain has this second effect because of the frightful alternative, the encroachment of sheer chaos, lingering traces and the persistent danger of which it continuously suggests. Any human pretension, as this chaotic surge should remind us, is preferable to the annihilation of all social tendencies, as Donne and

Hobbes described this; any human institution is preferable to the war of every one against every one.

*   *   *

It would be hazardous to take at face value everything Swift said in the Apology he affixed to the 1710 edition of the *Tale*. But his assertion that the primary foci of his satire were "Corruptions in Religion and Learning" seems to me to be accurate. In both these cases Swift has described two distinct institutions, a best human institution and that which is currently evident, giving much the more attention in both cases to the actual, "the modern," order of things. The best condition in religion can be defined as common faith and in learning as common sense. In the religious satire, which Swift develops as an allegorical fairy tale, he begins with the best condition, describing the agreement among three brothers in their attention to their father's will and to his gift of coats; and then he represents the modifications made first by Peter—Roman Catholicism—then Martin—Anglicanism—and finally Jack—the dissenting sectarianism of the other protestants. In the satire on learning, although the Author looks forward briefly to the inauguration of a formal academy, Swift has represented the current institutions aspectually, exposing their interconnections of genius and discipleship (or madness and credulity) first from one vantage and then another. The best possible state of learning, that is, a community of the sensible, he weaves incidentally into this largely analytical fabric. Religion and learning are emphatically united in the Digression concerning Madness; and there are connections between them more and less explicitly indicated throughout the *Tale*. But the two are best confronted separately as Swift himself suggested when he explained: "Abuses in Religion he proposed to set forth in the Allegory of the Coats, and the three Brothers. . . . Those in learning he chose to introduce by way of Digressions."[10]

Swift represented the integration of early Christianity, to begin with this the easier of his concerns, by the use of allegory describing a father on his death bed who gave his three sons a coat apiece, his will, and a little supplementary advice. The death of the father, by which Swift has indicated the earthly separation of mankind from divinity,[11] left the three brothers in as good a religious condition as is possible here. The will (the *New Testament* according to the notes of 1710), the coats (the doctrine and faith of Christianity), and the brothers (the Christian community) represent a complete and a sufficient religious organization. From any one of these, while this organization held, one might infer the contiguous elements: by consulting the will, for example, one might confidently describe the coats; and, vice versa, from the coats the directions in the will for maintaining them; from the shape of any coat, again, one might describe its wearer, and from the wearer, his coat. Each coat, moreover, resembled the others, and each brother, the other brothers, adding a metaphoric dimension to Swift's allegory. The entire organization, therefore, was deducible from the parts, all of them being united by resemblance or causation into a perfect whole.

This religious synecdoche persisted, to carry on the terms of the allegory, until the three brothers "came up to town and fell in love with the ladies"; and, perhaps, although this presents some painful implications, a little longer. Before this time, at all events, to quote Swift's laconic account, the brothers "travelled thro' several Countries, encountered a reasonable Quantity of Gyants, and slew certain Dragons." This is his complete representation of the great missionary age of the church, during which, to interpret it, humankind raised the assurances of Christian faith against certain frightful old superstitions; and it may somewhat reduce the dignity of religious history. The next paragraph, describing the brothers' actions after these "seven years," when they first got "to town," is unquestionably reductive.

> They Wrote, and Raillyed, and Rhymed, and Sung, and Said, and said Nothing; They Drank, and Fought, and Whor'd, and Slept, and Swore, and took Snuff: They went to new Plays on the first Night, haunted the *Chocolate*-Houses, beat the Watch, lay on Bulks, and got Claps: They bilkt Hackney-Coachmen; ran in Debt with Shopkeepers, and lay with their Wives: They kill'd Bayliffs, kick'd Fidlers down Stairs, eat at *Locket's* loytered at *Will's*: They talk'd of the Drawing-Room and never came there, Dined with Lords they never saw; Whisper'd a Dutchess, and spoke never a Word; exposed the Scrawls of the Laundress for Billet-doux of Quality: came ever just from Court and were never seen in it; attended the Levee *sub dio;* Got a list of Peers by heart in one Company, and with great Familiarity retailed them in another. Above all, they constantly attended those Committees of Senators who are silent in the *House,* and loud in the *Coffee-House,* where they nightly adjourn to chew the Cud of Politicks, and are encompass'd with a Ring of Disciples, who lye in wait to catch up their Droppings.

The problem with these fashionable practices is this: that they in no way offend against the father, the will or the coats and, thus, that they are allowable as religious activities and, representatively, as forms of Christian conduct. The brothers acted together at this time, as in their travels, and, as far as one can infer, they wore their coats clean and brushed them often, as the father had directed, and strictly followed the will concerning their "Wearing and Management." Thus all the original inferences metonymic and metaphoric are evident and the representation of Christian wholeness persists. The brothers do not "live together in one house," admittedly, as the father commanded them; otherwise, they would not have had to lie on bulks—or so I infer. But then, to look ahead, they would not settle into one house until after they had seriously abused the will and embellished their coats—when Peter took over the house of a Lord, ejected his rightful offspring, "and received his brothers in their stead."

Christianity, therefore, was not perfectly in compliance with divine mandate even in the best of times. But to lump the brothers' conduct against giants with their conduct in town, throughout which time they obeyed the will, apparently, and paid proper attention to their coats, allows interpretations of institutional Christianity even in the days of unity that can hardly be a source of religious satisfaction. In making such interpretations—in accordance with the allegorical implications—we are necessarily casting beyond the *Tale* proper and acknowledging an external, a material, world. All allegorical works—Dryden's *Absalom and Achitophel,* for instance, and Spenser's *Faerie Queene*—require this kind of acknowledgment. The external force of the present allegory is clear enough. During an early period of seven years plus, the brothers sufficiently observed the father's prime directives to maintain substantial unity. In the paragraphs on their travels and their first adventures in town, we should notice, Swift uses the third person plural: "They travelled . . . they kick'd Fidlers down Stairs . . . they constantly attended . . . Committees." Thus the inference of Christian unity in the external, material world, with all its problems, is readily available.

The developments to which Swift then turns and to which he has devoted most of his religious allegory may nevertheless seem to have been evident from the first. The very fact of three brothers implies the natural diversity of individual human kind. And the immediate admission of a possible eldest, that is, of a possible difference, although the midwife could not actually identify the different ones, recognizes the disruptive stresses of social and political life. The acknowledged possibility of the coats' being abused and the "Penalties [that the Father preordained] for every

Transgression or Neglect" also establish sin and punishment, that is, difference in conduct, within Swift's allegory. The very need of the brothers for coats, that is, for some distinguishable support, admits the imperfection of human kind. All these early aspects of the allegory foretell the eventual failure of the Christian institution. But the ideal of unity in religious organization and something like an original reality are, nevertheless, variously represented: in the perfect equality of the father's gifts to the sons, none of whom is distinguished from the others; in the fact of one will, which is equally relevant to all three gifts and all three sons; in the father's command (also inscribed in the will) "that you should all live together in one House like Brethren and Friends." Even here the impression of unity suffers a little explosion of cracks: they *are* brothers and so should hardly be ordered to live *like* brothers. The two terms, "Brethren and Friends," again, may remind us of a difference, of the fact that brothers are not always friendly. Nevertheless, these brothers are alike; so are their coats; and at least for a while, they act both in unison with one another and in compliance with the will: thus they constitute a single order. It is this emphatic religious unity which Swift has represented in the first paragraphs of his allegory, providing a vivid point of reference, that makes his exposition of the disintegration of the Christian community, its destruction of the proper connection between teaching and observance, and its inadequate institutional renovations so vivid and impressive.

Before describing the satire of learning, in which Swift has been forced to go a very different way to work, I must notice both the religious disintegration and the religious reconstruction that are represented in the allegory and thus projected in the material world. I begin with the most nearly precise metonymic joint, that between Martin's reformed coat and the father's will, recognizing that, even in this case, governed by the most sensible and observant human intelligence Swift can represent, humanity has not been able completely to reform the accumulated abuses of Christian history but only to reach back to an approximation of the original institution. All three coats had been extensively embellished by the brothers in their effort to maintain themselves in the world; and as time passed they wore on their coats, the Author explains,

> what ever Trimmings came up in Fashion: never pulling off any, as they went out of the Mode, but keeping on all together; which amounted in time to a Medley, the most Antick you can possibly

conceive; and this to a Degree, that upon the Time of their falling out there was hardly a Thread of the Original Coat to be seen, but an infinite Quantity of *Lace,* and *Ribbands,* and *Fringe,* and *Embroidery,* and *Points;* (I mean, only those *tagg'd with Silver,* for the rest fell off.)

This is the circumstance the two younger brothers had to reform when they took a copy of the will and confirmed their difference from their self-proclaimed elder, Peter. That "there was hardly a Thread of the Original Coat to be seen" obviously indicates the extent to which Peter—that is, the Roman Catholic Church—had obliterated the original connections and the scope of the task the two reformers faced.

They looked "some times on their Coats and sometimes on the *Will*" in making the attempt to re-establish this crucial contiguity. But when Martin "laid the first Hand," and "at one twitch" tore off "a large Handful of Points" and, at a second, stripped "ten dozen Yards of Fringe," he "very narrowly scap'd a swinging Rent" in the coat; and although he "gleaned out all the loose Threads" of gold lace with great care and "quite eradicated or utterly defaced" the embroidered human figures, he could not quite restore the coat. Utterly "defacing" the figures suggests imperfect success even here: he could not apparently "disembody" them. And some of the embroidery Martin had quite self-consciously to leave interwoven:

Where he observed the Embroidery to be workt so close, as not to be got away without damaging the Cloth, or where it served to hide or strengthen any Flaw in the Body of the Coat, contracted by the perpetual tampering of Workmen upon it; he concluded the wisest Course was to let it remain; resolving in no Case whatsoever, that the Substance of the Stuff should suffer Injury; which he thought the best Method for serving the true Intent and Meaning of the Father's *Will.*

The perfectly seamless coat, because of profound and perpetual tampering, cannot be restored to the condition in which it was first given to Martin: consequently, "the true Intent and Meaning" of the will can never again be strictly inferred from it. Primitive Christianity is irrecoverable.

The metaphoric as well as the metonymic links allegorically represented by Swift in the whole of institutional Christendom have also been destroyed. Martin, of course, carefully removed his coat and himself from any resemblance to Peter; and Jack, despite Martin's advice, broke the metaphoric connection between the two of them. Consider, moreover, the fortuitous resem-

blance that gradually became evident between Peter and Jack.
Jack tried harder than Martin, or so it seemed, to distinguish his
coat from Peter's detested finery. He ripped and tore it almost to
shreds in his effort to rid it of the embellishments that all the
brothers together had formerly attached.

> What little was left of the main Substance of the Coat, he rubbed
> every day for two hours, against a rough-cast Wall, in order to grind
> away the Remnants of *Lace* and *Embroidery;* but at the same time went
> on with so much Violence, that he proceeded a *Heathen Philosopher.*

Instead of attempting to recreate the metonymic connection between the will and his coat, as Martin had done, Jack struggled,
negatively, to break the metaphoric connection between his coat
and Peter's. The results of his efforts, however, proved very disappointing to him, because, after all, he came to bear a remarkable
resemblance to the detested older brother:

> For, as it is the Nature of Rags, to bear a kind of mock Resemblance
> to Finery; there being a sort of fluttering Appearance in both, which
> is not to be distinguished at a Distance, in the Dark, or by short-
> sighted Eyes: So, in those Junctures, it fared with *Jack* and his Tatters,
> that they offered to the first View a ridiculous Flanting, which assist-
> ing the Resemblance in Person and Air, thwarted all his Projects of
> Separation, and left so near a Similitude between them, as frequently
> deceived the very Disciples and Followers of both.

This resemblance in outward appearance represents a similitude
that Swift describes in inner nature, "Phrenzy and Spleen . . .
having the same Foundation." Both of these brothers—and thus
both of the sects they represent—are driven, not by a concern for
the will, that externally firm system of instructions, but by their
own individual whims—called variously "vapors," madness,"
"enthusiasm" and "inspiration" within the *Tale;* each one wishing
to be, in Donne's words, "the only Phoenix." Thus they eventually
presented outwardly similar, although not identical, public appearances, thrusting into public show their similarly private—
and to some extent privately similar—tendencies. Peter (with
Jack's original connivance, of course) had embellished his coat in
splenetic response to a variety of private urges, preeminently
pride, vanity, and greed (as the names of the ladies he hoped to
impress may suggest), whereas Jack ripped into his in the more
focused frenzy of zeal. But this zeal, composed crucially of Jack's
desire to destroy all resemblance to Peter, proved, as Martin

warned, to be a "Reflection" on Peter; and, like reflections, generally, it provided a sort of resemblance.

This latter day similitude does not, however, represent a recreation of the Christian community. In the first place, the likeness is only a flickering impression that close observation cancels. Jack seemed to resemble Peter "at a Distance, in the Dark, or [to] short-sighted Eyes." Zeal and pride, although both these passions constitute aberrations from Christian humility and obedience, can be easily enough distinguished from one another. In the second place, these brothers themselves disowned their resemblance: Jack's being mistaken for Peter, Swift explains, "was a mortifying Return of those Pains and Proceedings [he] had laboured in so long." Most important of all, the resemblance is one in disobedience and misconduct, that is, a disruption of the metonymic connection between the will and the coats. Peter's nature can be inferred from his coat and Jack's, from his; but the will, which one can at least glimpse by reference to Martin's reformed garment, is not evident from either one. Jack and Peter and thus the dissenting sects and Catholicism, as Martin's effort to reassert this connection shows by contrast, have gone similarly awry. The Anglican adjustment to the errors of early Christianity, although not perfect, is the best possible, Swift suggests, in the material world.

Swift's exposition of modern intellectual organization or what he calls "learning" is somewhat more negative than his representation of organized religion. The intellectual wholeness or common sense, as his age called it,[12] has never actually existed on this earth, or so he indicates; and he represents no likelihood for the achievement of this situation in which, as Marvell had put it (despairingly) in the previous generation, all agree. Swift is unable to detect or describe any good old days in the realm of learning.

The intellectual situation described in the *Tale* is not, however, quite so bad as this may suggest. Swift has been able to infuse his account of things, in the first place, with traces of common sense, that prevailingly metaphoric condition of community, in which different people hold resembling opinions based on resembling tissues of experience—or what Swift sometimes calls "Nature." In this passage from his celebration of madness and its successful dissemination in Section IX, for example, he recognizes such a condition:

. . . The Brain, in its natural Position and State of Serenity, disposeth its Owner to pass his Life in the common Forms, without any

Thought of subduing Multitudes to his own *Power*, his *Reasons* or his *Visions;* and the more he shapes his Understanding by the Pattern of Human Learning, the less he is inclined to form Parties after his particular Notions; because that instructs him in his private Infirmities, as well as in the stubborn Ignorance of the People.

This brief salute is no doubt shaky even in its mode of utterance. The explicit reason for a naturally sensible person's observing "the common Forms" is not, as it should be, a devotion to the vulgar dictates of sense and reason, but an awareness that the vulgar are stubbornly ignorant. The statement thus teeters on the brink of self-destruction. And whether "common Forms" are reflective of common sense is left in doubt. Swift explicitly recognizes "common Sense" as well as "the Senses" in the next sentence; but individual "Imagination," which is presented as being successfully "at Cuffs with the Senses," is the privileged actor of this sentence. Imagination "kicks common Understanding, as well as common sense . . . out of Doors"—somewhat as their crazy sibling kicked Martin and Jack out of the Christian brotherhood. Swift has nevertheless raised the possibility of individual persons, whose brains are in the normal position, sensibly shaping their understandings "by the Pattern of Human Learning"—that great repository of common sense—and drawing into intellectual similitude with a few others.

A few paragraphs before this relatively concentrated recognition of such intellectual unity, in his exposition of "new schemes in Philosophy," Swift presents it in a less emphatic but more pervasive way. The philosophical innovators, who act, he reports, "by a Method very different from the vulgar Dictates of *unrefined* Reason," very different, that is, in so many words, from common sense, were usually recognized—or "mistaken," to use the Author's actual term—"by their Adversaries, and indeed, by all ["by all"—there is the desiderated community of agreement], except their own Followers, to have been Persons Crazed, or out of their Wits." "Mistaken" no doubt resists the flow of the sentence; but otherwise the diction, that implicit undercurrent of English agreement, preserves it: "Crazed" and "out of their Wits" carry decisive negative force even if "vulgar Dictates" fails to furnish an altogether persuasive positive. Swift goes on to draw the consequences of this sentence: "all, except their own [credulous] Followers" would "tie . . . fast" these mad innovators and apply to them the commonly approved treatments for madness, "*Phlebotomy*, and *Whips*, and *Chains*, and *dark Chambers*, and *Straw*." Truly,

Swift's Author attributes such a response toward these crazy people "to this our undistinguishing age," but even he recognizes that the innovators resemble "for the most Part in their several Models . . . their undoubted Successors in the Academy of *Modern Bedlam*." Here diction clashes with diction: the noble implications of "successors" and "academy" are contradicted by "Bedlam." However, common sense still inhabits Swift's discourse: such philosophical innovators as Epicurus and Descartes, despite the armies of disciples that have gathered about them, deserve the "Name [of] *Madness* or *Phrenzy*," which are the only names "the Narrowness of our Mother-Tongue has . . . assigned" them.

By the time a reader reaches the Introduction, moreover, which is the Author's first full exposition of the order apparent in the current intellectual environment, he has been acquainted with such intellectual turbulency, especially in the Preface and the Dedication to Prince Posterity, that he should be able to face even the kind of institution described there, the kind characterized, that is, by genius and discipleship, with some tolerance. He should also be ready to endure the substantial instability at the heart of such an institution and to grasp the discursive instability with which it is exposed. In fact, however, I have found, in my experience as a teacher, that this doubled instability oversets even sophisticated readers oftentimes. Because of this, I will begin with an outline of the whole section.

Its argument, which emerges only by degrees, is this: that the *Tale* is a Grub-street and hence an intellectually profound work. This argument is developed as follows:

I. That it is a Grub-street work, that is, a piece of trivial entertainment
   A. That there are three kinds of oratorial elevation
      1. not the bar-bench (for two reasons)
      2. but these three
         a. the pulpit (for sermons)
         b. the ladder (for last words)
         c. the stage itinerant (for sales pitches)
[Digression explaining the necessity of elevation, that words have weight, and an application of this, the theater]
   B. That these elevations allegorically represent forms of writings
      1. the pulpit, religious writings
      2. the ladder, a) political and b) poetic writings

      3. the stage itinerant, the trivially entertaining writings of Grub Street: "under [which] Classis I list my present Treatise"

II. That Grub-street writings are not in fact trivial entertainments for the vulgar (as the Author himself has just asserted), but profound intellectual revelations for the few

    A. That they are closely related, despite contrary pronouncements by the interested parties, to scientifically and creatively profound works produced at Gresham and Will's

    B. That they square with "Wisdom"—that is, an understanding accomplished by an interpretive penetration beneath the surface of things—despite their apparent concern with external sparkle; illustrated by

      1. Reynard the Fox

      2. Tom Thumb

      etc.

III. Conclusion: that this "whole Work," like Grub-street productions generally, presents within a sparkling style of vulgar entertainment profound wisdom for the intellectually elite.

This section of the *Tale* is organized, appropriately enough, as a philosophical argument, that is, as a tissue of consequences and resemblances, and not, like the religious allegory in Sections II, IV, VI, and XI, as a representation of history. This is not to say, however, that it is intellectually coherent or unified—not by any means; but that an analysis of its intellectual connections and procedures will reveal its meaning and its validity. If the relationships between its parts are sound, if, that is, it makes a philosophically compelling case that Grub-street works are profound and that this is a Grub-street work, it establishes its own profundity; introduces a philosophy of profundity, that is, a philosophy confined to the few gifted members of the intellectual community, the "adepti," as the Author would call them; and divides this community of the few who know from the many who believe. With the outline of the Introduction before us we can calculate the success with which the Author achieves all this.

    The two major parts of the Introduction are, first of all, contradictory; or, rather, the second, that Grub-street works are profoundly mysterious, contradicts the first, that such works are superficially amusing. If we accept the second part, the first, that is, the identification of this work as a superficial production, obviously collapses. Thus the Introduction projects irreconcilably different judgments of the *Tale* as a whole: that it is relevant to society at large as light entertainment, or that, contrary to all vulgar apprehension, it is a dense work by an adeptus for adepti. The claim that the *Tale* is a work "of and for Grub Street," although made in the first part to exalt the *Tale*'s power to provide "pleasure and delight [to] Mortal Man," more nearly represents the contrary, which is developed in the second. Looking back from the second part, one recognizes, moreover, a serious contradiction within the first. The allegorical procedure it follows, first presenting at length a category of emphatically corporeal "machines" and then providing an altogether surprising intellectual interpretation, belies its contention that the *Tale* belongs in the same category as "Six-penny-worth of Wit," that is, as easy entertainment for the vulgar. However, even as it destroys its own argument, it provides an illustration of the contrary argument developed in the second part. It is a case, that is, of mysteriously buried meaning, except, perhaps, that it constitutes less a continually sweeter sack posset—one figure for "wisdom"—and more of a "Nut which [may] cost . . . a Tooth [and repay] nothing but a *Worm*." To enjoy this larger coherency, however, we must embrace the incoherency within the first part between its argument—that the *Tale* is superficial—and its procedure—an actual discursive profundity.

This instability in the structure of the Introduction is also evident in its texture. The Author follows the statement, "Of ladders I need say nothing," for example, by saying quite a lot about them. He follows the tactful reticence about the two upstart intellectual societies, "Their own Consciences will easily inform them whom I mean," by straightway announcing their names to "the World." And immediately after explaining that the challenge these societies have presented to Grub Street includes "an impossibility in the Practice," he accepts the challenge. More subtle discursive discontinuities are interspersed among these blatant contradictions. The author gives a vigorously analytical argument, for instance, against including the bar-and-bench among the oratorial machines; and then, as a climactic explanation, he admits, "if no other Argument could occur," his self-willed determination to preserve the number *three*, which the admission of this fourth machine would overturn. On the other hand, he himself overturns this number—although without noticing it—on two separate occasions within the Introduction. First, he allows the theater into the group of machines, thus introducing a fourth, and reveals by implication that it is a finer, a more sufficient, mode of elevation than any he has described. Again, when he comes to interpret the three machines he has explicitly nominated, it occurs to him that one of them, the ladder, actually represents two forms of writing, both political and poetic, so that, once again, although in a different way, he honors the hated number *four*.

There are also subtle tissues of diversity in the Introduction. The pulpit for example, adumbrates both a kind of writing and a kind of writer, being "a Type with a Pair of Handles," whereas the emphatically parallel stage itinerant is narrowly representative of certain kinds of "Productions." The pulpit, again, from which sermons are spoken, represents published sermons, the kind of audial discourse (which is metonymically represented by the pulpit) being substantially similar to the published discourse that it represents; whereas the last words projected from the ladder represent, not only two kinds of publication, but two, both of which, political propaganda and poetry, are quite different from it. The ladder's representations, moreover, are, unlike the pulpit's, primarily metonymic. It is true that climbing the ladder can provide a metaphorical representation of a poet's reach upward toward a poetic climax or his life-long ascent toward creative competence; but the ladder also represents poetry because "it is a Preferment attained by transferring of Propriety, and a confounding of *Meum* and *Tuum*." Poets, that is, deserve to be hanged for theft. And the same—that is, their deserving to be hanged—may well hold true of political writers too, although that is admittedly *my* inference: what one gets or ought to get from inciting "Faction" is presented actually by a "Hiatus in Ms."

Within the second part of the Introduction are other—I can hardly say similar—cases of imperfect and unstable discursive connectedness. The list of deep works is itself a tissue of anomalies. The connotations of "Whittington and his Cat," especially if one knows this popular old tale, stand in rigid opposition to the author's description of it as "the Work of that Mysterious *Rabbi, Jehuda Hannasi,* containing a Defence of the *Gemara* of the *Jerusalem Misna,* and its just preference to that of *Babylon,* contrary to the vulgar Opinion." One produced by vulgar English culture who recalls the echoing refrain, "Turn again, Whittington, thrice lord mayor of London," will surely question—indeed, reject—all interest in conflicting mysteries of the exotic middle east. "The Wise Men of Goatham," similarly, unless the announced "*Appendice*" is itself a perversion, can hardly pass, as the Author claims, for "a Treatise of immense Erudition." The force of his own diction and the connotations of his figures, as has been widely noticed,[13] persistently oppose the Author's positions. We might take the "turning back of Time's hour-glass" as an adequate expression of literary immortality; but at some point in the development of this personification, when we are told that the Grub-street writers have "clipt [Time's] Wings, pared his nails, filed his Teeth . . . blunted his Scythe, and drawn the Hob-Nails out of his Shoes," we will surely resist. Its concrete details come to dominate the figure's conceptual value, and the immortal writers are reduced to officious handy men or, rather, to silly nuisances. Such contradictions litter the second part of the Introduction. In recounting his literary life, to give a final example, the Author first allows that his "Conscience [is] Thread-bare and ragged with perpetual turning" and soon afterwards, when this relatively detached tone changes to one of self pity, he insists that "his Conscience [is] void of Offense."

The Introduction is not, for all these discrepancies, a *mere* jumble: its elements, however discrepant, are always vivid; and its diversities, if never subject to resolution, are always dynamic. If we take its first part as argument, honoring its sense, the second part contradicts it; if we take it as an illustration of the second part's argument, it contradicts itself; but it provides, in either case, some demanding argumentation or some lively evidence. Even if we reject it as both argument and illustration, it provides enough incidental sparkle to justify the Grub-street claim of entertainment value. If we reject the Author's espousal of the number *three*, again, we become more aware of his comical, crack-brained presence; if we accept this espousal, we find an analytical intensification of awareness and reject his fourth machine, the theater, and his four forms of literature; if, however, we accept the theater, we again reject the number. Every assertion, every figure, and almost every substantial term in the Introduction, in short, presents a range of arguable connections with other of its elements although no connection is firm. In recognizing or establishing one connection or one set of connections the reader deserts or denies another; but every denial is caused by some contrary connection, so that the Introduction, although never firm, is never chaotic: it is a tissue of continual intellectual becoming and as such a mirror image of the Lucretian universe.

And what is true of the Introduction is true of the whole *Tale*, in both its large and its small measures, and especially of its most intense moment, Section IX, the Digression concerning Madness.

The Digression is essentially, if not evidently, concerned with the same contiguity in the intellectual community between individual genius and social discipleship to which the Introduction was devoted. But this broadscale similarity, like all the *Tale*'s resemblances, is mutable and inexact. The most obvious difference between these two sections is the change in emphasis that comes in the second part of the Digression, its turning from the geniuses, or madmen, to their discipleship; but even the first part, which is chiefly concerned, like the Introduction, with the geniuses, is seriously incongruent with that earlier section. Simplifying the case somewhat to accommodate this large focus, we can discern two correspondent bodies of public genius in the two sections: religious and philosophical. Like the Introduction, moreover, the Digression also focuses on a third kind of genius. But instead of poetic-and-political genius represented by the ladder, the Digression presents imperialists, kings who wish to establish, not a society of proselytes, but "New Empires by Conquest."

The first pages of the Digression develop at some length this relatively impertinent kind of genius. Its difference from the other kinds does not add an enrichment, an extension, presenting a third, a fourth (or a fifth) kind of widely effective discursive power to that of philosophers and preachers. This madness is, rather, distractingly different from them, having no discursive ramifications at all. These madmen do not attempt to rise in a crowd or to sway an assembled auditory with cant or visions; their larger effects, rather, are "to take and lose towns; beat armies and be beaten; drive Princes out of their Dominions; fright children from their Bread and Butter; burn, lay waste, plunder, dragoon, massacre Subject and Stranger, Friend and Foe, Male and Female." This difference makes imperial madness seriously inappropriate to the Author's argument. He says he wishes to differentiate between the particular origins of the individual madness exhibited variously by "*Alexander the Great* [imperial madness], *Jack of Leyden* [religious madness] and *Monsieur Des Cartes* [philosophical madness]"; but this is not, as may be suggested by the great hiatus that occurs in the text where such an explanation was introduced, really the significant point of difference. The important difference is in the material effects of the three kinds of madmen: Calvin and Descartes, as the author elsewhere shows, persuaded multitudes by the eloquent dissemination of their delusions and inaugurated parties of belief and thought; Louis XIV and Alexander the Great merely butchered on a grand scale. The "blessings of

Conquest" are, then, despite the author's emphatic parallelism, seriously different from those of "Systems [and] Belief."

This grotesque irrelevancy significantly lightens Swift's satire of learning and religion, it seems to me: even while we deplore the effects of religious and philosophical madness, we must prefer the world they organize to one overrun with the madness of military conquest.[14] This apparent irrelevancy thus enforces the suggestion implicit in the Lucretian elements of the *Tale* and may further reconcile us to the present religious and intellectual organizations—bad as they are. I notice, to enforce this point, that the primary examples of military madness are two French kings, Henry IV and Louis XIV. Things are bad in England, as the visitor from Australia might recognize; but not as bad as they could be. English parties in religion and philosophy, if they can be confined to the absurd contiguity between the elevated and their auditory, as Swift describes this (and if a company of sensible Christian people can be maintained), are really quite tolerable. As Swift knew, the madness of a Catholic king or a Puritan parliamentarian could easily be transformed into the madness of conquest. Looking back and looking across the channel on this more brutal energy, as Swift implicitly invites us to do, serves thus, perhaps, as both a relief and a warning.

The material effects of religious and philosophical madness despite their fortunate difference from imperial madness are, of course, bad enough, as the exposition of "Happiness" in the Digression makes evident. The Introduction was chiefly focused on the eloquently mad, explaining how these pretenders to wisdom and inspiration exalt themselves above a credulous world. (Section VIII, on "the Aeolists," enriches this aspect of the case describing not "Wisdom," as in the Introduction, but its religious counterpart, "Enthusiasm" or "Inspiration.") The Digression is focused primarily on vulgar credulity. Here Swift develops with painful intensity the dispersive force of madness, explaining its enormous social success in terms both of resemblance and contiguity. Briefly, one way the mad organize a party of the credulous is the way one vibrating musical string sets in motion others of the same pitch: if a speaker, no matter how crazy his discourse, addresses the right audience, that is, an audience of similar convictions, he will enjoy the persuasive success Swift represents. Another way the mad organize their auditory is by describing either a splendid future (thus imposing on the auditory's understanding) or an embellished surface (thus imposing on its senses). In this case we can infer society's response—knowing its credulity—from the future glory or the present sparkle in the mad-man's address.

The discrepancy between emphatically parallel categories and the shifting understanding implicit in such discrepancy is evident throughout the Digression. The difference between the kings and the other two categories of madness provides a relatively easy example. To examine a more demanding one, consider the parallel "experiments" reported to defend the way the mad befuddle the senses of the credulous, experiments by which the Author attempts to demonstrate that "in most Corporeal Beings . . . the Outside [is] infinitely preferable to the In."[15] The illustrative similarity between the two experiments is enforced by the parallel temporal particularization with which they are introduced: "Last Week . . . Yesterday."

> Last Week I saw a Woman *flay'd,* and you will hardly believe, how much it altered her Person for the worse. Yesterday I ordered the Carcass of a Beau to be stript in my presence; when we were all amazed to find so many unsuspected Faults under one Suit of Cloaths: Then I laid open his *Brain,* his HEART, and his *Spleen;* But I plainly perceived at every Operation, that the farther we proceeded, we found the Defects encrease upon us in Number and Bulk.

The horrific quality especially of the first of these experiments has usually riveted the attention of readers and critics and destroyed both the intellectual detachment and the analytical attentiveness that the Author requires, thus compromising the discursive development in the cause of which the two experiments were introduced. Maintaining the appropriately scientific attitude and observing the argumentative whole, we see that the parallelism between "a Woman *flay'd*" and "the . . . stript . . . Carcass of a Beau," although evident, is seriously inexact.

It would be improved if the second member were revised to "a Beau stript." In both cases then the substance under attention would receive primary emphasis and the action, by which its surface was experimentally penetrated, would immediately follow. The beau's death, if we thus balance human male and female, is not relevant to the case; a living beau, that is, a fop sporting his characteristic surfaces, would fulfill the philosophical conditions, presenting a vivid parallel to the living woman and her characteristic surfaces. The statements, however, even if they are refined in this way, are still very different from one another, since "Woman" and "Beau" are themselves very different terms. A feminine person finely dressed or stark naked fits under the category "Woman"; so does such a person from any historic age, any race, or any social class. "Beau," on the other hand, is remarkably narrow: to qualify, a man must be, not only dressed, but finely dressed; and he must enjoy some social standing in English—or maybe French—society of the seventeenth or eighteenth century.[16] A closer resemblance would be that between coquette-and-beau or woman-and-man. In those cases the resemblance might be too close, admittedly, for the two cases to constitute two "experiments," especially if the same verbal, "stript" or "flay'd," were used for each case. A coquette stripped and a beau stripped, that is to say, might merely duplicate the point. The intellectually appropriate parallel, then, should perhaps be between a woman flayed and a beau stripped.

The difference between these two cases, nevertheless, would be so great as to compromise the argument: the indicated offense to the woman would be pain and possibly death, depending on the interpretation of "flay'd"; that to the beau, mere embarrassment. (The extended attention to the beau's carcass can be seen as an attempt by the Author to bring the two cases into a closer resemblance, answering death with death.) The term *"flay'd"* is, of course, part of the problem. It may be a hyperbolical form of "whipped"; understood in this way, it more nearly balances the emotional effect of "stript," constituting a similar kind of embarrassment. But this understanding, that is, the leaving of most of the woman's skin in place, would queer the parallel substantively and ruinously weaken the experiment: whipping would reveal very little of the woman's inside, very little, that is, of what lay inside her whole skin. "Flay'd," however, is more precisely and more normally a term for total removal of the skin and thus congruent with "stript," which represents total removal of the clothes. "Woman *flay'd*," understood in this way, is, however, strongly metaphorical, the woman being reduced to a fox or a rabbit or a victim of butchery; and this puts the term "Woman" under a strain to which nothing in the second experiment is quite analogous. Although "Carcass" undermines "Beau," it hardly reduces it beneath "man" to "animal"; whereas that is the effect of *"flay'd"* on "Woman" and—in case we missed it, as Swift seems to have feared—on "Person."[17]

As this difference between the two cases should suggest, there is a larger difference, as well, one between each case in turn and the general contention that they illustrate, that is, again, that the outside of natural substances is preferable to the in. Does the flaying of a woman reveal a womanly inside less attractive than the womanly outside, as the experiment should demonstrate, or does it reveal an altogether new substance, reducing the living woman to a dead animal and thus destroying the natural integrities on which the Author wishes to comment? Does not such treatment—like the treatment of babies in a "A Modest Proposal"—simply disallow the apprehension of human personality, making an altogether different general point or complex of points from the one the Author intended? "Beau" was reduced, on the other hand, only to "Man" (a human corpse) by "Carcass." But is not that reduction excessive in its own way? Once the human body is pronounced dead, all its pretensions—surely all those to beauty and acclaim—become irrelevant. (I recall the frightful ambition enunciated by the youthful hero of a naturalistic novel of the fifties: "Live hard, die young, and have a good-looking corpse.") The "unsuspected Faults," which the Author goes on to reveal in the carcass, are undoubtedly excessive, formally speaking, to any analysis of a beau. The beau's finery was not meant to hide deformity but—rather like the mask at a play—to cover mere nature. The naked man alive or dead, is thus the proper and the sufficient exposure of the "Beau."

This inappropriate dissection of the beau may be, however, appropriate to a different general argument from that in support of which the two experiments were produced, an argument the Author *now* states: from these experiments he concludes, not merely that the outside of things is preferable to the inside:

I justly formed this Conclusion to my self; That whatever Philosopher or Projector can find an Art to sodder and patch up the Flaws and Imperfections of Nature,[18] will deserve much better of Mankind and teach us a more useful Science, than that so much in present Esteem, of widening and exposing them.

This is apparently a more appropriate conclusion to the revelation of the carcass's constitutional defects, but I must question it too: what is needed is not a cosmetician, but a doctor or, more truly, an undertaker. Not only does this new point leave the explicitly contested generality behind, therefore, but it requires in itself some serious scrutiny. The best alternative to stripping or flaying or dissecting may not be soddering and patching up, although such faults and defects as the Author found within a certain beau's carcass might indicate this to him; but something quite different from this. One alternative, one which Martin's rediscovery of his coat might recommend, is a lively acceptance and a gracious adjustment to things in their mere normality, to a woman, for example, in one kind or another of her ordinary, un-adorned condition.

Such dynamically irreconcilable differences as these, which are evident throughout the *Tale*, disallow wholeness not merely in the human society to which it refers, but, as my own analytical efforts may suggest, in the individual minds of its readers as well. The common faith and the common sense that are variously embedded as cultural desiderata at no point actually crystallize, at no point are allowed to crystallize, either in the Author's matter or in a reader's mind. No tissue of metaphoric or metonymic connections in the *Tale*, large or small, allows the chance for a comprehensive understanding any more than it allows the hope of a coherent society. The *Tale* is, as I have suggested earlier, a literary analogue of the material universe. This is not to say, how-ever, that the *Tale* is chaotic—whatever the state of its reader's understanding may be. Its separate indications of likeness and contiguity are sufficiently enforced so that every atom of the dis-course is attached somewhere—somewheres. Parts and particles rebound from one kind of relationship to hook into another, shift-ing from relevance to relevance, but never simply falling into the void of nonsense. The discursive mass never quite disintegrates. And the body of awareness that we may cautiously assemble, as our minds adjust to such turbulent circumstances, is this: that the great cultural unities, which can be glimpsed now and again, will never exist in the material world; but that we must endure—and perhaps improve from time to time—the absurdly deficient institutions that we have. This state of things, despite its recalci-trant imperfections and its incurable mutability, is, in contrast with the threatening chaos of strictly atomic purposes and colli-sions that Hobbes and Donne and Swift all recognized, at least something we can laugh at.

*   *   *

In the *Essay Concerning Human Understanding*, which was pub-lished about ten years before Swift composed the *Tale*, Locke pre-sented a paradigm of language that precisely conformed to an external world of restless material things such as that projected by Swift's Author. The ends of linguistic discourse, were three: "to make known one man's thoughts or ideas to another . . . to do it with as much ease and quickness as possible . . . and thereby to convey the knowledge of things." These "things," as Locke's distinction between "ideas" and "things" makes clear, are material things in the external world. The discursive chain that Locke's pronouncement indicates involves a writer (like Swift's Author) in establishing a linkage, first, between material things and his own ideas of them and, second, between his ideas and his words; and a reader (or listener) in making a correspondent linkage of words to ideas and of ideas back to material things. The Author, whose allegories point insistently outward to the material world, assured his "Learned . . . Reader" that he had provided him with "sufficient Matter to employ his Speculations for the rest of his Life."

Locke apparently had mixed feelings about this communicative chain. The neat statement of principles just quoted suggests confidence and, indeed, complacency: if a writer is only quick and easy, Locke seems to feel, the passage between his own knowledge of material things and his respondent's should be smooth and reliable. Elsewhere in the same book of the *Essay* in which he has rung off this formula for linguistic communication, however, his tone is different. Consider, for instance, this reference to the first link in the chain: "Because men would not be thought to talk barely of their own imaginations, but of things as really they are; therefore they often suppose their words to stand also for the reality of things." And he is sometimes almost as skeptical of the link between words and ideas: "though words, as they are used by men, can properly and immediately signify nothing but the ideas that are in the mind of the speaker [he observes]; yet [speakers] in their thoughts give them a secret reference to two other things"—that is, of course, to ideas in the respondent and to things in the external world. Locke's skepticism about the separate links in his own communicative chain has here led him to skepticism about the whole linguistic enterprise; and as the great *Essay* in which these statements are embedded shows, he had good reason for this skepticism. The *Tale* may no doubt be seen at one point and another to confirm such a feeling.

In the *Principles* (1710) and the *Dialogues* (1713) that Berkeley published ten or fifteen years after Swift composed the *Tale* and ten or fifteen years before he produced *Gulliver's Travels*, this friend and colleague of Swift worked out a radical simplification of Locke's chain. By turning ideas into things, as he sometimes expressed it, Berkeley formulated the following system of linguistic discourse: he described in a writer or speaker one link only, between ideas and words; and in a respondent, correspondingly, a single link between words and ideas. This linguistic representation of Berkeley's perceptualism, it should be noticed, reduces both the complexity and the presumption of Locke's proposal. Locke's paradigm is circular, leading from certain external things through two sets of ideas and words, as just indicated, back to the very same things. Berkeley contents himself, on the other hand—in accordance with his philosophical position, of course—with two relatively similar sets of ideas, the writer translating his own ideas into words, the reader turning from those shared words to ideas of his which, although they may and should closely resemble the writer's ideas, are strictly his own. Both writer and reader have their separate responsibilities: the writer to represent his ideas as clearly as the conventions of language will allow; the reader to entertain and judge for himself those ideas of his which the writer's language has occasioned in him.

There were two especially troublesome problems in Locke's communicative chain, as Berkeley considered this, both of which he believed that his discursive paradigm abolished. One of these is the discrepancy between one's perceptions of material things, as entertained by the five senses, and the things themselves, a discrepancy accommodated throughout the history of materialism with the doctrine, to which I referred briefly in chapter 1, of primary-and-secondary qualities. Berkeley confronted this problem at length in the first of his *Dialogues*. The other, the discrepancy between the incorrigible particularity of things and the necessary generality of words, he tackled in the Introduction to his *Principles*. Whatever the philosophical merits of Berkeley's arguments against these two Lockean positions may be, they constitute tremendous benefits to the interconnected activities of literature and, most immediately, to the responsive activity a reader practices in trying to make sense of Captain Gulliver's discursive activity.

Locke denied that perceptions of color, sound, taste, or smell represent anything in the external world; only touch, which acquaints us with size and shape and mass, tells the truth. Such a teaching, seriously entertained, prompts a writer to believe that in describing even such persistent human interests as colors and smells and sounds he is not dealing with reality and thus that such concerns deserve little or no attention. Since my horse, according to Locke, is not really grey or sorrel—nor any other color, of course—it hardly matters what color I attribute to it; since the smell of my stable in no way represents the stable itself, being merely the effect of certain insensible particles somehow or other emanating from it, I need not recognize the seeming difference in smell between that and my house. In describing my horse as grey and in distinguishing between the smells of my house and my stable, I would not be telling a respondent anything about the real, the material constituency of my possessions. But when Berkeley denied that any perceptual qualities inhere in matter and argued that all alike were entertained by the mind, he abolished the distinction that makes sound and color and smell "secondary," and he established all the contents of sensation, all perceptions, on the same level of reality, that is, on the level of total reality. Every sense impression, he taught, is neither more nor less than the impression it is. A writer who was concerned with reality, therefore, faced the same responsibility, that is, an absolute responsibility, in describing any and all elements of his experience. His entire tissue of experience was his reality. In describing it, a writer was not, like a disciple of Locke, presenting a mixture of real and imputed qualities and thus a dubious image of some world lying altogether beyond him; rather, he was describing reality. Berkeley confidently called this reality "Nature."

If, however, this reality was strictly a writer's own, and if he must endure full responsibility for it, the reader, who drew his own ideas from the words he shared with any writer, must endure his own full responsibility as well. Because he interpreted the words he read and translated these into ideas, the ideas, which enjoyed no support from any material realm, were obviously and inescapably his ideas, his reality. This consequence of Berkeleian immaterialism pervades both the *Dialogues* and the *Principles*. In the Introduction to the *Principles* Berkeley thus advised his reader:

> Whoever therefore designs to read the following sheets, I entreat him to make my words the occasion of his own thinking, and endeavor to attain the same train of thoughts in reading, that I had in writing them. By this means it will be easy for him to discover the truth or falsity of what I say. He will be out of all danger of being deceived by my words, and I do not see how he can be led into an error by considering his own naked undisguised ideas.

There are a couple of observations that must be made about this candid attribution to the reader of the full responsibility for his own understanding. First, the word "same" here is, as Berkeley well knew, a courteous overstatement: at most the reader might entertain ideas of his own that were closely analogous to those which the writer had originally consulted. Second, the confidence in perfect understanding that Berkeley expresses is painfully off the mark, as he himself was soon to find out. Readers resisted

Berkeley's words bitterly, and held him altogether responsible for teachings they absolutely refused to acknowledge: Swift would have understood this. Berkeley has, nevertheless, indicated exactly the right attitude for a reader of *Gulliver's Travels* to assume or, at least, to attempt. The reader of the *Travels* should hold himself responsible for the naked, undisguised ideas Gulliver's discourse arouses in him and judge both them and himself accordingly—no matter how vexatious that may prove.

This point is reinforced by Berkeley's correction of a second troublesome doctrine of Locke's, that concerning linguistic generalization. Locke taught that the mind composes general ideas by abstraction from the concrete particulars of experience and that words represent these strictly synthetic properties. Once again, then, according to Locke's understanding of nature and language, a writer simply cannot truly represent reality. The generality of terms stands necessarily at odds to the particularity of things. And there is standing between the two, moreover, a tissue of abstract ideas, to which the words refer, a tissue that is itself remote from the concrete particulars of experience. Such a teaching further prompts the writer to be vague and careless and to blame any failure of understanding on the impossibility of the communicative conditions. A reader, correspondingly, who is no more able than a writer to move from the generalities of language to the particularity of things, will accept solace for his confusions in the imperfection of language. I am not here describing Locke's own sentiments, of course, but the prevailing effects of his materialism, as Berkeley recognized and opposed them. Berkeley's simplification, once again, both makes communication possible—as Berkeley described it—and focuses all responsibility for the fulfillment of this possibility on the writer and the reader.

Ideas, that is, primarily sensations, Berkeley taught, are strictly particular. There is no such thing, no such idea, contrary to what Locke suggested, as that of a triangle "which is, neither oblique nor rectangle, equilateral, equicrural, nor scalenon, but all and none of these at once."[19] There cannot be the idea of a horse, again, that is at once sorrel and grey. According to Berkeley, consequently, a word becomes general merely by standing indiscriminately for any one of a number of particular ideas. The term "horse" is general in our linguistic usage by standing indiscriminately for a large number of particular impressions, each of them of an equine cast, certain ones of which may be grey, others sorrel, and others of still different colors. More adequately, the term refers back to such a congeries in the writer's (or speaker's) mind;

and forward to a quite different congeries, but one the separate cases of which similarly conform to some equine awareness or other, in the reader's mind. A writer who had a sufficient command of his own equine ideas would use the term *horse*, within the limits of linguistic efficacy, with adequate precision, perhaps describing "a small, bay horse." A reader, correspondingly, having his own stock of ideas, would entertain that one—or one of those—that "a small, bay horse" raised in his consciousness. He would then, if he followed Berkeley, judge the "naked undisguised ideas" of his own that reading about "a small, bay horse" had aroused in him, enduring the sole or at least the primary responsibility for these ideas.

Gulliver's Travels is a dramatization of such a perceptual model of literary communication. Virtually its complete realm of reference is "remote" from normal human life and experience, so remote, indeed, that an Irish bishop, as Swift wrote Pope, professed that "he hardly believed a word of it." In the *Travels* Swift has presented a discourse that derives strictly from the avowed experience of Captain Gulliver and strictly appeals to the reflections on that by its reader: this work has no other sanction. Such a remoteness of reference cuts the book off from what Swift's anxious friends described as "particular reflections,"[20] forcing the reader to decide strictly about the ideas herewith aroused in him and rendering all external applications, all efforts to reach out into the material world, adventitious or, at least, secondary. This strongly urged sufficiency of Gulliver's discourse—its detachment from events in England or Ireland, say—is enforced by the penumbrae of mendacity and madness with which Swift has variously hedged Gulliver's whole story and, especially in the narrator's direct references to European society, by what both Swift and Gulliver recognize as Gulliver's tendency "to extenuate the Vices and magnify the Virtues of Mankind." The *Travels* is, as the bishop said, "full of improbable lies." The sufficiency of the discourse is assured, finally, by its expository mode, its emerging, even when encountering events which once produced a sense of excitement, as the calm, circumstantial recollection of an irrevocable past. The *Travels* is in its totality an account of events, that is to say, which a reader may judge with no feelings of physical involvement, calculating with confident detachment the train of particular ideas it raises immediately in his own mind.

Each reader brings to the *Travels* his own stock of ideas answering to such general words as *great, small, human,* and *horse*. He becomes acquainted here and here only with the general words

struldbrugg, yahoo and *houyhnhnm* and with the particular representations of the creatures (or, more rigorously, the impressions)
from which these words have derived and to which they refer.
His unavoidable activity simply in reading the *Travels* is to test
the "naked, undisguised ideas" herewith aroused in him by these
words.[21] If he is an appropriately Berkeleian reader, he will give
individual attention to the narrator's complacent assertion that
he could "easily creep" into his Lilliputian quarters; to the "Activity" with which he responded to the Brobdingnagian cow dung;
to the "Honour" he attempted to derive from his conduct toward
the Brobdingnagian monkey; first to the charge of adultery raised
against the narrator in Lilliput and then to the response he made
to this charge. Such a reader will continually struggle to identify
and to judge the train of ideas such trains of language raise in
his mind, ideas he can never attribute to and thus never blame
on an external nature of things. He may reject all those ideas he
can attribute to Gulliver and/or condemn as foolish; he must accept responsibility for the rest.

*   *   *

None of the chapter headings, which occur in a group at the
beginning of the *Travels* and are also deployed, each in its proper
place, at the top of every chapter, gives an adequate indication of
the coming events, except possibly for the suggestiveness of the
odd names of Gulliver's hosts. These headings, although strictly
correct in general, might, except for the names, introduce the
particular exposition of an altogether credible and, indeed, ordinary travel story. Thus pressing into the details of each chapter
presents a contrast that illuminates the remote particularity of
Gulliver's adventures. One heading announces, for example, that
Gulliver "is made a Prisoner, and carried up the Country" in
Lilliput; another, that he "is seized by one of the Natives, and
carried to a Farmer's House" in Brobdingnag. The verb "carried"
is, however, ludicrously different in its particular meaning in the
two cases as a consultation of the different chapters shows.
"Seized" is comically apt for Gulliver's apprehension in Brobdingnag, as one comes to see; "made a Prisoner" is, on the other
hand, hardly indicative of Gulliver's first contact with the might
of Lilliput as one will come imaginatively to understand this.[22]
"The Author instrumental in saving from fire the rest of the [Lilli-
putian] Palace" makes a nice retrospective joke, especially with
what we may come to see as its play on the term "instrumental."

Or consider this heading to one of the Brobdingnagian chapters: "He makes a Proposal of much Advantage to the King; which is rejected." How strange that reads until one looks back from the particular advantages of the proposal Gulliver actually made. This diversity between the general headings and the particular developments of the chapters gives a recurrent emphasis to the stress between the generality of language and the particularity of experience—or, as Gulliver sometimes calls it, "adventure"—that Swift has occasioned throughout the *Travels* in the mind of his reader.

To examine this point of stress, I will focus on the voyage to the land of the houyhnhnms and test the three general terms, two of them unique to Gulliver, that stand at the center of its particular adventures: these terms are *yahoo*, *houyhnhnm*, and *human*.[23] By sifting the first and to some extent the second chapter of Gulliver's account, the relevant portions of which are presented as both clear-sighted and philosophically significant, I can establish definitions of these terms that have the virtues, first, of distinguishing sharply between them and, second, of enjoying—or so I hope it will prove—wide agreement. Here, then, are my definitions:

    I. *human:* a creature
        (A) of anthropoid physique
        (B) of sufficient intellect
            (1) to employ a language
            (2) to organize a society
            (3) to use tools for physical convenience;
    II. *yahoo:* a creature
        (A) of anthropoid physique
        (B) of insufficient intellect
            (1) to employ a language
            (2) to organize a society
            (3) to use tools;
   III. *houyhnhnm:* a creature
        (A) of equine physique
        (B) of sufficient intellect
            (1) to employ a language
            (2) to organize a society
            (3) to use tools for physical convenience.

Generally speaking, *human* resembles *yahoo* physically and not intellectually; whereas it resembles *houyhnhnm* intellectually and not physically: each of the three being, however, substantially distinct from the others. There is no doubt some warrant in the *Travels* for making *human* a sub-category of *yahoo* and, contrariwise, *yahoo* a sub-category of *human*. I would, however, suggest, as a preliminary caution, that although *tiger* may be a sub-category of *cat* or *shark*, of *fish*, one would be well advised, before plunging into a dark woods or a murky pool where one may expect to find cats and fish, respectively, to make the kind of study of those situations that I propose now to make of the land of the houyhnhnms.

Gulliver simply carries his anthropoid form, his discursive and social capacities, and his hanger (not to speak of his garments with their various fastenings) into Houyhnhnmland. That the roaring and howling anthropoids soon to be called "*Yahoos*" lack the use of what Gulliver describes in the letter to Sympson as "a sort of Jabber," that they merely "herd" together, and that they lack tools is dramatically declared in Gulliver's first encounter with them. Their "perfect human Figure," admittedly, *he* is first forced to recognize in the second chapter, in which he is placed experimentally, as it were, in comparative proximity with a yahoo. In the first chapter, during which the reader may have decided on the strength of Gulliver's meticulous description that yahoos have an anthropoid physique, Gulliver found their shape on the one hand "singular" and on the other hand "deformed." "Deformed from what?" one may have asked. At all events, by the middle of the second chapter, at which point Gulliver has declared the physical similarity between *human* and *yahoo*, the elements of my definition have been forcefully assembled. The involvement of the houyhnhnms, whose experimental efforts were described as "not unlike those of a Philosopher, when he would attempt to solve some new and difficult Phaenomenon," underscores the definitive value of these early experiences.

The houyhnhnms, which Gulliver studies with something like the same intellectual concentration they focus on him, judging them at one point to be sorcerers and modifying this by degrees as houyhnhnm evidence mounts up, are made philosophical objects too in the first two chapters. Gulliver, who has just been through a looking-glass confrontation with a yahoo, goes through a like routine with a houyhnhnm. In the first case the yahoo "lifted up his fore Paw" toward Gulliver; in the second Gulliver reached his hand out to stroke the houyhnhnm's neck: mirroring processes of examination that give the two situations comparable definitive force.[24] Gulliver's raising his hand to stroke the houyhnhnm, "using the common Style and Whistle of Jockies," declares the houyhnhnm's equine shape; it was clear enough, however, from the first moment when Gulliver saw "a Horse walking softly in the Field." Both houyhnhnm sociability and discourse also emerge in the first chapter when a second horse appears and the two, after a courteous striking of right hoofs, begin "to confer together" as "Friends" in a language that "expressed the Passions very plainly." This early description of the houyhnhnms' tongue may present a problem since, as Gulliver learns, houyhnhnms have in fact no passions to express. But the language is nevertheless quite evident as Gulliver shows by himself straightway beginning to learn it. Significantly the words he first practices are *yahoo* and *houyhnhnm*, the two new terms that Gulliver and his reader must chiefly attempt to understand. In the next chapter, when Gulliver enters a houyhnhnm "House," he discovers some houyhnhnms busy "in domestic Business," notices the "elegance" with which their "Rooms" are furnished, and receives some milk "in Earthen and Wooden Vessels," from which we may infer the houyhnhnm capacity to use tools and begin to discover, perhaps, that in this capacity they lag far behind the human race. The elements of the definition of *houyhnhnm* are also evident, therefore, before the end of the second chapter.

I begin testing the scope of these definitions by recalling the young yahoo female who no doubt found in Gulliver a perfect yahoo figure. Although Gulliver did not instinctively recognize a perfect human figure in her, to say the least of it, he eventually neglected his own sense and took hers as authoritative. His first yahoo contacts followed the same pattern: immediate, unquestioned discrimination was followed by an expressed identification. When the houyhnhnms put Gulliver next to a yahoo, however, he acknowledged the resemblance with horror—surely the sign of some reservation in the identification—and noted certain small differences in face and feet that suggest vast differences in physical conduct. When Gulliver actually described naked savage people, human beings, that is, of the least sophisticated kind, on the island he visited after leaving Houyhnhnmland, he immediately identified them as "Men, Women and Children round a fire." Although his mind can be led to emphasize the physical similarity between himself and all human beings, on the one hand, and yahoos, on the other, then, these two kinds of anthropoid nevertheless differ in evident and unmistakable ways. No one who first sees a yahoo, we may infer, would expect him—like the first human creature Gulliver saw in Lilliput—to have a bow-and-arrows.

The resemblance is there, however, in much of the body, the disposition of the limbs, and even the kinds of hair. Humans and yahoos are also both omnivores, although the difference in diet is enough to allow Gulliver to maintain some distance at table—as he no doubt does. Yahoos eat roots of all kinds—like yams and radishes and potatoes, perhaps—but no oats; they devour several kinds of meat: beef, dog, ass, and cat—all quite raw, of course. Although Gulliver catches an occasional fowl or rabbit—with "Springes made of *Yahoos* hairs"—and cooks them for his supper, his main fare is oats and milk, houyhnhnm food. Soon after seeing an old houyhnhnm eat a warm porridge of oats boiled in milk, Gulliver made an oatmeal cake for himself which he likewise ate warm with milk. Gulliver prepared his food with some care, while the yahoos merely snatch and gnaw. There is nevertheless enough physical similarity to describe both humans and yahoos—along with Brobdingnagian monkeys and Brobdingnagians—as anthropoid specimens. But the exact degree of resemblance is indeterminable, seeming sometimes to Gulliver and the houyhnhnms to be perfect and at other times to Gulliver, if not to the houyhnhnms, to be too slight to acknowledge. The houyhnhnms' naming of the yahoo appendages that correspond to human hands "forefeet" suggests that yahoos normally scramble on all fours although Gulliver once remarks that "they often stood on their hind Feet." When Gulliver uses yahoo skins to make his sails one feels the resemblances more strongly, I take it, and directs his satiric sense that way; when Gulliver accepts the yahoo female as an authority for likeness or labels himself *yahoo*, one endures the strong pull of the differences.

The degree of likeness between human and houyhnhnm intellect is also both various and subject to interpretation. I note the closeness by recognizing the remarkable degree to which Gulliver fit into houyhnhnm society. He quickly learned the language, often took part in conversations, and in time found a place—if a humble one as "Fellow-Servant" of the Sorrel Nag—in a household. He held many talks with the houyhnhnm Master. He was admitted into wider reaches of houyhnhnm society as well—if under somewhat insulting conditions—and, unlike his fellow servants (not to speak of any yahoo), participated in discussions among its more elevated ranks. Gulliver's technological skills were much greater than those of his hosts, of course. The houyhnhnms had fire to heat their oatmeal, flint knives, clay and wooden bowls and extremely simple houses (or, as I would call them, stables). They lacked the wheel and were pulled along in sledges.[25] (I have never been able, by the way, to imagine four yahoos, as reported by Gulliver, actually pulling a full-grown horse in such a vehicle.) Gulliver, who brought his metal hanger and his complicated clothes along with him to Houyhnhnmland, developed "Springes . . . of *Yahoos* hairs" and made "two Chairs" (why two?); he also repaired his clothes. He both designed and built his own "*Indian* Canoo" and furnished it with four paddles (why four?). He thus seems like a technologically advanced houyhnhnm or what one might call a "wonderful" houyhnhnm. The houyhnhnms themselves celebrated his departure from Houyhnhnmland much as human beings mark the departures of their great explorers, with public honors (of a kind) and personal regrets.

The difference between houyhnhnm and human intellect can best be indicated by recalling western culture both as it is in our experience and as Gulliver and the Master apprehend it. The English language, first of all, is much more complex in form and extensive in diction than the houyhnhnm tongue, containing ways of expressing doubt, hope, opinion, and passion as well as facts; and requiring terms for an enormously wider range of activities than the houyhnhnms ever conceived. This difference, or so the convert to houyhnhnmism would claim, constitutes the measure of human depravity. Speaking with anthropological detachment, however, I suggest that each language is broadly adequate to the various socio-political needs of its users. Since "vast Numbers of our People are compelled to seek their Livelihood by Begging, Robbing, Stealing, Cheating, Pimping, Forswearing, Flattering, Suborning, Forging, Gaming, Lying, Fawning, Hectoring, Voting, Scribling, Star-gazing, Poysoning, Whoring, Canting, Libelling, Free-thinking and the like Occupations"—not to speak of many perhaps more respectable activities not mentioned by Gulliver such as teaching, peddling, sewing, preaching, printing, painting, sailing, horse-training, and hunting, we need all these terms. The houyhnhnms, of course, do not. Both cultures are centered, however, in family life and responsibility; both present socio-political hierarchies with upper and lower classes; both depend on large-scale organization with a representative assembly. The two are thus similar enough for a human being to accommodate himself both to the houyhnhnm language and to houyhnhnm ways and to describe these to the rest of us so that we can judge and, where relevant, apply them.

That the houyhnhnm way of life is preferable at every point of difference I deny. I personally like clothes, French cuisine (which the houyhnhnms—and Swift?—would abhor), travel, and books—despite all their disadvantages. And after some consideration, I find that I cannot modify my way of adjusting to a death in my family so as to conform to houyhnhnm stoicism, nor to the birth of two offspring of the same sex so as to achieve houyhnhnm social economy. I simply reject the example Gulliver offers of the houyhnhnm response to procreation and the younger generation:

> When the Matron *Houyhnhnms* have produced one of each Sex, they no longer accompany with their Consorts, except they lose one of their Issue by some Casualty, which very seldom happens: But in such a Case they meet again; or when the like Accident befalls a Person, whose Wife is past bearing, some other Couple bestows on him one of their own Colts, and they go together a second Time, until the Mother be pregnant.
>
> ....
>
> [At the grand assembly] the Regulation of Children is settled: As for instance, if a *Houyhnhnm* hath two Males, he changeth one of them with another who hath two Females: and when a Child hath been lost by any Casualty, where the Mother is past Breeding, it is determined what Family in the District shall breed another to supply the Loss.

Nor can I give my support to Gulliver's recommendation that humankind should imitate the houyhnhnms in the nurture and rearing of the young:

> In educating the Youth of both Sexes, their Method is admirable, and highly deserveth our Imitation. These are not suffered to taste a Grain of *Oats*, except upon certain Days, till Eighteen years old; nor *Milk*, but very rarely; and in Summer they graze two Hours in the Morning, and as many in the Evening, which their Parents likewise observe; but the Servants are not allowed above half that Time; and a great Part of the Grass is brought home, which they eat at the most convenient Hours, when they can be best spared from Work.

I am determined to keep my own children, no matter how excessive in their number or unbalanced in their sexes they may be; I will be—have been—fond of each of them in special, personal ways; and I will raise them according to the traditions of humankind and my own best lights. I will not even consider denying them oats or milk for the first eighteen years of life, nor of regulating their grazing at all. And if one dies, I will mourn him as my nature prompts me to mourn. There is no evidence that Gulliver differed from me in this: he never seems to have tried any such houyhnhnm practices on his family as he here recommends despite the fact that he was, like me, excessively encumbered with offspring. Each culture, then, the houyhnhnm and ours has a body of practices and a language to fulfill its own nature and its own situation. And these situations are, for all their differences, close enough—both of them being organizations of linguistically capable mammals—so that they can be compared in many ways.

Before actually making comparisons and thus testing my general definitions against the particulars of Gulliver's account of things in Houyhnhnmland, I must recognize and, at least for now, set aside the traditional notion that humans are somewhat superior to yahoos and somewhat inferior to houyhnhnms—a notion that the placing of Gulliver's domicile in Houyhnhnmland and certain abstract houyhnhnm judgments seem to support. This notion has been challenged by Donald Keesey, who points out several ways in which humans are significantly worse or lower than yahoos.[26] This would mean, perhaps, that wherever traditionalists came upon the word *human*, they would argue for such a formulation as "wonderful" or "gentle" *yahoo*; and that Keesey would substitute something like "odious" *yahoo*. My definitions will not allow either of these moves, of course, since *yahoo* does not contain the capacities of speech, tools, or true sociability. No modification, neither "wonderful" nor "odious," can bridge the substantive difference between *human* and *yahoo* except, of course, for such expressions as "speaking, sociable, and technically gifted," which would simply contradict the definitions and the weight of the particular evidence supporting them.

No identification, no substitution of different terms, seems to me to be justified. Although humankind may resemble yahoos very closely at certain points, as Swift once suggested to Thomas Sheridan, the categories are sufficiently different so that every substitution must be seriously inexact. When, for example, Gulliver describes himself to the Portuguese seamen—in Portuguese—as "a poor *Yahoo*," he has, by definition, contradicted himself or, as he would put it, said the thing which was not since yahoos do not possess the linguistic capacity to say anything: they only howl and roar. One who speaks must be either a houyhnhnm, as Gulliver's accent and many aspects of his conduct toward the Portuguese seamen proclaim him to be, or a human, "a poor Englishman," say, as he had informed the first linguistically gifted creatures that he met on his arrival in Houyhnhnmland. One may test this case most precisely, perhaps, by substituting the definition of *yahoo* in the proper place: "I am a poor naked anthropoid, unable either to speak or to make such things as boats and clothing."

Consider, again, Gulliver's refusal to wear any of Pedro de Mendez's garments on the grounds that he would abhor "to cover myself with anything that had been on the Back of a *Yahoo*"— worn on the back, that is to say, of a naked anthropoid creature. Gulliver's attitude here reflects that of the houyhnhnms, who are indignant at the mere proximity of a yahoo. But as a houyhnhnm, Gulliver should have simply rejected all clothing whatever— something he never does. He should also do so, of course, if he is the poor yahoo he just announced himself to be. But taking Gulliver as an articulate anthropoid creature who fastens himself up in garments, what does one make of his statement? Since Pedro de Mendez also has clothes, he is immediately different from *yahoo:* one cannot wear a garment that has been on the back of a yahoo. Nor would one discuss this topic, as Gulliver has done with the Portuguese captain, with a yahoo. Actually, one could wear something that had been on the back of a yahoo, it occurs to me, if, like Gulliver (ironically), he had created some of his clothing from yahoo skins. I need hardly labor the fact that Gulliver eventually accepts, as man from man, two of the captain's clean shirts to show that the use of the term *yahoo* and the implicit identification of the captain are ridiculous. In another case, similarly, that one in which Gulliver describes a rich English "*Yahoo*" and makes this creature's first interest "to purchase . . . the finest Clothing," he also undermines his own usage. The yahoos have neither the dexterity to don nor the social vanity to enjoy hooks and laces and satin.

This rigorous application of my definition of *yahoo* is possible because Swift has preserved the concrete evidence on which it is based with considerable care. When he extends yahoo nature at all—as in the Master's discourse on certain odd yahoo practices— he carefully hedges the discourse. In the first place, the Master claims merely to have heard about some of these practices—if we can believe him—from "some curious *Houyhnhnms.*" Other odd yahoo activities were "discovered," he says, by "his Servants." And in all the activities by which the Master, having heard about human civilization, draws yahoo life into an approximation with it, Gulliver himself allows, "my Master might refine a little in these Speculations." This stretch in the concept *yahoo* is always rendered, finally, so as to preserve my definition: yahoos never speak or use tools; and even their most apparently communal activities need not be described as either social or organized.

The definition of *houyhnhnm,* although it clarifies any particular discussion of the *human-houyhnhnm* equation, will not give immediate results—except, of course, in the few but amusing instances when human and houyhnhnm physiques are at issue.[27] Both humans and houyhnhnms almost always show "sufficient" intellect, as the definitions assert, to speak, socialize, and use tools. The issue in studying both human and houyhnhnm discourse is how "sufficient," how adequate, is this intellect? The houyhnhnms' general definition of themselves, *The Perfection of Nature*," is sheer nonsense. No creature can be perfect. That the equine body is actually better than any other, the anthropoid, say, is also subject to serious question,[28] especially when what Gulliver describes as "Dexterity" is at issue. The houyhnhnms have no need to thread a needle, whether we believe that they can do so or not. But it might be well worth their while to make two blades of corn grow where only one grew before and, having done so, to be able efficiently to harvest the crop; and to hammer out wheels with iron rims to put on their sledges.

That the houyhnhnm intellect is, like all created intellect, imperfect in experience, in sense, is revealed again and again. Before Gulliver showed up in Houyhnhnmland, the Master had no conception of clothing, weapons, boats, or horsemanship; and he had a terrible time, even with Gulliver's help, in getting an imaginative grasp on such things. Having never seen a boat nor, of course, the sentient anthropoids who might build and sail it, he could hardly believe in such a contraption even when he was ordering Gulliver to make one. He wished, as he put it, "I would contrive some Sort of Vehicle resembling those I had described to him, that might carry me on the Sea." The Master has no term for such a "Vehicle," no certainty that Gulliver can make one, and, apparently, little confidence that the thing will float. When Gulliver reels off a list of vile European practices in his discourse with the Master, one can hardly help laughing at the lurid flicker of light that one can imagine to be playing across this houyhnhnm's beautifully innocent mind.

The Master, for all Gulliver's praise about his ability "daily [to point out] a thousand Faults in myself" (what an ability!), has serious trouble absorbing even the particular human evidence which he himself beholds. He has seen how clean, how busy, and how picky in his food Gulliver is; he has remarked his aversion to yahoos. But when the representatives in the houyhnhnm assembly attack Gulliver because, as Gulliver reports, "I might be able to seduce [the yahoos] into the woody and mountainous Parts of the Country, and bring them in Troops by Night to destroy the *Houyhnhnms* Cattle, as being naturally of the ravenous

Kind and averse from Labour," he has apparently nothing to oppose. The syntax of this charge is fuzzy no doubt: is it the yahoos or Gulliver or both who are being described as "naturally . . . averse from Labour"? Is Gulliver, again, being pointedly charged with "the natural Pravity of those Animals," or merely with the ability seductively to prey on this "Pravity"? But, taking that into account, it is still inconceivable that Gulliver, whose education as an anthropoid houyhnhnm the Master has superintended and observed—as the paragraph immediately following the assembly's charge against Gulliver declares—should act as the assembly speculates that he might; and equally inconceivable that a sensible intelligence should not recognize this and, out of sheer houyhnhnm devotion to truth and honesty, bring up the relevant facts to combat such a charge. But the Master does not combat this charge; he merely carries out, if reluctantly, the demand for Gulliver's removal that arises from it.

Take a simpler case of this houyhnhnm imperviousness to particular experience, one in which a number of these creatures were involved:

> The *Houyhnhnms* who came to visit my Master [as Gulliver reports] out of a Design of seeing and talking with me, could hardly believe me to be a right *Yahoo*, because my Body had a different Covering from others of my Kind.

These houyhnhnms, who came pointedly to see *and* converse with Gulliver, could not know that he had, in fact, exactly the same covering as others of his kind since, unlike Gulliver's reader, they had never seen any other such beings. But by talking with Gulliver, they surely should have recognized that he was capable of talking and, thus, clothed or not, that he was crucially remote from any yahoos they had ever encountered. It was the intelligence each houyhnhnm recognized in the other's speech, after all, and not any covering, that prompted each one to infer rationality in another and in all the houyhnhnms at large. Not even Gulliver could infer rationality—that source of houyhnhnm complacency—from the two stone horses (why not one stallion and one mare?) that he purchased when he got back to England; whereas he was forced to recognize and respond to the discursive, argumentative rationality of Pedro de Mendez. And yet the houyhnhnms, who visited the Master expressly to talk with Gulliver, totally neglected the force, the implications, of Gulliver's talk—

and his houyhnhnm talk, at that. Instead, they reasoned about his clothes.

I have now reached the vexing problem of houyhnhnm reason or, rather, the problem of what I have called its sufficiency and of what others, among whom are the houyhnhnms themselves, call its perfection. That it is at least sufficient to allow speech, society and some technology I do not question. I am as willing to imagine a horse having such intelligence as the next fellow. But that this intelligence as shown in the *Travels* is adequate to pronounce on such topics as human reason, human pride, and human nature in general, I do question. If we practice the minute particularity of attention which Johnson described as characteristic of Swift's mind and analyze the processes of houyhnhnm discourse, we will have to augment the complaint against their sense, I believe, with a further complaint against their reasoning. Consider, for instance, the Master's conduct in this discussion of human capacity:

He said, if it were possible there could be any Country where *Yahoos* alone were endued with Reason, they certainly must be the governing Animal, because Reason will in Time always prevail against Brutal Strength. But considering the Frame of our Bodies, and especially of mine, he thought no Creature of equal bulk was so ill-contrived, for employing that Reason in the common Offices of Life; whereupon he desired to know whether those among whom I lived, resembled me or the *Yahoos* of his Country. I assured him, that I was as well shaped as most of my Age; but the younger and the Females were much more soft and tender, and the Skins of the latter generally as white as Milk. He said, I differed indeed from other *Yahoos* being much more cleanly, and not altogether so deformed; but in point of real Advantage, he thought I differed for the worse. That my Nails were of no Use either to my fore or hinder Feet: As to my fore Feet, he could not properly call them by that Name, for he never observed me to walk upon them; that they were too soft to bear the Ground; that I generally went with them uncovered, neither was the Covering I sometimes wore on them, of the same Shape, or so strong as that on my Feet behind. That I could not walk with any Security; for if either of my hinder Feet slipped, I must inevitably fall. He then began to find fault with other Parts of my Body; the Flatness of my Face, the Prominence of my Nose, my Eyes placed directly in Front, so that I could not look on either Side without turning my Head: That I was not able to feed my self, without lifting one of my fore Feet to my Mouth: and therefore Nature had placed those Joints to answer that Necessity. He knew not what could be the Use of those several Clefts and Divisions in my Feet behind; that these were too soft to bear the

Hardness and Sharpness of Stones without a Covering made from the Skin of some other Brute; that my whole Body wanted a Fence against Heat and Cold, which I was forced to put on and off every Day with Tediousness and Trouble. And lastly, that he observed every Animal in this Country naturally to abhor the *Yahoos*, whom the Weaker avoided, and the Stronger drove from them. So that supposing us to have the Gift of Reason, he could not see how it were possible to cure that natural Antipathy which every Creature discovered against us; nor consequently, how we could tame and render them serviceable. However, he would (as he said) debate the Matter no farther. . . .

The very fact that Gulliver's account of human activity has drawn the Master into a highly contentious "debate," one that is also intellectually speculative, upsets the houyhnhnm notion of reason as unproblematical and of truth as strictly factual.

But the debate itself is laden with difficulties of both sense and reason.[29] The Master's dislike of Gulliver's face, to start with sense, is very puzzling. In attacking the prominence of his nose, the Master may seem to be thinking with satisfaction about his own perfect "Countenance" and its mere nostrils: he is surely remembering his eyes with some complacency when he attacks Gulliver for being able to look straight before himself. But is not a horse's face, in a truer sense, at least from the eyes on down, one great proboscis, a nose so prominent, indeed, that it splits the horse's gaze? And this is just the beginning of the Master's nonsense. His doubts about even entertaining the notion that creatures such as Gulliver might possibly be "endued with Reason" is another failure: it shows the Master's difficulty in acknowledging the very presence of Gulliver, an obviously rational creature, who uses the same logical forms of speech as the Master and, as their discussions develop, comes to make the same deliberate judgments about the same intellectual materials. The Master's last point against Gulliver as a physical specimen toward which "every Creature discovered . . . a natural Antipathy" is similarly ludicrous. It is not merely that the Sorrel Nag would eventually show a tenderness for Gulliver; but at this very moment, the Master is in a close, confidential meeting with him, gaining "Advantage [and] Pleasure" from his intimate company, as the houyhnhnm assembly will eventually complain. But the Master's discussion of Gulliver's "fore Feet" is the most blatant piece of nonsense in this remarkable debate. The Master has quite recently been described closely observing Gulliver undress himself, an experience he actually refers to in this passage; as this passage also suggests, he has beheld Gulliver feed himself. And he must have noticed Gulliver's manual dexterity in trapping and dressing the game and in making the bread, which his elbows allow him to carry to his mouth. But all that here occurs to the Master is how poorly adapted his hands are for walking—and dear, dear! how Gulliver totally neglects to use them for this. He is unable to call Gulliver's hands "fore Feet," he says, not because of what Gulliver does with them, but because of what he does not do. I acknowledge some validity in the Master's suggestion that Gulliver walks with relative insecurity (although how often, in fact, has he seen Gulliver fall down?); but this is such a tiny grain of sense in such a heap of foolishness.

The errors of reason in the Master's statement, in so far as these can be separated from the errors of sense, are equally destructive of houyhnhnm perfection. How can the Master both complain against the prominence of Gulliver's nose—whatever we may judge about the sense of this—and, in almost the same breath, against the flatness of his face and hope to be judged logically consistent? I have already discussed the Master's reason for not calling Gulliver's hands "fore Feet," a point he introduces with the logical term "for." His unwillingness to see any reason for the clefts in Gulliver's hind hoofs, furthermore, recalls his failure to notice the reasons Gulliver has found for such clefts in his hands. Notice also the error in the parallelism indicated by "And lastly" toward the end of the passage: the earlier statements have been pointedly distinguishing between Gulliver and the yahoos; this one implicitly lumps the two together—unless *we* insist, "another difference, for whereas yahoos are abhorred, such humans as Gulliver are not." To do this, of course, disallows the "So" of the Master's grand conclusion. This statement, "consequently," that reasonable anthropoids could not "tame and render . . . serviceable" any other animals, is his greatest failure of reason. Apparently because of his dislike of Gulliver's anthropoid physique, the Master here rejects his own universal principle, that reason will always prevail: it is not applicable to "us." "So that [how impressively rational] supposing us to have the Gift of Reason, he could not see how it were possible to cure that natural Antipathy which every Creature discovered against us." Even if we allow the Master to disbelieve Gulliver's account of human horsemanship (and never to have heard about man's best friend), he has seen with his own eyes a reasonable *and* sociable anthropoid: he is at this moment in a close conversation with one. But the Master has fooled himself with his own nonsense into contradicting the premise of this very debate and, with the same stroke, denying the first principle of houyhnhnm life.

Nor is the Master a uniquely foolish houyhnhnm. The statement of the general assembly, at least as the Master recounts this to Gulliver, presents an equally unacceptable discourse:

> In the Midst of this Happiness, when I looked upon my self to be fully settled for Life, my Master sent for me one Morning a little earlier than his usual Hour. I observed by his Countenance that he was in some Perplexity, and at a Loss how to begin what he had to speak. After a short Silence, he told me, he did not know how I would take what he was going to say: That, in the last general Assembly, when the Affair of the *Yahoos* was entered upon, the Representatives had taken Offence at his keeping a *Yahoo* (meaning my self) in his Family more like a *Houyhnhnm* than a Brute Animal. That, he was known frequently to converse with me, as if he could receive some Advantage or Pleasure in my Company: That, such a Practice was not agreeable to Reason or Nature, or a thing ever heard of before among them. The Assembly did therefore *exhort* him, either to employ me like the rest of my Species, or command me to swim back to the Place from whence I came. That, the first of these Expedients was utterly rejected by all the *Houyhnhnms*, who had ever seen me at his House or their own: For, they alledged, That because I had some Rudiments of Reason, added to the natural Pravity of those Animals, it was to be feared, I might be able to seduce them into the woody and mountainous Parts of the Country, and bring them in Troops by Night to destroy the *Houyhnhnms* Cattle, as being naturally of the ravenous Kind, and averse from Labour.

This is a formal "*Exhortation*" and, as an accompanying paragraph suggests, it should be notable for its reason. But it is, in fact, as defective in both sense and reason as the Master's debate. Members of the assembly, as the statement shows, have had a substantial experience of Gulliver: they know the extent of his relationship with the Master; they know, from individual observation, that he is unsuited to yahoo employments; some of them have both visited with him in the Master's house and entertained him in their own. They must have noticed like the Master, who admits as much in the very next paragraph, that Gulliver is in fact clean, moderate in his diet, busy, and extremely obsequious. Yet they lump him—in a construction that does not even qualify as good grammar—with the filthy, ravenous, lazy, and treacherous yahoos.

If Gulliver is lazy, to turn from questions of sense to those of reason, he could hardly be expected to engage in the enterprises of seduction, training, and leadership that would be required to transform the yahoos into an organized threat; and if *they* are lazy (to mention only one pertinent quality), the yahoos can hardly be expected to participate in such vigorous, demanding, and organized activity. If Gulliver is too delicate for yahoo work, as has been explicitly acknowledged, he can hardly be expected to "swim back to the Place from whence [he] came." And, finally, to reason against the Master's conversation with Gulliver because it was "a thing never heard of before" is absurd: it prompts one to question, furthermore, what the assembly can mean by labelling as unnatural and unreasonable such a discursive employment of the houyhnhnm tongue by two such self-consciously rational intellects: surely the Master has himself spoken as reasonably during their conversation as a houyhnhnm can. Once again there is the machinery of reason—the parallel "That" clauses and the strategic use of "therefore" and "because"—but not the substance.

I am not arguing that all houyhnhnm discourse is nonsensical and irrational;[30] nor will I argue this about all of Gulliver's discourse. Often when he and the Master confine themselves to the general ideas of such topics as yahoo existence or human life they present descriptions and judgments that are, not only impressive, but apparently just. This is so in part, however, because of the discourse's very generality, which provides a tolerance, a vacant intellectual ground, between the discourse itself and all particular embodiments. This vacant ground, this intermediate realm between general words and real things, to which the actual experiences of life may be added, sometimes provides merely an intellectual buffer. Such is virtually always the case, of course, in the general expositions of yahoo modes of conduct. And even the comments on Europe that Gulliver makes, being aimed at the Master, who lacks any particular European knowledge, may simply be observed at the distance of broadly relevant generality. Thus when Gulliver describes European conflicts over "whether *Flesh* be *Bread* or *Bread* be *Flesh*," one may leave it at that, as the Master must do: in this case, he recognizes the essential triviality of our religious conflicts. Or he may—and probably will—go on to fill in the arguments of transubstantiation and consubstantiation from his own knowledge, no doubt preserving his own opinions of these arguments. This will flavor his primary sense of Gulliver's discourse with a secondary sense—with a sense, however, that he might be wise to mistrust—and give him a full impression of its propriety. Thus the reader, himself supplying particulars—as Berkeley explains—or merely entertaining general applicabilities, finds considerable satisfaction in these discourses. But when Gulliver and the Master confront the particulars of Gulliver's houyhnhnm adventure or Gulliver himself or Gulliver as an example of humanity, their talk is deprived of the tolerance, the vagueness of application, that surrounds and protects their general discussions. In these talks they share the details of their intelligence with the reader and become vulnerable to his detailed analysis. Certain of these talks, I am arguing, can be shown to be seriously at fault. And since they are faulty, I would suggest further, everything the houyhnhnms say should be examined with intellectual caution; and their general claims of special intelligence should be viewed with suspicion.

Gulliver's elaborations on these claims must also raise doubts, and his rationality must, consequently, be suspect. To consider it in particular, I turn toward his response to the assembly's charge against him. Gulliver fainted when he heard that he must quit Houyhnhnmland; and, when he came to, the Master, who had been observing this phenomenon, reported that he had "concluded I had been dead"—another case in which truth turns out to be problematical. Gulliver then responded to the assembly's "*Exhortation*":

I answered, in a faint Voice, that Death would have been too great an Happiness; that although I could not blame the Assembly's *Exhortation*, or the Urgency of his Friends; yet in my weak and corrupt Judgment, I thought it might consist with Reason to have been less rigorous. That, I could not swim a League, and probably the nearest Land to theirs might be distant above an Hundred: That, many Materials, necessary for making a small Vessel to carry me off, were wholly wanting in this Country, which however, I would attempt in Obedience and Gratitude to his Honour, although I concluded the thing to be impossible, and therefore looked on myself as already devoted to Destruction. That, the certain Prospect of an unnatural Death, was the least of my Evils: For, supposing I should escape with Life by some strange Adventure, how could I think with Temper, of passing my Days among *Yahoos*, and relapsing into my old Corruptions, for want of Examples to lead and keep me within the Paths of Virtue. That, I knew too well upon what solid Reasons all the Determinations of the wise *Houyhnhnms* were founded, not to be shaken by Arguments of mine, a miserable *Yahoo*; and therefore after presenting him with my humble Thanks for the Offer of his Servants Assistance in making a Vessel, and desiring a reasonable Time for so difficult a Work, I told him, I would endeavour to preserve a wretched Being; and, if ever I returned to England, was not without Hopes of being

> useful to my own Species, by celebrating the Praises of the renowned
> *Houyhnhnms*, and proposing their Virtues to the Imitation of Mankind.

Gulliver has sandwiched between the assembly's charge and this response his note on houyhnhnm "*Exhortation*," explaining that, as the houyhnhnms see things, a rational creature can never be "*compelled* but only advised or *exhorted;* because no Person [a lovely term here] can disobey Reason, without giving up his Claim to be a rational Creature." This seems to me to be Swift's hint that we should be especially alert in testing the arguments immediately before us, that is, the houyhnhnm exhortation, the intellectual adequacy of which I have just discussed, and Gulliver's response.

Gulliver's response is a parody of houyhnhnm reasoning and, more particularly, of the very exhortation to which he is responding. He employs the same paraphernalia—a series of "That" clauses and a liberal sprinkling of logical terms such as "although . . . yet," "however," "therefore," "for"—and commits the same kind of failures. If we place my definition of *yahoo* in the statement about the "arguments of . . . a miserable *Yahoo*," noting not only the yahoos' lack of speech but, *a fortiori*, of argumentative capacity, we see that Gulliver is practicing in an exaggerated form the kind of nonsense he will soon try on the Portuguese—and something like the same nonsense in the exhortation that underlies the houyhnhnm fear of Gulliver's organizing a rebellion. His horror of returning to Europe as an ordeal of "passing my Days among *Yahoos*" is similarly foolish: it is only in Houyhnhnmland that he may—that he must, to some degree—be so accompanied; only there do yahoos truly worthy of such a name exist. Gulliver's assertion that the houyhnhnms are "renowned" is simply false: the houyhnhnms may become renowned eventually through Gulliver's authorial exertions—if he can make anyone believe in their existence at all; but as he speaks, they are absolutely unrenowned.

The consideration of possible materials for his boat reveals Gulliver to be, in line with his houyhnhnm discipleship, not only nonsensical but irrational as well. If necessary materials are simply unavailable, as Gulliver asserts, no matter what motives of obedience and gratitude may press him, his attempt to build a boat is foolish. Consider also Gulliver's complaint that the assembly's exhortation was too rigorous. Either they are right in describing Gulliver as a dangerous yahoo and thus justified in expelling him or wrong and thus silly to do so: reason cannot be too rigorous. If the Europeans are yahoos, again, as Gulliver insists, his plan to teach them is strictly irrational for, as he knows, yahoos are quite unteachable. This whole discourse, finally, shows the same kind of intellectual flip-flop I described in the Master's debate. It begins in abject despair: "Death would be too great an Happiness." But as Gulliver discusses the perils of travel and the horrors of life on the other side, his understanding shifts about; and it does so, moreover, against the extremely negative tendency of his discourse. He "was not without Hopes," he concludes, of a useful life back home where he would not merely live in the corrupting environment of yahoos but, although an unteachable yahoo himself, teach those unteachables.

The fact that the Master made a "very gracious Reply" to this effusion should remind us that, in respect to discursive rationality, the perfect houyhnhnm Master and his miserable human disciple are very much alike. In making this close identification between Gulliver and the Master we are, as it may please us to recognize, distinguishing between Gulliver and ourselves.

*   *   *

We have now examined enough of the voyage to Houyhnhnmland in enough detail to question the houyhnhnms' characterization of themselves as "the *Perfection of Nature*," to doubt their inclusion of Gulliver in the category of *yahoo*, and to suspect the returning Gulliver's attitude toward his family, his neighbors, and his countrymen. The rest of the *Travels* is subject to a similarly skeptical attention. We should have accumulated enough evidence of human nature within and without Gulliver's account of his voyage to Brobdingnag, for instance, to resist in general and to analyze in particular the judgment of the usually intelligent King that "the bulk of [Englishmen are] the most pernicious Race of little odious Vermin that Nature ever suffered to crawl upon the Surface of the Earth." The Lilliputian Emperor's "lenity"— not to speak of his imperial pretensions—and the ambitions of the Lagadian virtuosi we should, on the basis of experiences presented in the *Travels* and our own store of sense, also be ready to question. Swift has submitted one complete case (his exposition of the struldbruggs) of the kind of study that is indicated, with varying degrees of insistence, throughout the book.

In the *Travels* at large he has confronted his readers with an array of perceptual problems, projecting a wide range of generalities—in headings, categories, accounts, judgments, professions and terms—and opposing these with a remarkable train of par-

ticular events, situations, and involvements. With the variety of
his adventurer-narrator's responses to these problems, he has
prompted his readers to test each and all of them for themselves.
If we react to this prompting, we must consider the opinions
and attitudes impressed on us by Swift's fiction and attempt,
by reference to the particularities he has provided and our own
preliminary understanding, to comprehend and to judge them.
In the process we may compose ourselves to understand and
judge the things impressed upon us by nature.

As we thus improve our sense of particular moments in the
train of ideas Gulliver's words occasion in us—in each of us separately—and revise (and keep on revising) our own general sense
of things, we should also see that we are, individually, the primary focus of this satire.[31] As we come to recognize that these
remote, mendacious events occur only in our responsive awareness, we should also recognize our unique propriety of all accompanying generalities as well. We are incidentally concerned, no
doubt, with politics, science, religion, and law in the external
world. The descriptions of these institutional conditions, however, are all projected as elements of Gulliver's individual awareness and become focused, as I have tried to explain, as elements
of ours. In accepting all the things occasioned in us by Swift's art
and in struggling by turns to analyze and to synthesize them,
therefore, each of us may discover that he is himself an *animal
rationis capax*, to the exposition of which Swift once suggested
that he had dedicated his book. As one's grasp of the *Travels*
improves, that is to say, one recognizes in himself a giddy intelligence that must always be ready to improve itself.

This makes the satire of the *Travels* very different from that of
the *Tale*. In reading the earlier work we were prompted by its
allegorical representations, its journalistic references, and its Lucretian emergencies to judge an external, material world. Even the
Author, for all his crack-brained particularity, stood for something
outside us, for allegiances and activities at which we could safely
point. But the *Travels* seldom gives its reader such comfort. One
is both the victim and the judge of this satire. And, paradoxically
perhaps, the less aware one is of this perilous eminence, the more
peril one endures, the more of a victim he becomes. To grow
conscious of former follies in apprehension and judgment, on the
other hand, and to recognize one's persistent intellectual fallibility
in all its variety is to be less foolish, less of a satiric victim. But,
or so my experience indicates, one is never completely free. Not
only must a reader recall how blind or prejudiced or inattentive

or credulous he was just a little bit ago—a memory that should keep one humble enough; but this awareness of follies past should prepare each reader—as he acknowledges it—for follies to come. Such an attitude, such a live awareness of one's susceptibility, allows a reader—taking here what comfort we can—to endure his intellectual giddiness, that is, his being *animal rationis capax*, not as a definitive truth, but as a persistent challenge.

Such an attitude, such a critical sensitivity to the details of things as these pass through the consciousness, is also the right one with which to confront the flickering variety of Gay's poetry and the inductive ambitions of Pope's.

3

Gay's Jests

John Gay, in gathering particular items of his observation and in honoring their individuality, is the most like Swift of any other eighteenth-century writer. His description of London streets, *Trivia* (1716), bears an obvious resemblance in this respect to Swift's two London poems of 1710. But Gay both narrows and suppresses the procedures of composition and analysis that Swift encourages, advocating rather a cheerful encounter with life's separate experiences and observations as these rise and pass before us.

Gay honored, as perhaps no other poet has ever done, the pre-eminence of the perceptual present, distinguishing with the utmost emphasis between what Hume, later in the century, would exalt as "Impressions" and what he demoted as mere "Ideas":

> All the perceptions of the human mind resolve themselves into two distinct kinds, which I shall call IMPRESSIONS and IDEAS. The difference betwixt these consists in the degrees of force and liveliness with which they strike upon the mind, and make their way into our thought or consciousness. Those perceptions, which enter with most force and violence, we may name *impressions*; and under this name I comprehend all our sensations, passions and emotions, as they make their first appearance in the soul. By *ideas* I mean the faint images of these in thinking and reasoning. . . . I believe it will not be very necessary to employ many words in explaining this distinction. Every one of himself will readily perceive the difference betwixt feeling and thinking. The common degrees of these are [so] easily distinguished that no-one can make a scruple to rank them under distinct heads, and assign to each a peculiar name to mark the difference.

For Gay any impression was incalculably more interesting than any idea. He is thus the least reflective of our great poets, fastening individual attention, rather, on this and now this and now this. He embraced with the least possible reservation the principle that each thing is particular and delighted himself with the pres-

90

ent particular, enjoying all things as they emerged in the train of consciousness. The past, on the ideological compositions of which generalization is based, and the future, to the ideological possibility of which generalization is applied, he emphatically depressed, attending with the purest possible devotion to those perceptions entering now with the most force and violence upon his awareness. Swift, often without acknowledging it, requires his reader to reflect, to test the contents of his understanding, bringing his present impressions into some kind of relationship with his accumulated ideas, and composing larger realms of experience and understanding; Gay—to speak a little extravagantly—only wishes us to attend and to behold.

Swift's most random "Inventories" bristle with general implications and usually carry a general intellectual sting as well. The mere list of "Treatises wrote by the same Author" that the satirist appended to his *Tale of a Tub*, which represents virtually as many genres as titles, suggests that this "Author," if we take his bibliography as a whole, possesses an extremely slap-dash kind of creativity. Between the different items of the list, we endure opportunities for subordinate syntheses: we may infer, as we advance from title one to title two, for example—contrary to the Author's opinion?—that there are only "THREE . . . Wits in this Island"; and that "Zeal" in title six is reducible to "Ears" in title seven. Individual titles in the list have the opposite effect, prompting us to practice, not synthesis, but analysis: determining finally that a "panegyrical Essay" on even so splendid a number as "THREE" is a little anthropomorphic; that crediting "Grub-street" with any "principal Productions" is questionable; and that describing the activities of "the Rabble" as "Proceedings" is almost a contradiction in terms. This mere inventory of titles presents in its parts, its relationships, and its totality a suggestion of responsive procedures, variously synthetic and analytical, reaching toward orders and confusions as great as the Author will expose in the *Tale* at large.

Swift's 1710 poem on London, the "Description of a City Shower," also provides wide-ranging inductive opportunities.[1] To illustrate Londoners' conduct during the actual shower, Swift presents five separate cases, the first three each deployed in its own couplet, and each of the next two in a pair. Every case is different in its organization, obviously enough, "Females" coming at the end of the first line of that couplet, for example, and "The Templer" coming at the beginning of the first line of that one; but all taken together suggest a range of general opinions. Only one of these cases, the sempstress, escapes some kind of moral condemnation; just as she is the only one who simply braves the shower to go on about her work. The first two, the "Females" and the "Templer," engage in fakery, the first pretending to shop, the second, to summon a coach. The difference between the sempstress and these two allows a number of general inferences: that it takes very little to make most people hypocritical—and very little attention to detect it; that most Londoners have little or nothing to do; that human kind, unless driven by some practical purpose, is so feeble that any little thing will determine its conduct. The degree of generality to which we carry such inferences is not strictly marked: although there are both men and women idlers, the specificity of "Templer spruce" (especially since we may imagine a particular concern with his clothes) may inhibit the inclusion of all men in the opinion. On the other hand, we may sympathize with "the dagged Females" and broaden our opinion simply on the basis of this case to include everybody— at least until the sturdy sempstress emerges. Thus, despite the meticulous definition he gave to the different cases, Swift's poem teases us to test various syntheses and analyses, travelling up and down the inductive road that Bacon and Sprat had constructed.

In *Trivia*, a more extended and ambitious description of London than Swift's, Gay actually claims an inductive purpose. He has explored the streets of London, he says by way of introduction, to teach others "how to walk clean by day, and safe by night," giving a great catalogue of particular cautions of such things as "when to assert the wall [for instance], and when [to] resign." And at the end of the poem he takes credit for accomplishing a general lesson: "Mankind / Their future safety [will] from my danger find" and "bless my labours." He reasserts this purpose at one point after another throughout the poem, advising the "prudent walker" to provide the right shoes for himself, to avoid dirty tradesmen, butchers, sweeps and chandlers, to circumvent certain alleyways especially at night, and always to guard his belongings. But this general application of his "labours" is not only in itself pointedly particular and practical; it is continually overwhelmed by Gay's particular descriptions of the passing scene.

In the very first paragraph of the poem, for instance, the one in which he announces his general ambition, Gay describes how he can himself "securely stray / Where winding alleys lead the doubtful way" and "explore . . . the silent court and op'ning square." The solicitous guide, that is to say, has even here been replaced by a mundane Aeneas. And when he describes the scenes of his exploration, they emerge as scenes, that is, as interesting impressions. Addressing the goddess, Trivia, whose spirit invests his poem—and not the innocent traveller—Gay reports:

> To pave thy realm, and smooth the broken ways,
> Earth from her womb a flinty tribute pays:
> For thee the sturdy pavior thumps the ground,
> Whil'st ev'ry stroke his lab'ring lungs resound.

Any chance generalization—that earth is bountiful; that the streets are good; that the work of a pavior is hard—is irrelevant if not contrary to the actual force of this description. Gay provides, rather, a vivid representation of the streets and their maintenance or, more truly, the pavior's strokes and the heaving of his breath.

This focus on the poet's observations in their details is, despite incidental claims of general application, the continually reasserted center of the poem. In this description of a thief, for example, a preliminary warning is almost immediately lost in the excitement of the event:

> Where the mob gathers, swiftly shoot along,
> Nor, idly mingle with the noisy throng.
> Lur'd by the silver hilt, amid the swarm,
> The subtil artist will thy side disarm.
> Nor is thy flaxen wig with safety worn;   5
> High on the shoulder in a basket borne
> Lurks the sly boy; whose hand to rapine bred,
> Plucks off the curling honours of thy head.
> Here dives the skulking thief, with practis'd slight,
> And unfelt fingers make thy pocket light.   10
> Where's now the watch, with all its trinkets, flown?
> And thy late snuff-box is no more thy own.
> But lo! his bolder thefts some tradesman spies,
> Swift from his prey the scudding lurcher flies;
> Dext'rous he 'scapes the coach with nimble bounds,   15
> Whilst ev'ry honest tongue *stop thief* resounds.
> So speeds the wily fox, alarm'd by fear,
> Who lately filch'd the turkey's callow care;
> Hounds following hounds, grow louder as he flies,
> And injur'd tenants join the hunter's cries.   20
> Breathless he stumbling falls: Ill-fated boy!
> Why did not honest work thy youth employ?
> Seiz'd by rough hands, he's dragg'd amid the rout,

And stretch'd beneath the pump's incessant spout:
Or plung'd in miry ponds, he gasping lies,   25
Mud choaks his mouth, and plaisters o'er his eyes.

Lines three to five present a dogmatic prediction, the thief will get away with your "silver hilt," thus making the near future into a virtual present. And at line six the description shifts to the present itself: "the sly boy . . . lurks [and] . . . plucks." Thus Gay observes the event he was professedly determined to prevent. Nor does he seem to mind: first he notes calmly enough that "thy flaxen wig" is in danger; and then he calmly watches it vanish. And now something altogether different catches his eye, the pickpocket, whose cleverness clearly delights him. This rascal's "practic'd slight" emerges first as a kind of trick: "where's now the watch, with all its trinkets, flown?" Gay thus invites the victim to join him in a fascinated enjoyment of the thief's practice. And then comes a good joke on you: "And thy late snuff-box is no more thy own." The adjective "late" denies the victim's ownership even before the object, "snuff box," is mentioned; and "no more" thus becomes an amusing redundancy. Very funny. The advocacy of prudence has obviously dissolved in a fascination with the thief's dexterity and the victim's discomfiture.

Gay has no general allegiance, neither to you nor—now—to the clever thief. Each shift in his impressions justifies, or so Gay sees it, a shift in feeling. For now the thief is noticed by a tradesman, he flees, and is suddenly transformed from a subtle artist to a "scudding lurcher." It is not his dextrous hands but his dextrous feet Gay notices now. Actually, "Dext'rous" is misplaced, belonging rather with the handy fellow above than with the runner, to whom it is actually attached, a misplacement that defines the sudden shift in Gay's attention: this is and is not the light-fingered thief above. After a total diversion, in which Gay focuses attention on a Chaucerian countryside, he turns back to the thief, but with yet a different attitude. In one line, twenty-one above, he provides first a merely visual apprehension of the thief, "Breathless he stumbling falls"; and then, using the caesura to rationalize the shift, he addresses the thief with accents reminiscent of the *Aeneid:* "Ill-fated boy!" The sympathy suggested here lasts through the next line, although it is developed in a less heroic key; and then comes a vivid description quite devoid of personal feeling that details the thief's punishment. "Choaks" and "plaisters" give first what we may call the medical facts of the thief's state and then a neat reduction of him to a mere object in the city scape: he is rendered by the artful use of indigenous materials into one more item of the London scene. Notice first the remarkable range of attitudes with which Gay invests the succeeding impressions of this one figure and second the total neglect of pedagogical purpose. This purpose is reasserted at the beginning of the next paragraph—"Let not the ballad singer's shrilling strain / Amid the swarm thy list'ning ear detain"—to suffer almost immediately the same neglect. The scene, the spectacle, is all.[2] And the spectacle is, of course, a train of diverse and essentially discrete impressions, each one uniquely compelling both in its visual and in its emotional value.

Even his cautionary exposition of prostitutes and their wiles, which naturally bristles with general morality, Gay develops as an object of observation. It is introduced under the heading, "various city frauds," along with gambling tricks and the picking of pockets. But each of these preliminary frauds enjoys its brief moment of descriptive eminence and gives way. Gay then introduces prostitution in characteristic style: "O! may thy virtue guard thee" through "the harlot's guileful paths" so that the town in general may be healthier "And city cheeks grow warm with rural red." But then comes a highly particularized exposition of the harlot's artful conduct and a story of a certain incautious "yeoman."

Here is the exposition:

> 'Tis she who nightly strolls with saunt'ring pace,
> No stubborn stays her yielding shape embrace;
> Beneath the lamp her tawdry ribbons glare,
> The new-scowr'd manteau, and the slattern air;
> High-draggled petticoats her travels show,   5
> And hollow cheeks with artful blushes glow;
> With flatt'ring sounds she sooths the cred'lous ear,
> My noble captain! charmer! love! my dear!
> In riding-hood near tavern-doors she plies,
> Or muffled pinners hide her livid eyes.   10
> With empty bandbox she delights to range,
> And feigns a distant errand from the 'Change.
> Nay, she will oft the Quaker's hood prophane,
> And trudge demure the rounds of *Drury-lane.*
> She darts from sarsnet ambush wily leers,   15
> Twitches thy sleeve, or with familiar airs
> Her fan will pat thy cheek; these snares disdain,
> Nor gaze behind thee, when she turns again.

The warning comes (without warning) in line seventeen at the caesura—"these snares disdain"; its very abruptness shows how far Gay has strayed from his professed didacticism or, rather, how deeply he has plunged into his real concern. Even though the description is couched as a general representation, it continually verges on particularity, especially as details of the harlot's appearance and conduct accumulate; and the final strokes, the twitch of "thy sleeve" and the pat on "thy cheek," have an inescapable tactile immediacy. The description is so seductive, indeed, that, despite the cautionary terms—"flatt'ring," "hide," "prophane," "ambush"—Gay is altogether justified, it seems to me, to warn the susceptible traveller not to "gaze behind thee, when she turns again." The particulars of dress, conduct, and location with which he has embellished her have transformed this she at last from a figure of general and remote relevance to this very she whose base touches are almost too seductive to resist. The fascinated gaze predominates in this passage and not the moral danger.

Then follows the story of the yeoman who needed but would no doubt have ignored Gay's warning: it proves, indeed, the gaze's predominance.

> I knew a yeoman, who for thirst of gain,
> To the great city drove from *Devon's* plain
> His num'rous lowing herd; his herds he sold,
> And his deep leathern pocket bagg'd with gold;
> Drawn by a fraudful nymph, he gaz'd, he sigh'd;   5
> Unmindful of his home, and distant bride,
> She leads the willing victim to his doom,
> Through winding alleys to her cobweb room.
> Thence through the street he reels, from post to post,
> Valiant with wine, nor knows his treasure lost.   10
> The vagrant wretch th' assembled watchmen spies,
> He waves his hanger, and their poles defies;
> Deep in the round-house pent, all night he snores,
> And the next morn in vain his fate deplores.

This account is revealingly disjunctive: two couplets describe the victim's success in his business; then after a narrative leap at the couplet break, two more disclose his visit to the prostitute's "cobweb room"; another leap lands the victim, now a mere public nuisance, in a brawl, an episode that has no necessary narrative or didactic connection with the prostitute; and then the last couplet finds him in jail: in the first line he snores, and in the second he deplores. The passage is thus not so much a story as it is a series of vivid impressions. One can no doubt connect the gold with the harlot (something Gay does not do) and then yoke one kind of debauchery with another. But in poetic fact, the different segments are sharply separated by syntax, meter and substance: no mention of money clouds the vividness of the sexual indulgence; nor does any mention of alcohol; and although a reader may supply these narrative connections as each is needed by retrospective imagination, one does not do so to the blurring of each moment in its explicit force. The didactic supply is fainter still although "fraudful," "doom," and "fate" no doubt stir a certain moral awareness. Nevertheless, we are chiefly directed and chiefly concerned, I believe, to behold the yeoman's vulnerability, his seduction—he would gaze again—his public misconduct, and his incarceration each one in its turn as an item of observation. It's hard to think, for instance, of enduring drunken snores except from a distance of comfortable distaste.

The next paragraph, which might well provide explicit moral judgment and general moral instruction, goes like this:

> Ah hapless swain, unus'd to pains and ills!
> Canst thou forego roast-beef for nauseous pills?
> How wilt thou lift to Heav'n thy eyes and hands,
> When the long scroll the surgeon's fees demands!
> Or else (ye Gods avert that worst disgrace) 5
> Thy ruin'd nose falls level with thy face,
> Then shall thy wife thy loathsome kiss disdain
> And wholesome neighbours from thy mug refrain.

This paragraph focuses on separate elements of the victim's situation: his health, his finances, his face, and his ostracism, each one disclosed in a sharply individuated couplet. As in the case of the young thief, different attitudes invest the different points of disclosure. The first couplet turns the address upon the victim—a new departure from the lines above; it projects a sympathy, moreover, that echoes from the realms of pastoral elegy. The second, from which sympathy has been cancelled, begins, at least, with a religious note; but shifts to the harsh question of money. The third plays epic horror against medical prognosis, turning probability into reality by the very force of description, in such a context the fallen nose being held in grotesque similitude, perhaps, with the fallen towers of Troy. The fourth couplet, as in the account of the thief above, concludes this anecdote with hardhearted detachment. "Mug" here has something like the power to distance readers that "snores" had at the end of the paragraph just above. At no point does Gay mitigate the report on this victim's fate—least of all at its close, of course—with moral generalization although, once again, we may derive a cautionary warning while laughing from a pretty safe distance at his "loathsome . . . mug." We feel chiefly our comfortable solidarity with the "wholesome neighbors," however, and behold the harlot's victim, as we beheld the thief, as one more lively item in a passing parade.

Trivia over all presents the kind of movement that these passages suggest, indicating general inferences of judgment or caution or concern and then, as things develop, neglecting these in favor of the liveliest, most flexible possible responsiveness to the developing sights in their shifting particularities. At one point Gay says, "I remark each walker's diff'rent face, / And in their look their various bus'ness trace"; and, indeed, this tireless attention to differences and variety is the essence of his poem. Even when he seems most determined to organize a system of general advice, the differences prevail:

> If cloth'd in black, you tread the busy town,
> Or if distinguish'd by the rev'rend gown,
> Three trades avoid; oft in the mingling press,
> The barber's apron soils the sable dress;
> Shun the perfumer's touch with cautious eye,   5
> Nor let the baker's step advance too nigh:
> Ye walkers too that youthful colours wear,
> Three sullying trades avoid with equal care;
> The little chimney-sweeper skulks along,
> And marks with sooty stains the heedless throng;   10
> When small-coal murmurs in the hoarser throat,
> From smutty dangers guard thy threaten'd coat:
> The dust-man's cart offends thy cloaths and eyes,
> When through the street a cloud of ashes flies;
> But whether black or lighter dyes are worn,   15
> The chandler's basket, on his shoulder borne,
> With tallow spots thy coat; resign the way,
> To shun the surly butcher's greasy tray,
> Butchers, whose hands are dy'd with blood's foul stain,
> And always foremost in the hangman's train.   20

Gay here devotes himself explicitly to a schematic pattern of advice, organizing the dangers to garments presented by London streets under three headings, dark garments, colorful ones, and all shades with, respectively, three, three, and two particular cautions. But each danger, as Gay encounters it, receives strictly unique exposition; and, although some are couched as points of advice ("Shun"; "Nor let"; "guard"), others are just described— as if, indeed, all caution is useless. "Oft in the mingling press," he reports with perfect diffidence, "The barber's apron soils the sable dress"; and, again, "The chandler's basket, on his shoulder borne, / With tallow spots thy coat." No matter how much care one takes, it seems, his garments are going to get soiled and spotted—and he (you) might as well like it. This is a general inference, truly, but one, it should be noticed, that precisely opposes the professed theme of care and caution. The passage ends with a vivid representation of butchers as unavoidable elements in the London scene and thus concludes, in accordance with Gay's unquenchable instinct, in attention to the rapidly shifting show.

This lively, engaging poem has no doubt a general meaning or, at least, a general implication. It suggests the preeminence of particular impressions in human pleasure, if not human understanding, and consequently espouses an individual alertness and responsiveness of mind. Reflection and imagination, although not cancelled, are radically diminished by Gay, who presents individual happiness as primary and locates that in the enjoyment of one's impressions, that is, of the show. "All things" constitute a "jest" for Gay, as he wrote in his own epitaph, and the pleasure of the jest consists in the individual's susceptibility to "all things." Gay thus brought consciousness and experience into the closest equation of any writer before Hume, who would describe personal identity, we may recall, as "a bundle or collection of different perceptions which succeed each other with an inconceivable rapidity, and are in a perpetual flux and motion." Gay's emphasis on perceptual furniture in its shifting detail may well have weakened his apprehension of the underlying mental substance—or so it could be argued—and thus made individual personality vulnerable to the forces he would himself unleash in *The Beggar's Opera*. The narrator of *Trivia* is virtually a conduit, at any rate, through which a perpetual flux of London impressions flows with something approaching inconceivable rapidity: he is thus a preliminary illustration of Hume's shocking but challenging teaching.

* * *

In *The Beggar's Opera* Gay developed his advocacy of individual human awareness and of individual human life. This remarkable work teaches, to recall William Empson's somewhat romantic words, that "only the individual can be admired."[3] Empson is referring, of course, to the individual person, not the individual percept; but the two, as a consideration of the *Opera* will illustrate, are tightly bound together. Throughout the *Opera* Gay has subjected personality to the inhospitable environment of society, the various customs, manners, and pressures of which oppose all personal differences; and he describes, finally, the obliteration of both the different people people see and the different people people are. Society, as Gay encountered it in the *Opera*, can dissolve the most recalcitrant aspects of personality—personal love, personal honor, personal grievance—reducing each human being to an indistinguishable atom in the body of the human commonalty. It is a force for human generalization—or metaphor unrestrained—and thus inflicts on the people of the *Opera* what Gay might call "a down-right deep tragedy." *The Beggar's Opera*, which is undoubtedly one of the most amusing works in English literature, provides the fullest possible exposition of this tragedy.

In the *Opera* as a whole, Gay has composed an emphatic metonymic fabric. The strict differentiation of discourse from song, which the beggar, the putative author, insists on by boasting of his avoidance of recitative, forces Gay's audience to live with two continually interrupted and interruptive literary modes and thus endure—much as in reading *Trivia*—a relentless tissue of expressive contiguities.[4] To enforce this point, I recall that the work makes use of sixty-nine airs—all but a few late ones being separated from one another by passages of prose discourse. This persistent generic strobe, which should keep metonymic sensibilities on the alert, is enforced by the meta-dramatic (or meta-operatic) frame, in which the beggar and a player discuss the work, indicating its difference, as both drama and opera, first from formally contiguous works and second from all of nature. In this frame Gay indicates a broad discrepancy between high life and low, to which the *Opera* itself often alludes:

> *Beggar.* Through the whole Piece you may observe such a similitude of Manners in high and low Life, that it is difficult to determine whether (in the fashionable Vices) the fine Gentlemen imitate the Gentlemen of the Road, or the Gentlemen of the Road the fine Gentlemen.—Had the Play remain'd, as I first intended, it would have carried a most excellent Moral. 'Twould have shown that the lower Sort of People have their Vices in a degree as well as the Rich: And that they are punish'd for them.

This resemblance the beggar would have modified, as he says, maintaining the difference, the definable contiguity, between high life, whose membership is not punished for its vices, and low life, whose members are. By sinking this difference in accordance with the absurd principle of opera, that the story "must end happily," Gay has it both ways; thus, at the close of his work, emphasizing the stress between metaphor (or resemblance) and metonymy (or difference) and, since Macheath is brought back—just as a rich man would be—in triumph, suggesting the deplorable prevalence in this world of the metaphoric way.

At the very opening of the work, in its first song and an immediately succeeding commentary, Peachum, the virtual epitome of the world it depicts, describes a series of explicit similitudes by which he undermines the difference, the definable contiguity, between different professions and different estates:

> Through all the Employments of Life
>   Each Neighbor abuses his Brother;
> Whore and Rogue they call Husband and Wife:
>   All Professions be-rogue one another.
> The Priest calls the Lawyer a Cheat, 5
>   The Lawyer be-knaves the Divine;
> And the Statesman, because he's so great,
>   Thinks his Trade as honest as mine.

A Lawyer is an honest Employment, so is mine. Like me too he acts in a double Capacity, both against Rogues and for 'em; for 'tis but fitting that we should protect and encourage Cheats, since we live by them.

The switch from song to statement, which might jar—and alert?—an audience, has no effect on Peachum's train. Throughout this passage, he likens priests to lawyers, statesmen to informers (his trade), and lawyers to informers, primarily on the grounds of such categories as *employment, trade, profession,* and *cheat,* the evidently financial implications of which I will soon examine. The details of Peachum's virtually universal equation, which includes "each" neighbor and "all" professions, echo throughout the opera.

Peachum's corival, Lockit, the prison warden, who, like Peachum, carries about an account book, includes himself in this system and, by likening himself first to an innkeeper and then a tailor, extends it. He greets Captain Macheath, who has just been arrested, as "a Lodger of mine," enforcing the figure by de-

manding "Garnish, Captain, Garnish." And in finding the "fit-
test" fetters for him, becoming more-and-more accommodating
in getting just the right fit as the Captain pays more-and-more
money, he becomes almost indistinguishable from his commercial
counterpart: "—How genteely they are made!—They will fit as
easy as a Glove." Dealers in salvation, in justice, in freedom, in
power, even in death are recognized, like those in goods, by the
denizens of this world as "honest" professionals. Peachum and
Filch agree, for instance, that their profession and that of medicine
are equally beholden for opportunities of remunerative employment to women. Macheath asserts that for recruiting such women
to the ranks of "free-hearted ladies," "The Town perhaps hath
been as much oblig'd to me . . . as to any Recruiting Officer in
the Army." And, before joining these ranks as a freehanded ad-
mirer of women, he equates his particular devotion to Polly with
that of a courtier to a pension or a lawyer to a fee—figures of
speech that Polly apparently finds assuring. Love and lovers are
generally included, along with husbands and wives, in this metaphorical stew. Males are likened to thieves, perjurers, and courtiers; females—when not simply reduced to free or saleable
"whores," "sluts," "hussys," and "wenches"—are likened to lawyers, who must "be fee'd into our arms," to smugglers, to tradesmen, and thieves. Macheath's doxies, however, even while
conducting a commercial seminar, evidently appropriate, indeed,
to whores, sluts, and thieves, carefully maintain the polite forms
of address: they are all like ladies, that is to say, and like ladies
all the time. The actual thieves of Macheath's gang are, similarly,
like gentlemen except when they observe, somewhat sourly, the
similarity between gentlemen and gamesters.

This wholesale figurative erosion of professional and social differences is extended in the *Opera* by the equivalencies between
one person and another that gradually overtake and degrade
every one of the characters, even the major ones, and by the
characters' pervasive habit of describing their conditions and their
conduct in conventional generalities.

Again and again, the *Opera* presents the illusion of personal
substance, of particularity in nature and purpose, only to undermine it. Both Polly and Lucy seem strictly themselves, strictly
different, when each one is first introduced: Polly is a fresh young
thing with a spice of canny self-interest; Lucy, a frail maiden
wronged and embittered. Each one has songs specifically suitable
to herself, or so it seems, and her own characteristic sentiments.
In her first appearance Polly sings the originally touching but

increasingly cynical song about virgins whose careers, to the very end, parallel those of *"the fair flower in its Lustre"*; another, innocent in tone but crafty in its message, explaining why she married; and, somewhat later, the shocking if sentimental one that informs her parents, *"on the Rope that hangs my Dear / Depends poor Polly's life."* These songs enforce Polly's discourse, delineating her own special grasp on her particular domestic circumstances. But certain songs of Lucy's, which echo these, gradually flatten and reduce Polly, transforming her into an approximation of her rival. Polly explained to her parents how Macheath *"so closely prest"* her in so *"sweet"* a fashion that she must have *"comply'd"*; Lucy explains to her father in almost the same words how Macheath *"so closely . . . prest her"* and in so *"sweet"* a fashion that she did comply. Polly's figurative representation of herself as a ship *"tost"* in storms that fears to be *"lost"* Lucy also echoes in both figure and rhyme. Even Polly's pun on *"Depends,"* by which she relates her fate with Macheath's, is echoed, if in a crude form, by Lucy's father, who assures his daughter, *"I hang your Husband, Child, 'tis true, / But with him hang your Care."*

Lucy's personality suffers, of course, the same fate as Polly's, describing virtually the same curve of development. She is also introduced as a unique person with appropriately descriptive songs. The bitterness with which she likens the imprisoned Macheath to a trapped rat and herself to the housewife that caught it—partly because she chiefly desires to be a wife, and the wife of this very rat—gives her an identity quite separate from Polly's. Her nature is further removed from anything Polly has yet had to express in her second song, when she generalizes Macheath's inconstancy, describing the *"cruel . . . Traytors, / Who lye and swear in jest."* She is, however, soon echoing Polly, as I have indicated; and as the story develops, these rivals for public possession of Macheath become virtual reflections of one another. When they are squabbling over him, for instance, they sing two duets, *"I'm bubbled"* and *"Madam Flirt,"* in both of which they parrot one another. The effect of this is eventually reinforced by the entrance of their fathers, themselves mirror images, and by the establishment of a visual tableau with Macheath focused between the two father-daughter pairs, a situation his song, *"Which way shall I turn me?"* makes evident. In this late scene (III, xi), the two women once again sing a duet in which they parrot one another: *"'Tis Polly sues—'Tis Lucy speaks"*; *"Must I—Must I."* This song is followed by analogous appeals of each daughter in turn to her father. Polly on her knees asks Peachum to *"sink the . . . Evidence"* against

Macheath; then Lucy begs Lockit on her knees to repress "the Evidence"; both plead for "Compassion." Each one completes her request, moreover, with a song, each of which in turn closes on an expression about *"every Month* [being] *May."*

This developing identification of his two heroines Gay drives home by actually wrenching his story at one point, making Lockit speak about Macheath, quite inaccurately, the same way that the Peachums did, that is, as the "Husband" of his daughter. This allows him moreover, to echo attitudes and advice that the Peachums expressed. Peachum, who had seen widowhood as Polly's only deliverance from Macheath, was seconded by his wife, who advised their daughter, "Away, Hussy. Hang your Husband, and be dutiful." Lockit, likewise, argues that "no Woman would ever marry, if she had not the Chance of Mortality for a Release," and advises Lucy, "Do like other Widows—Buy yourself Weeds, and be cheerful." At the work's end, despite the fact that Lucy has tried to poison her, Polly suggests to her erstwhile rival, "Let us retire, my dear Lucy, and indulge our sorrow." And in the trio of farewell that they sing with their joint husband, they dwindle to mere aspects of one another: *"Would I might be hang'd! And I would so too;" "No token of Love? No token of Love?"* The tragedy, although its operatic reversal will require a sort of discrimination at last—"I take *Polly* for mine"—has made interchangeable female ciphers out of Gay's two heroines.

The same is true of his villains, Peachum and Lockit. Each one begins in his own profession although he immediately equates that, primarily on the basis of finance, with others. Peachum is concerned with the impeachment of his criminal subordinates: he books Tom Gagg, a "lazy Dog," for the forty-pound reward; leaves Black Moll to plead her belly, knowing that she and Filch are taking the necessary measures; determines to try Wat Dreary for a session or two longer; and, indeed, takes the actions a Peachum should take. Lockit also begins in a distinctively professional way, furnishing Macheath with the lightest fetters he can afford and locking him away. But the circumstances of the *Opera*, both the romantic and the professional, whittle away their separate identities, making them, like their daughters, subject to virtually metaphoric substitution, one for the other. Lockit's concern with the mutuality of their "Friendship" implies this:

> *Peachum* is my Companion, my Friend—According to the Custom of the World, indeed, he may quote thousands of Precedents for cheat-

ing me—And shall not I make use of the Privilege of Friendship to make him a Return?

Each one, informer and warden alike, enjoys "the Privilege of Friendship," and thus becomes the mirror image of the other. Their actual fight, during which they are displayed "collaring each other," intensifies the equation. And they end as strictly balancing figures in the domestic tableau that surrounds Macheath: their predatory concern with him has reduced them finally to the two halves of one "honest" in-law, an effect that is epitomized by their agreement "to go halves in *Macheath*," that is, to divide the bounty for his impeachment.

Macheath is the one figure who comes through the *Opera* with significant integrity: no other peg can fit his place in Gay's board. And, in so far as he preserves a self, even when it is no thicker than his red coat, he illuminates the collapse of individuality in the others. Standing among the commercial ladies; standing between Lucy and Polly; and, later, between the father-daughter pairs: Macheath gives visual force to their lack of particular personality. Being one cock among several hens, as Jenny Diver describes him, he enforces their merely categorical existence as "Women," to whom his attentions, as both the song and his own statements declare, are merely wholesale. Polly and Lucy, similarly, are both wives—along with "four Wives more," who show up at the end; and Peachum and Lockit are, in Macheath's words, a couple of "infamous Scoundrels." He is, on the other hand, always "the Captain." But even Macheath suffers in this pathologically metaphoric atmosphere. For one thing, he can be reduced to forty pounds, the same value as Tom Gagg or any other malefactor, and divided into halves: he can be transformed, that is, to just another entry in Peachum's and Lockit's books. Into this category, of course, Peachum and Lockit may also be fitted since, as Peachum recognizes, "Macheath may hang his . . . Father-in-law." Macheath himself reminds his comrades, who may escape the same fate for a few months longer, of this fact: Peachum's and Lockit's "lives are as much in your Power, as yours are in theirs."

Macheath is further blurred and diffused as a unique presence by his apparent sensibility—that is, the feelings and principles that emerge from his speech. His tendency to equate women with one another and with money, for instance, dilutes the identity as Polly's lover that his apparent affection for her originally conferred on him. His admission, "Women, I love the sex," undermines the kinship with Romeo that was established in the scene of his and Polly's parting, and includes him in his world's prevailing sensibility, an effect that is augmented when he sings, "*How happy could I be with either, / Were t'other dear Charmer away.*" His dependence on wine for courage, again, lumps him with the rest of the gang who also found that "*Wine inspires us . . . / With Courage.*" Macheath does retain a certain singularity throughout the *Opera*: he is generous and true to the gang in a distinctive way. However, although he never betrays anyone to the law, he insists at last on the vengeful betrayal of his villainous opposites. His previous tolerance of Peachum on the grounds of usefulness, likewise, and his prevailingly utilitarian view of women, which is especially evident when he sacrifices Polly as a "Wench" practicing a "Fetch" to assure Lucy's connivance in his escape, reduce Macheath to a proper citizen of Peachum's world.

The fleeting allusions to Christ, like whom this Son-of-the-Heath is betrayed (and by the *Ju Das*, *Jenny Diver*) to "*suffer . . . at the Tree,*" do not actually preserve the figure, or so it seems to me. If he is also surrounded by two thieves, as once he is no doubt, these two are essentially undistinguishable. The pervasive threat of death does provide something like an enduring halo for Macheath; but death is a strong presence throughout the *Opera*. In the first act, for example, Peachum puts a member of the gang named "Tom Gagg" on what he later describes to Mrs. Peachum as the black list; and at the opening of the second, two members of the gang have this macabre little exchange about a fellow member named "Tom":

> *Ben Budge.* But pr-thee, *Matt*, what is become of thy Brother *Tom*? I have not seen him since my Return from Transportation.
> *Matt of the Mint.* Poor Brother *Tom* had an Accident this time Twelve-month, and so clever a made Fellow he was, that I could not save him from those fleaing Rascals the Surgeons; and now, poor Man, he is among the Otamys at *Surgeon's Hall.*

Is this the same Tom? (Gay has made a similar double reference to Black Moll, who was reported to need insemination—so that she could plead her belly—in the first act and represented in the second as having just received it.) If so, this little digression endows the obvious horror of this "Otamy" with terrible efficiency. Such signs of death, often represented as hanging, all focus on Macheath and thus illuminate him. But, when we view the *Opera* at a distance and see that mortality is swiftly overtaking almost everybody, we find that it has included the Captain as a mere example in one more of its categories.

The effects of actual figures of speech and of the developments of the plot in dissolving the outlines of personal individuality in the *Opera* are reinforced by the characters' persistent habit of generalizing, of lumping one another together into categories of appetite or fashion or mortal susceptibility or financial convenience. Lucy should not mourn for Macheath, Lockit tells her, for instance, because "Tis not the fashion nowadays." In considering his friendship for Peachum, again, Lockit invokes "the Custom of the World," himself determining to follow this custom; and he sings a song of general import about "Gamesters united in Friendship." Many of the songs have a prevailingly general significance: Lucy's about traitors in love; Jenny Diver's about the similarity of lawyers to gamesters; Macheath's on the effects of love and on the swiftness with which youth passes; and the gang's on the various inspiriting effects of wine. Polly, even when she is appealing for personal sympathy, explains that *"Virgins* [in general] *are like the fair Flower in its Lustre."* She herself does not strictly belong to the general category of *"Virgins,"* but her use of the plural nevertheless generalizes *"Flower"* when that is metaphorically substituted. Polly begins another song defending her own actions by enunciating a general principle, *"Can Love be controul'd by Advice?"* Although during the shock of discovering Polly's marriage, Mrs. Peachum notes particularly, *"Our Polly is a sad Slut,"* she more normally generalizes, as in the song, *"A Maid is like the golden Oar."* Peachum, too, generalizes first about *"all the Employments of Life"* and, later, even when he is confronted with what Mrs. Peachum condemns as Polly's "particularity," about the capacity of lawyers to steal one's *"whole estate."*

The general principles recognized in Gay's world, such as the equivalency of love with possession, the dishonesty of almost everybody, and the necessity of observing fashion, contribute significantly to its inhabitants' tendency to neglect or deny the particularities of their conditions, their commitments and their acquaintance. But the "Fuller's Earth," which takes the stain of individual existence from almost everything, is money, as Peachum, the master alchemist, proclaims. Money reduces the qualities Gay introduces in the *Opera* to quantities—to "stock" as Moll Flanders might put it; and thus allows the materialistic equation of anything with anything and of anyone with anyone. ("You cannot add apples and oranges," as my old arithmetic teacher used to warn his pupils; but reduce them both to fruit or on down

to items in an account book and they figure quite smoothly.) It is
not merely that all relationships in this world can be resolved into
business arrangements, love into "fees" and "debts"; freedom
into "garnish" and "perquisites"; thievery into a cure for "ava-
rice"; and marriage into a tissue of fortunes, pay, jointures, con-
tracts, and legal dispute—although that is bad enough. When
Mrs. Peachum berates Polly for not choosing a husband with
money; when Lockit advises Lucy to impeach Macheath because
she "can't have the Man and the Money too"; when Jenny Diver
and Suky Tawdry make "a private bargain" to betray their host
and lover; when Peachum lets Betty Sly escape transportation
simply because he can get more money by her staying in England:
Gay has apparently composed, if in highly concentrated form, a
conventional attack on greed. But considering these in connection
with a prevailing figure in the *Opera*, that in which specified
amounts of money are metaphorically substituted for actual persons, we face a still more terrible situation: that is, the virtual
obliteration, partly owing to greed no doubt, of human beings in
their particular natures and human experience in its particularity
of sensation.

In the world of Gay's *Opera*, in which money can rationalize
any metaphor at all, the experiential, the natural, tissue of lively
identities and interesting differences has been cancelled. It may
seem paradoxical to all of us who have considered metaphor as
a way of sharpening and clarifying our sense of things, but the
logical end of this procedure is the reduction of all things to the
same thing, to interchangeable counters in a strictly undifferenti-
ated field. To Peachum any thief is or may become a forty-pound
entry in the book and thus a substitute for any other. Even Macheath, whose value to Polly is strictly particular, strictly incom-
mensurable, Peachum can reduce to forty pounds and thus halve
equitably with Lockit. (This may explain, I suppose, why Macheath, who perfectly understands the *Opera*'s arithmetic, sets
twenty *guineas* as the perquisite Lockit may require for his escape.)
Peachum is forced sometimes to acknowledge the particular
qualities of things. He once advises Polly, who is going to wait
on customers for her father's goods,

> . . . If 'tis the Gentleman who was here Yesterday about the
> Repeating-Watch; say, you believe we can't get Intelligence of it, till
> to-morrow. For I lent it to *Suky Straddle*, to make a Figure with it to-
> night at a Tavern in *Drury-Lane*. If t'other Gentleman calls for the
> Silver-hilted Sword; you know Beetle-brow'd *Jemmy* hath it on, and

he doth not come from *Tunbridge* till *Tuesday* night; so that it cannot
be had till then.

But this observance of particularity is, as Peachum understands,
a hindrance to trade. Mrs. Trapes complains to him about a certain stolen item, for instance, "that Watch was remarkable, and
not of very safe sale." He himself once directs Mrs. Peachum to
"rip out the Coronets and Marks of those dozen of [stolen] Cam-
bric Handkerchiefs"—thus obliterating their "remarkable" qualities and reducing them to undistinguishable and therefore safe
items of stock.

Money, as the "Fuller's Earth" that can remove all particular
traces from things, is most impressively focused by Peachum and
others on women. Consider, for example, Mrs. Peachum's general
discussion of her daughter's present and future social condition:

> A Maid is like the golden Oar,
> Which hath Guineas intrinsical in't,
>   Whose Worth is never known, before
> It is try'd and imprest in the Mint.
> A Wife's like a Guinea in Gold,   5
> Stampt with the Name of her Spouse;
>   Now here, now there; is bought, or is sold;
> And is current in every House.

A maid—Polly, for instance, as *we* may recall—is like a lump of
ore that will make an uncertain number of guineas, the number
and hence the full and actual worth of the lump being determined
when it is minted, that is, I take it, when the marriage settlement
is concluded. The glamorous expression, *"golden Oar,"* may disguise this unmitigated materialism; so may its being presented
as a pretty song: but this mother's evaluation of her maiden child
her general, metaphoric representation makes pretty clear. The
second quatrain is worse: in the first one Polly can be imagined
at least as a particular lump of ore and one, furthermore, who is
worth a specific number of guineas—more or fewer than another
maiden. In the second quatrain, a wife, that is, any wife in general, is like a single golden guinea; every wife, according to the
figure, being, except for her stamp as "Mrs. Peachum" or "Mrs.
Macheath," precisely interchangeable on the market with every
other. And the stamp, as Mrs. Peachum's introductory remarks
make clear, is itself only of general importance. It doesn't matter
which wife this one is, only that she is a wife, or, as Mrs. Peachum
puts it, "another's property." The reduction of wives to properties

is, however, not the worst of this business: the worst is this, that in being reduced to items of property, they are deprived of their individual substance. Every wife, like every guinea, is strictly interchangeable with every other.

This figure occurs at several points in the *Opera*. Macheath likens his parting from Polly to a miser's surrender of a shilling:

> *The Miser thus a Shilling Sees,*
> *Which he's obliged to pay,*
> *With Sighs resigns it by degrees,*
> *And fears 'tis gone for aye.*

I'm not sure whether we should note that Polly seems like a smaller coin to her husband than to her mother. But that Polly's closest connections agree in reducing her to an object that is indistinguishable from thousands of others constitutes a point of decisive importance. Polly responds to Macheath's figure by likening herself to a boy who sees his pet sparrow escape:

> *The Boy, thus, when his Sparrow's flown,*
> *The Bird in Silence eyes;*
> *But soon as out of Sight 'tis gone,*
> *Whines, whimpers, sobs, and cries.*

This conclusion to their scene of parting maintains a distant allusion to the romantic separation of Romeo and Juliet, both of whom conceived of Romeo as "a wanton's bird, / That let's it hop a little from his hand / Like a poor prisoner in his twisted gyves, / And with a silken thread plucks it back again, / So loving-jealous of his liberty." But Polly earlier has conceived of Macheath, quite in line with the general tendency of the *Opera*, as "contreband . . . Treasure" of which she finally has complete "*Possession.*" In a few minutes Macheath, while waiting on a company of women, draws the logical conclusion of his metaphor for Polly: "a Man who loves Money, might as well be contented with one Guinea [with one shilling?] as I with one woman." Lucy also connives at this corrosive figure: the only difference between a man who cheats young maidens and "whoever steals a shilling," she sings, in another of the *Opera's* general expositions of love, is that the thief in love, unlike the other, "*With Boasts the Theft reveals.*"

The inhabitants of the *Opera* then, who characteristically reduce everything and everyone into financial terms, deny the particular, the individual, qualities of things and persons. Once he is dead, Macheath advises both Polly and Lucy, if a husband is what they want: "Ship yourselves off for the West Indies, where you'll have a fair chance of getting a Husband a-piece; or by good Luck, two or three, as you like best." Once again, the furthest thrust of Gay's jest is not that husbands and wives are mere commodities;[5] but that, in being reduced to commodities ("ship yourselves"), they are further reduced to strictly interchangeable items: advice to one wife is exactly appropriate to the other as well; and any husband (or set of husbands) will fill the vacancy left by any other. Lockit accounts for this reduction of human individuality by distinguishing between mankind and the other animals:

> Lions, Wolves, and Vulturs don't live together in Herds, Droves, or Flocks.—Of all Animals of Prey, Man is the only sociable one. Every one of us preys upon his Neighbour, and yet we herd together.

The point is that among mankind, that sociable animal, predator and prey "herd together"; that is to say, they cannot be told apart. The predators Lockit mentions may recall a cluster of figures in the *Opera* that has been recognized by Patricia Spacks,[6] a cluster of animals variously disposed as predators and prey: foxes steal hens; fishermen (or women, actually) catch gudgeons; hunters kill ducks; housewives trap rats. Implicit, however, in the *Opera*'s reduction of all society to oppressors and victims is a worse: that one can't tell which is which. The animal figures, reductive as they are, are thus relatively cheery in this context. At least when we see a fox in a hen house or a housewife with a rat, we can identify and perhaps sympathize with the victim. But the misadventures of a guinea—*"now here now there; [now] bought or . . . sold; / And . . . current in every house"*—we can hardly even follow. It is to this that the individual differences, in which Gay has located human happiness, have been reduced.

*   *   *

In *Trivia* Gay accepted Berkeley's teaching that perception is and ought to be the total concern of humanity, and he submitted himself without reservation to what Hume, following Berkeley, would describe as an inconceivably rapid procession of different things: with the result that Hume might have predicted. He virtually became the things that he beheld. In the *Beggar's Opera*, on the other hand, Gay gave personal identity in the form of his dramatic personages an emphatic presence, making it much more resistant to the effects of perception and making its erosion much more impressive. He submitted his personages first to the effects of perceptual resemblance, as this works in the habits of culture and the conventions of society, and thus described the absorption of Polly in a caldron of categories. He submitted all the *Opera's* personages secondly to the radically material realm of trade, reducing them to pounds and shillings. Even Macheath, as I have explained, has been comprehended in these terms and melted down in a commercial computation. In the *Opera*, individual personal substance is thus vulnerable to—has, indeed, thus been destroyed by—perception, on the one hand, and matter, on the other.

Pope would largely avoid the second of these dangers, that is, the depredations of matter, creating his world inductively from the perceptual resemblance of things. His meticulous observance of the differences between things saved—for a time at least—the different substances. But perceptual differences proved, finally, to have as reductive an effect, Pope discovered, as Gay had found in perceptual resemblances. Once Pope acknowledged "that each one differs from himself," he would be driven, like Gay before him, to describe the dissolution of individual personality. Since Radcliffe and Austen were determined to establish sufficient personal substances to justify marriage and a sufficient array of characters to maintain society, they confronted this complicated threat to human identity that the poets had represented as their primary challenge. How might their heroines reconcile such perceptual fragments as one mind encounters and compose from them such a thing (in Sterne's comic words) as a married man? Better perhaps, to what extent might they do so?

First, however, to proceed in good order, we must examine the full power of inductive composition and the full awareness of perceptual diversity as these emerge in the essays of Pope.

4

Pope's Essays

Alexander Pope devoted himself throughout his career to a study of the different things of his experience in their particularity, believing, however, that these things were naturally organized as integral substances and coherent developments and that a poet could reconcile them accordingly in reliable generalizations. This was what it meant for a poet to follow nature.[1] Because of its limitations in experience and comprehension, however, as Pope vividly recognized, the human intellect, poetic or otherwise, must follow nature from a good way behind especially if it aspired, as Pope did, to reach the most stupendous natural organization of all, that is, the universe. Like Berkeley, Pope had an intense confidence in this ultimate organization and, beyond that, in its divine support; but representing it in poetic essays was, as he well knew, another matter:

> Thro' worlds unnumber'd tho' the God be known,
> 'Tis ours to trace him only in our own.

A poet, who, like everybody else, had to rely on his senses, could not behold how worlds on worlds compose one universe nor even observe how the finer nerves and vessels compose one human body. It was but a part or, more precisely, a few parts that he saw and to which he must refer in making his poems.

This insufficiency of human intelligence to carry out tasks of composition that it could nevertheless conceive Pope recognized throughout his life. In his youthful *Essay on Criticism*, he explained:

> Thus in the *Soul* while *Memory* prevails,
> The solid Pow'r of *Understanding* fails;
> Where Beams of warm *Imagination* play,
> The *Memory's* soft Figures melt away.

The chiasmus here, indicating a little turn toward and then away from memory, is significant: even so basic a creative exercise, it implies, is too hard to be altogether accomplished by the individual human mind. As one consults memory, one's understanding diminishes; and the assemblage of memorabilia, on which understanding might have worked, dissolves as one attempts, by an exertion of imagination, to weld together the remembered elements. The different actions that human intelligence must take to compose its experience and establish natural patterns seem indeed to be both necessary and impossible. Nor is this the full story of our creative limitations.

> One *Science* only will one *Genius* fit;
> So *vast* is Art, so *narrow* Human Wit;
> Not only bounded to *peculiar Arts*,
> But oft in *those* confin'd to *single Parts*.

Nevertheless, thus confined in both capacity and range, the human mind may yet attempt, Pope has asserted, to bring some of its ideas into order:

> Each might his *sev'ral Province* well command,
> Wou'd all but *stoop* to what they *understand*.

If separate minds would share their individual provinces with one another, moreover, and draw on the knowledge that Western culture has accumulated, practicing the politeness and invoking the learning that Pope's age insistently advocated, they might in time achieve a general sense of nature entire and, by beating over this ample field together, reach at last up through nature toward nature's God.[2]

I have shown in Swift and Gay a skepticism and even a hostility to generalization both as an intellectual practice and as a product of social institution. These older contemporaries of Pope focused human happiness in separate persons and based human understanding on separate impressions; the processes of intellectual composition and social observance, which threaten the individuality of people and experience, they viewed therefore with relentless suspicion. Gay indicated this attitude positively in *Trivia* by illuminating the immediacies of perception and negatively in *The Beggar's Opera* by describing the erosion of personality. Swift developed it in many ways, making the multifarious forms of generality available and at the same time challenging them with an impressive range of particular circumstances. Pope, on the other hand, although he paid steady attention to people and to things in their differences, embraced the challenges of generalization both in human understanding and in human society. As he grew older, admittedly, he became intensely sensitive to the particularity of things and skeptical of even our most habitual and necessary inductions. "General Satire in Times of General Vice," he once explained, "has no force. . . . 'Tis only by hunting One or two from the Herd that any Examples can be made."[3] This is only the first step in Pope's analysis of individual character, moreover, as examination of the epistle *To a Lady* will show. And yet, once again, he was at the same time deeply committed to "the Herd," that is, to general representations and general judgments.

The more fully one accounts for the parts, Pope always believed, the more adequately one can represent the whole;[4] and although he seems finally to have given up the effort to reach agreement with the whole of human society,[5] he never gave up the attempt to represent the whole human situation. Understanding Pope's creative commitment in such a way, I suggest that his leading principle was this: he who generalizes is a poet.

*   *   *

Pope's dedication to the likenesses and differences among separate things and to the general orders that might be inductively composed from them can best be demonstrated, perhaps, by studying extreme examples: the first epistle of *An Essay on Man*, in which his confidence in the composition of things comprehended the universe; and the epistle *To a Lady*, in which he discovered the composition of an individual person to be virtually inconceivable.

To represent Pope's exposition of the perceptual universe as "one stupendous whole" in the *Essay*, I return to Berkeley, a friend with whom the poet is known to have consulted.[6] In his *Three Dialogues* the philosopher had enunciated a proof of deity and an image of the world to which the poet's is closely similar. This theology was, moreover, precisely congruent with Berkeley's basic principle, *esse* is *percipi*, and thus very compelling.

. . . It is evident . . . that sensible things cannot exist otherwise than in a mind or spirit [that is, *esse* is *percipi*]. Whence I conclude, not that they have no real existence, but that, seeing they depend not on my thought, and have an existence distinct from being perceived by me, *there must be some other mind wherein they exist*. As sure, therefore,

as the sensible world really exists, so sure is there an infinite omnipresent Spirit, who contains and supports it.

This wonderfully terse proof, with which Berkeley has replaced
the old-fashioned argument from design, a version of which he
himself had formulated in his *Principles*, precisely fits his radical
philosophy. It is no doubt *ad hominem*, depending on the apparently immovable human tendency to believe in a world of nature
external to its own consciousness. That is what Berkeley means
by asserting that "the sensible world really exists": it exists, as
Johnson's famous kick illustrates, in the firm belief of each and
every human being. Given this belief and given Berkeley's basic
principle, to the establishment and development of which the
Three Dialogues is devoted, the conclusion clearly follows: there
must be a universal mind which supports the sensible universe.
And Berkeley can therefore describe a world as vast and as splen-
didly organized as he can imagine:

> How sincere a pleasure is it to behold the natural beauties of the
> earth! To preserve and renew our relish for them, is not the veil of
> night alternately drawn over her face, and doth she not change her
> dress with the seasons? How aptly are the elements disposed! What
> variety and use in the meanest productions of nature! What delicacy,
> what beauty, what contrivance, in animal and vegetable bodies! How
> exquisitely are all things suited, as well to their particular ends, as to
> constitute opposite parts of the whole! And, while they mutually aid
> and support, do they not also set off and illustrate each other? Raise
> now your thoughts from this ball of earth to all those glorious lumi-
> naries that adorn the high arch of heaven. The motion and situation
> of the planets, are they not admirable for use and order? . . . Yet, if
> you take the telescope, it brings into your sight a new host of stars
> that escape the naked eye. Here they seem contiguous and minute,
> but to a nearer view immense orbs of light at various distances, far
> sunk in the abyss of space. Now you must call imagination to your aid.
> The feeble narrow sense cannot descry innumerable worlds revolving
> round the central fires; and in those worlds the energy of an all-
> perfect Mind displayed in endless forms. But neither sense nor imagi-
> nation are big enough to comprehend the boundless extent, with all
> its glittering furniture. Though the labouring mind exert and strain
> each power to its utmost reach, there still stands out ungrasped a
> surplusage immeasurable. . . . Is not the whole system immense,
> beautiful, glorious beyond expression and beyond thought!

That is, of course, beyond *our* thought.
An understanding of this stupendous "contrivance," Berkeley's
representation of which approaches the very threshold of Pope's

Essay, sanctions and encourages the tireless exercise of experimental science—or what Pope and Berkeley called "natural philosophy"—with its mechanical aids to the "feeble narrow sense" and its meticulous measurements of areas and times. Its practitioners consider the "connexion of ideas" great and small that they can gather and record; and, by careful induction, describe "the laws and methods of nature." And for the most part, as the example of Newton suggested, they would find what in the *Principles* Berkeley called "an admirable connexion" in things great and small. But even the detection of rude, shapeless, and jumbled natural elements—what Pope would acknowledge as "plagues or earthquakes . . . a Borgia or a Catiline"—fails to weaken Berkeley's proof:

> You may now, without any laborious search into the sciences, without any subtlety of reason, or tedious length of discourse, oppose and baffle the most strenuous advocate for Atheism; those miserable refuges, whether in an eternal succession of unthinking causes and effects, or in a fortuitous concourse of atoms; those wild imaginations of Vanini, Hobbes, and Spinoza: in a word, the whole system of Atheism, is it not entirely overthrown, by this single reflexion on the repugnancy [that is, the contradiction] included in supposing the whole, or any part, even the most rude and shapeless, of the visible world, to exist without a mind? Let any one of those abettors of impiety but look into his own thoughts, and there try if he can conceive how so much as a rock, a desert, a chaos, or confused jumble of atoms; how anything at all, either sensible or imaginable, can exist independent of a mind, and he need go no farther to be convinced of his folly.

The whole of the perceived and of the conceivable universe then, both in its normal regularity and in its incidental confusion, must necessarily be comprehended by a mind or spirit—*esse* is *percipi*—and thus the existence of a universal, omniscient mind is certain.

This represents, I believe, the appropriate background of the *Essay.* Pope, like Berkeley, is devoted to human experience, insisting that we can trace God only in our own perceptions, reasoning strictly from what we know. He is vividly aware at the same time, as Berkeley was, of the "finer nerves and vessels, the conformations and uses of which will for ever escape our observation,"[7] that is, of the conceivable tissue of experiences lying only within the range of telescope and microscope; and on beyond only within the range of imagination; and on beyond that: a totality the existence of which necessitates a mind of all. The first epistle of the *Essay* is devoted throughout its course to these two realms, the perceivable and the conceivable; and it develops its image of universal nature and of nature's God by enacting upon its readers an imaginary voyage or—more precisely, perhaps—a series of imaginary elevator rides between them. The first epistle of the *Essay* thus constitutes a refinement and an intensification of Berkeley's argument. The philosopher proved to the vulgar, the ordinary folk (or, better, to the ordinary in all people), that, since there was an ordinarily apprehensible tissue of perceptuality lying beyond individual human perception, there must be a mind of all; the poet proves to the intellectually arrogant, the scientifically ambitious people (or, better, to that strain of intellectual pride in all people), that, since there is an intellectually apprehensible tissue of perceptions lying beyond its actual (and augmented) power of perception, there must be a mind of all.

This epistle of the *Essay* is characterized throughout its course by its pointed presentation of politely shared experience and understanding and thus constitutes a fabric of what Pope and his age quite appropriately called common sense. Its verbs, which cluster around the activities of seeing and saying, enforce this complex intention to observe and to share. Among these verbs, these activities, are, first, see, eye, look, shoot, explore, expatiate, trace, guess, comprehend, weigh, judge, think, find, mark; and, second, say, tell, reason, ask, wrangle, call, cry, answer, reply, charge, acquit, name, blame. Pope has created this situation of polite intellectual exchange, moreover, precisely in keeping with his intentions as I have been deducing these. His opening invitation draws his friend, St. John, from the realm of public involvement, an obviously natural human vantage point, to that of unnaturally detached observation from which the two of them can behold all things with an equal eye. This dichotomy of vantages is suggested in the very first lines with Pope's urging that he and his friend should rise above all "low," "meaner" things. And it is quite sharply defined in the line, "A mighty maze! but not without a plan," the first half of which represents the world as human beings involved in the stresses of present employment endure it, the second half disclosing the view, the understanding, that the retirement, to which Pope invites his friend, will allow: as one draws back from a maze, rising above it on trembling pinions, he immediately recognizes its orderly coherence. In the next lines, similarly, "A Wild, where weeds and flow'rs promiscuous shoot, / Or Garden, tempting with forbidden fruit," one moves from a sense of confused, entangling details enunciated in the first line to the sense, defined by the second, of a highly organized—indeed, divinely instituted—whole, the detachment from personal involvement again allowing a view not merely more complete but different in kind: what looks like a wild while one is entangled in it is revealed to an elevated view to be a garden.

Pope rejects for his present purposes the old story in recounting which Milton attempted to justify God's ways. He recognizes temptation as a persistent aspect of the scene, but does not acknowledge a fall.[8] The different scenes he invites his friend to observe and share constitute not a historical but a continuous situation, one that makes all observations everlastingly valid: he reasons not only from what he can observe at this time, but from what humankind have always and will always be able to observe; and thus he stands as a candidate for a common sense that reaches to the very edges of human culture. We will no doubt reject his "headlong lioness"; but we do so, with his approval, on scientific grounds: Pope's expert source was simply in error in this case.[9] We would never ask Milton's avuncular lion, his inattentive whale or his eloquent serpent to pass scientific muster, whereas most of Pope's animals will do so quite brilliantly: from the half-reasoning elephant and the sagacious hound to the intricately skilled spider and the fly with his microscopic vision.

The evil change that Milton imagined as the consequence of human presumption Pope denies, replacing it with a difference, although no doubt compatible sometimes with human presumption, in vantage point. Instead of early purity and later corruption, that is, the story of the fall,[10] Pope presents—as both concurrently and everlastingly available—the personally involved apprehension of things and that revealed to personal retirement. In imaginatively developing the latter, to which Pope invites his friend and, by implication, all of society, he creates the means of representing God's universe to humankind. On occasion, Pope will condemn us—if not St. John—for "soaring" or "rushing" into the skies, but in the epistle's introduction he pointedly advocates such a removal, even if the advocacy is rationalized as offering (the displaced politician?) all or almost all that "Life can . . . supply."

Pope prosecutes this different viewpoint throughout the epistle, describing actually unexperienced likenesses and contiguities among the diverse orders of creation. He enjoys, even while mocking them, Epicurus's peculiar perspicuity and, at another time, the high notions of anthrocentrism as a general attitude; in each case providing the view from this height in the very process

of rejecting it. On the other hand, he lowers us (with scientific
diffidence) to the hopes of the poor Indian, to the bemusement
of the horse and the ox, to the qualities and capacities of various
lower animals—down at certain points to the minute susceptibili-
ties of the insects. He rushes us up and drops us down with
remarkable economy, an economy achieved in considerable part
by the employment of tropes: metaphor, generally speaking,
provides the motive energy for these shifts, metonymy both a
visionary discrimination and the assurance of one's eventual establishment in his own specific place. These excursions are articu-
lated with a wide variety of positive tones, sympathy, admiration,
and exhilaration (in representing the spider's fine touch, for example), and with an equally wide range of negative tones, from
irony to sarcasm to pious outrage. But from all, the negative no
less than the positive, Pope derives an active and poetically compelling exposition of the difference between the universe which
humankind can naturally experience and that which, under ordinary conditions, we can only imagine.

In the first lines of this passage there is a metaphor that works
to such an effect:

> Heav'n from all creatures hides the book of Fate,
> All but the page prescrib'd, their present state;
> From brutes what men, from men what spirits know:
> Or who could suffer Being here below?

The development of time into the future, as creatures must cope
with this, has been likened to a book and the emerging unknown,
delimited as separate pages that have been withheld from those
to whom they refer. This metaphor, which implicitly likens
"Heav'n" (itself a tactful metonym) to a benevolent tutor, subtly
modifies the difference between the creatures listed in line three,
uniting brutes, which cannot in fact read, of course, with men,
who can, and men, who must read to extend their knowledge,
with spirits, who need not do so. On the one hand then, this
metaphor unifies the three different orders on the consideration
of which this passage is chiefly focused. On the other hand, by
dividing the seamlessly evolving future into contiguous entities
of ignorance-and-revelation, that is, into separate pages, this
metaphor enforces the difference between these orders that requires the imaginative inference which is the passage's primary
effect.

In order adequately to represent this effect I must also acknowledge two transparent metaphors, two assertions of similitude embedded in diction. First, each of the general terms, "brutes," "men," and "spirits," represents as similar—similar, that is, in the knowledge of their fates—every particular member of that category. Pope's practice here is no doubt normal and, therefore, unobtrusive; but its consequences for his argument are nevertheless enormous. (Every general term is a metaphorical black hole, attracting millions of particular items or, if you will, proper names and many intermediate terms into a vortex of sameness and constituting in itself, as the Nominalists balefully insist, a philosophical move of great significance.) Pope has made serious use of this linguistically normal assertion of similitude throughout his *Essay.* Tentatively taking "brutes" in the present case as synonymous with "beasts," which Pope has distinguished elsewhere from birds, fish, insects, and the microscopic myriads, I recognize as strictly similar in the way indicated such creatures as the groveling swine, the dull ox and the faithful dog. Under "men" I list indiscriminately (for this moment) Catiline, Newton, the poor Indian, and Lord Bolingbroke; and under "spirits," the nine heavenly hierarchies, seraphim, cherubim, thrones, dominations, virtues, powers, principalities, archangels, and angels, which were enumerated by Denis and subtly recognized in this very poem by Pope. What is being established in this passage, therefore, holds the same, whatever their individual differences may be, for every brute, every human, and every spirit. The term "creatures," emphasized by "all," is categorically analogous but a stage up in generality, holding as similar in the indicated way, not only all brutes, men, and spirits, but all birds, fish, and insects, right down to the green myriads. Owing to this sharply delimited pyramid of likeness and difference, the statement, the theological force of which I will soon deduce, pertains alike—allowing for the differences asserted by the three subordinate generalities— to all creatures. Pope's meticulous use of normal linguistic generality has allowed him, without the employment of obtrusive tropes, to organize a full system of similitudes and contiguities, the combined elements of which constitute a universal synecdoche.

Before considering the statement Pope has made about this whole system of created beings, I must recognize the strains in it which emerge in the fourth line of the passage. "Here below" conventionally means here on this earth, exempting all spirits from the position; but not in this case. Here it becomes metaphori-

cal, likening the empyrean right up to the foot of God's throne
to mundane ignorance: the "spirits," being creatures too, as Pope
has indicated, also remain "here below" with men and brutes.
This usage, like the book metaphor, modifies the partition dividing the human realm from that of angels and thus makes the
spheres of heaven accessible, if not to the invasion of human
intelligence, at least to a speculative excursion. "Who" is under a
similar strain, pulling, however, primarily the other way. We have
little trouble saying, "Gabriel who"—a recognition that further
diminishes the angelic partition; but in the present context brutes
may also herd under this pronoun since their "Being," like that
of men and spirits, is made sufferable by their ignorance of their
own fate. "Who" pulling one way and "below" another thus
strengthen the coverage of "creatures" and facilitate the passage
of human intelligence both up and down the great chain of being
that Pope enacts on his readers again and again in this epistle.

Prosecuting the book-of-fate metaphor, we see that the line,
"From brutes what men, from men what spirits know," presents
two separate pages, one of which is hidden from the brutes even
while men are reading it and one of which is hidden from men
while the angels read. The first of these pages, a radiant example
of which Pope will present in the very next lines of the epistle,
is, unlike the second, totally accessible to humans as a fulfillment
of the stated conditions: we enjoy at once a sense of it as hidden,
that is, from brutes, and as revealed, that is, to us. It recalls
thousands of individual pages, moreover, looking back on which
we see to have been both hidden and revealed at once: pages, for
example, on which the fate of the swift trout became legible to
the tyrannic pike and others on which that of the pike became
legible to the skillful fisherman. Thus opening around this page,
which we behold as both hidden and revealed at once, are innu-
merable illustrative instances: and an enormous pattern, a system
of unexceptionable similitudes, emerges. Every page in the book
of fate, we infer, is like every other, being at once hidden from one
being and evident to another. And this compels us to augment the
partially completed pattern of the second page that the line offers,
inferring a being to know this page—this kind of page—of which
we are now ignorant. (This precisely reflects the Berkeleian inference that I have recently noticed.) The mere fact of this hidden
page in *our* fate, a fact that has been subtly particularized with
the elliptical suspension of the term "know" in the very line that
is presenting it, requires us to infer the spirits, the intellectually
higher creatures, who must exist in order to know this page and

thus to allow its inclusion in the pattern of fateful pages that our own experience—as animated by Pope—has presented to us. And once the inference of these next higher spirits has been made, the existence of a higher tier of being that must (in order to avoid an infinite regress) end in total sentience has been established. Above the highest creature, who endures a succession of hidden pages, must be the master intellect, to whom every page is always already available, an intellect that contains and supports the whole tissue of time and fate that includes every creature. Thus by following the equivocal nature of fate as Pope has tropically illuminated it, we find ourselves led up from "what we know" to what we did not know, from "nature up to nature's God." All this Pope has enacted upon us by drawing our attention to that one apparently exceptional page of fate, the existence of which but not the contents of which we know.

In the very next lines of the epistle, Pope provides a luminous instance of the first page above, one drawn, that is to say, from human experience:

> The lamb thy riot dooms to bleed to-day,
> Had he thy Reason, would he skip and play?
> Pleas'd to the last, he crops the flow'ry food,
> And licks the hand just rais'd to shed his blood.

Recognizing the lamb as a "brute" presents a challenge to human sympathy that will inform the development of this instance. Having absorbed it, however, if with reservations, we see that the lamb can suffer his "Being here below" because the page of his fate, which we are now reading (that is, his being doomed to bleed today), has been hidden from him: the lamb is thus similar to every other brute and a representative for brutes as a whole. While enforcing the brutal specificity of this case, however, Pope develops it to extend our knowledge, again representing by implication the whole chain of creatures. The lamb itself radiates with both human and sacred meanings, its "blood" especially suggesting a similitude both with human beings in general and with a certain one of them, the crucified Christ. This upward reach of the case is enforced by "dooms" and "hand," as I will soon explain. It also reaches downward: in bending to crop "the flow'ry food," the lamb is reading a page on which is written the fate of the surrounding verdure even while that unknowingly fulfills itself in blossoms. "Flow'ry food" presents this page of fate in both its aspects, the adjectival reduction, "flow'ry," enacting the lamb's preeminence: although flowers in themselves, these lowly items on the scale of created being are, according to the hungry doom of the lamb, becoming food to him—just as he is, because of our riotous doom, becoming food to us. Although "skip" and "play" intensify his likeness to a certain group of humankind, again, the fact that he "licks," rather than kisses, the hand that deals him his fate strongly specifies his situation, making contiguity dominate similitude, as it has throughout this whole section of the poem.

The "you" Pope addresses enforces the human difference, but it is also subjected to metaphorical expansion. "Riot dooms" is an oxymoronic expression, for example, somewhat like "flow'ry food": "dooms" reaches upward, linking "you" to God, on whose final doom, as the word reminds us, all the creatures wait; but "riot," possibly recalling the prodigal son, anchors "you" inescapably in the rowdy, appetitive world of humanity. (Man is, in one sense, more of a brute than the lamb is.) The figuratively radiant "hand" also reaches both ways: it is a metonym for knife, since the unaided hand can hardly shed blood, and thus intensifies human butchery; but it is also a synecdoche, in the first place, for "you," no doubt, but also—especially since it is, not "thy hand," but "the hand"—for some divine intervention. The synecdoche of "hand" for God, which is a common cultural property, Pope actually employs in this poem, insisting that mankind should feel "Safe in the hand of one disposing Pow'r." Once again, however, the insistence on riot and butchery as the motives of this "hand" preserves as the primary intention the difference between carnivorous humans and the whole spiritual realm and, beyond this, the contiguity of the separate created orders.

Both line three in my first quotation from the *Essay* and the extended instance of the lamb constitute synecdoches, each of them in its own way representing the whole chain of created being. They thus unify the different realms of creation and facilitate movement up and down its separate tiers, the practice of which has, as I have explained, a decisive benefit for Pope's theology. It is crucially important, on the other hand, to recognize that in both the logical inference and in the illustration, Pope has established a plane of being which, unaided by his poem, we can, as he has made us recognize, only conceive. It is his use of metaphor and metonymy, again, that both illuminates the limits of our natural vision and allows us throughout the poem to soar "on trembling pinions" into this realm of greater illumination. The opportunity for such an excursion Pope makes spectacular use of in the immediately following lines.

Another challenging transition, bridging between the prophecy of the lamb's butchery and the announcement of the divine kindness, propels his readers into the empyrean of insouciant observation:

> Oh blindness to the future! kindly giv'n,
> That each may fill the circle mark'd by Heav'n;
> Who sees with equal eye, as God of all,
> A hero perish, or a sparrow fall,
> Atoms or systems into ruin hurl'd,   5
> And now a bubble burst, and now a world.

The proffered view, which we enjoy from the vantage of divine equity, transforms a variety of created states into a synecdochic tissue for the whole created universe or, rather, for its eventual destruction. The completed circles of hero, sparrow, atoms, systems, bubble, and world, modified individually by details of allusion, grammar, and diction, stand as a selection of parts for the fate of creation as a whole. We here view each and all with the "equal eye" that our normal perspective disallows, having soared to the heavenly situation Pope has made temporarily available to us. The items themselves, the differences of which impress ordinary human awareness, are rendered "equal" in that divine view to which we are here admitted, our normally metonymic sense being replaced (or modified) briefly by the metaphoric diffidence of deity.

This illuminated situation Pope defines in the first three lines with elaborate tact. The passive voice in the first line, which withholds identification of the responsible agent; the spatial term, "Heav'n," in the second, which accommodates all spiritual conditions, and in the third the simile (or optional simile) that represents the "equal eye" through which we now see as resembling—not identical with—that of God: these practices broaden the present metaphorical indications and aid our removal to the divine vantage, allowing us an excursion somewhere beyond the angelic partition but not providing us a seat on the throne of God. Still, of course, we see quite enough and with quite enough equanimity for Pope to enact his point. The sparrow's fall, because of the biblical allusion, we may see as God sees it although it is well within normal human range; so is the death of the hero, which, being a human end, comes closer to home. The balance of the hero with the sparrow, nevertheless, and the governance of both with the quasi-divine "seeing" keep them remote from ordinary human sympathy. Both the atoms and systems, the difference between which is adequately indicated by the terms, are new to—that is, beyond—human seeing, the one more minute than a microscope, the other more vast than a telescope, can accommodate. This line not only forces into brief imaginative accessibility universally tiny and universally vast things, however; in doing so it suggests the universe according to Epicurus and that according to Newton, holding before the backdrop of divine awareness all human cosmologies and reducing them all, finally, to an equal transience before the eye, through which we now briefly see, of omniscience.

The first line of this complex synecdoche for the whole of creation presented natural things that humans can see; the second, things that we can only conceive; the third presents in dynamic opposition a spherical object normally accessible to our sight, the destruction of which is available to us, with a spherical object beyond our vision, the destruction of which is almost too frightful even for us to imagine; both, like the items above, presented before the "equal eye" of heaven. This climactic pairing has been specifically prepared for with the metaphoric language used just above to describe the destruction of all created things, that is, "filling the circle marked by heaven." The bubble, which expands to fill a circle that increasingly taxes its cohesive power, precisely concludes this subtle trope, which, obviously enough, represents both a fulfillment of being and its extinction. This trope thus enriches the sense of fate to which Pope has been attending throughout this whole section of his poem and especially suits the instances—two explosively ripe spheres—he is now describing. A bubble, which reaches its greatest extent and its disintegration at the same moment, is the normal experiential example. The climactic line that describes it, however, requires us, after merely beholding this complex fate of a bubble, to participate in that of a world—our world? the only one we know?—ourselves supplying the necessary verb. It thus implicates us creatively in the similitude which, although unthinkable to normally situated human beings, precisely fulfills this visionary moment, enacting upon our understanding the difference between divine apprehension, with its comprehensive insouciance, and ours.

The difference between human and divine apprehension Pope has developed throughout this epistle of the *Essay* by representing again-and-again a difference between naturally perceived and naturally unperceived perceivables: between a wild and a garden; a bubble and a world; the whispering zephyr and the thunderous music of the spheres. The epistle is thus emphatically founded on the third category of things I described in chapter 1, that is, the things of sense experience. *Gulliver's Travels*, although chiefly concerned with the same category of things and with the intellectual vexations they present, allowed its readers to test it and indeed to attack it on the grounds of its reference to a material world, that is, on the grounds of what Gulliver calls truth. A bishop of Swift's acquaintance did so, as I have noticed, dismissing the whole book as a pack of lies. This allows readers, further, to misapprehend and indeed to neglect the *Travels*'s problems of personal experience, as many persons besides the bishop have apparently done. But the first epistle of the *Essay* is as candidly focused on perceptual experience, on what human beings can see and say and know, as Gay's *Trivia*. With this difference: whereas Gay was strictly devoted to particular percepts and separate perceivers, Pope wishes to generalize, extending his own sense of things to cover all of nature and to satisfy all of humankind.

Lucretius, his great rival in the poetry of theological demonstration, had represented the universe, as Pope often subtly acknowledges, as a strictly material system, a vast, occasionally retarded flow of atomic seeds. To know this universe was both easy—now, at any rate, that Epicurus had described it—and of secondary importance, useful, indeed, only in so far as this would allow mankind to free itself from the observances of superstition and achieve a more humane and rational mode of conduct. This appropriate conduct was exemplified by Epicurus, in his retirement to his garden, and—better still—by the remote and indifferent gods. Pope, who drew heavily on both the cosmological and ethical teachings of Lucretius throughout his career, had, as this epistle itself shows, great sympathy with the quasi-divine retirement that Lucretius advocated. In this epistle, however, which is devoted to "the nature and state of man with respect to the universe," he prompts humankind to consider the universe, not as a material system, as Lucretius had done, but as an object of insouciant observation, that is, as he recognizes with a variety of tones, as a concern of intellectual pride.

In thus focusing on the universe, not primarily as a material entity, but as a topic of observation—of science—he precisely agreed with his friend, Berkeley, whose masterpiece is entitled appropriately, "*The Principles of Human Knowledge.*" When Berkeley advised Pope to excise from the *Essay* an address to Christ parallel to Lucretius's address to Epicurus, he cancelled a scheme that was, except for the fact that Christ himself had not been primarily concerned with human knowledge, altogether suitable. Lucretius's master was a sage, a philosopher, one whom Lucretius properly praised for his intellectual penetration, for his having pierced the vast immensity of the universe and discovered its secrets. Pope's contemplated address would not, of course, have been suitable to Christ, whose emphasis was on faith, hope, and charity not on sense, reason, and understanding; but Pope's grasp of his own interest and of his response to Lucretius was perfectly correct. And he got it right in this epistle, moreover, by neglecting Christ altogether, as Berkeley advised, and inviting his philosophical friend St. John to join him in withdrawing to a point from which they could, like Epicurean gods, observe the world, reach as full a knowledge of it as human faculties would allow, and explore for possible knowledge in the latent tracts and giddy heights beyond. He also got it right, although in a different vein, with his mockery of the Lucretian apostrophe, satirizing all such human presumption as that of Epicurus to pierce beyond the world that is actually apparent to us and consider "worlds on worlds." In this address he defined, as at many other points in the epistle, the difference between the knowledge humankind can have and that, always lying beyond it, which, in its intellectual pride, it will imaginatively conceive. From this discrepancy, this irremediable difference between what we can know and what we can know about, a discrepancy Pope has dramatized with unique poetic genius, he derives the necessity—at least for the presumptuous human psyche—of a being, a presence, that can know all of this. Thus he demonstrates a deity whose comprehensive awareness supports the whole natural frame, a God in whom, as Berkeley describes it, all that is lives and moves and has its being.

Pope has presented the knowledge that requires such a deity with great tact and solidity, avoiding both the speculative and the superstitious, and paring down supernatural evidence to the immediately analogous—a world with a bubble, a maze with a garden, an odor that kills with one that thrills—and to the immediately probable. From the vantage of his tropical elevator, he directs our gaze down and in: upon the stolid ox, the cunning spider, and the green myriads in the peopled grass; that is, on sensual, even if unsensed, images. He does refer once to a seraph, truly, and once to the music of the spheres (subjunctively—satirically); but he focuses upon unquestionable natural existents: the mite, which hardly requires comprehension, the bear's own fur, and the apparently tainted green. His super human awareness of these things, the natural existence of which all of us accept, thus carries virtually experimental weight; and the demonstration of knowledge reaching just beyond our knowledge is consequently concrete and persuasive. The knowable atom, aroma, and world have a presence in Pope's poem equally as vivid to us as the known ox and lamb and hero. And the inference of "an equal eye" that beholds both and thus supports the stupendous unity of nature we can affirm because, at least briefly, we have participated in its view.

*   *   *

Pope was a philosophically ambitious poet. Supported as he was by spectacular British accomplishments in both science and philosophy, he believed that he might enforce a coherent natural system of universal scope. He was, on the other hand, because of his very ambition, no doubt, vulnerable to serious disillusion. *Dunciad* IV, with its conclusion in "universal darkness," is the most explicit announcement of this disillusion; but the most intellectually compelling exposition of it is provided by the first two *Moral Essays*, that is, the epistle *To a Lady* and the epistle *To Cobham*.

In the *Essay on Man* (ca. 1730–1733) Pope fully explicated the universal order in variety that he had believed in since the beginning of his poetic career—a belief that profoundly informs his practice as a poet. Throughout these years (ca. 1704–1733), the tensions from which his style develops are prevailingly reconciled in general unity, the disparate elements of his experience cohering finally in a representation of reliable developments and firm substances. But thereafter (ca. 1733ff.)—partially owing, perhaps, to the very stretch required by the *Essay*—the emphasis shifts; and the skepticism that necessarily dwells near the heart of all inductive ambitions becomes predominant. In his studies of character (ca. 1730–1735), even the firmest of all human substances, that is, the named beings of one's acquaintance, begin to come apart: most people, as Pope recognizes in analyzing the experiential constituency of his companions, have no characters at all.

In examining his feminine acquaintance in the epistle *To a Lady*, Pope acknowledged what he had begun to recognize in examining his masculine acquaintance, that the perceptual pieces simply could not be reconciled: "How many pictures of one Nymph we view, / All how unlike each other, all how true." And thus the very designation, "one Nymph," will not hold up. We are a long way here from the certainties of *Windsor Forest*, "Where Order in Variety we see, / And where, 'tho all things differ, all agree." We are for that matter crucially divided from the second epistle of the *Essay on Man*, on the basis of whose abstractions, reason and self-love, Pope deduced the psychological doctrine of the ruling passion, a doctrine that was still functional, if shrinking in its validity, in *To Cobham*. Pope is still—quite properly—concerned with "all"; but whereas once all the different elements in his view composed one harmonious world, now not even all the perceptions he must attribute to one acquaintance compose an integral character.[11]

In considering the characters of women—as of men in *To Cobham*—Pope struck one of those rude shapeless patches he had mentioned in passing in the *Essay*. Since this patch is the heart of the human world, however, it presents a dreadful anomaly. He has given it the attention, therefore, that it deserves. Most women—maybe all and, indeed, maybe all persons—are, as nice observation reveals, bundles of incongruity, jumbles of differences that virtually belie the claim of unity in their names. Flavia, Calypso, Philomedé and the rest, each and every one, are so diverse in their perceptual manifestations that their names become elements of irony and deception. They may as well, Pope implies at certain points, be identified as "Simo's Mate" or "her" or "who." Major figures he introduces in the genitive case, directing us to "Narcissa's nature" and to "Atossa's mind," a deflection of focus that reminds us that the contemplation of a name—that virtual guarantee of personal substance for a Platonist—offers delusion and distraction to the nice observer. It is by no means insignificant that Lady Mary Wortley Montagu was baffled by the different experiences and observations that Pope—here and elsewhere—attributed to Sappho; nor that a storm of controversy has raged for centuries about the identification of Atossa. The actual details, as the wealth of scholarship has shown, will not quite attach to any of Pope's acquaintance. In snatching the atoms of personal conduct from the quick whirls and shifting eddies of his experience, missing much that another might notice and all that takes place in the dark, as Pope suggested in the epistle *To Cobham*, any one observer can catch at best "the Cynthia of this minute." Pope was neither the first nor the only author to acknowledge the diversity of the impressions that may gather around a single proper name: Swift's Gulliver is—in often dizzying rapidity—now a clever human being, now a professing yahoo, and now a practicing houyhnhnm;[12] Gay's Macheath is in one situation a devoted lover and in another a cynical lecher. But

Pope is by far the most explicit and the most candid expositor of this painful insight.

The first paragraphs of the epistle *To a Lady* render with remarkable intensity the limitations of human observation and human identification. In the set of cases to which no one name is assigned we can hardly be sure that one name would do:

> How many pictures of one Nymph we view,
> All how unlike each other, all how true!
> Arcadia's Countess, here, in ermin'd pride,
> Is there, Pastora by a fountain side:
> Here Fannia, leering on her own good man,   5
> Is there, a naked Leda with a Swan.
> Let then the Fair one beautifully cry,
> In Magdalen's loose hair and lifted eye,
> Or drest in smiles of sweet Cecilia shine,
> With simp'ring Angels, Palms, and Harps divine;   10
> Whether the Charmer sinner it, or saint it
> If Folly grows romantic, I must paint it.

Are all these shows attributable to a certain "one Nymph"; or do the particular disparities require us to infer more than one? We know each impression is "true"—possessing the unquestioned reality that Hume has explained; but the difference between them, to one after another of which Pope has affixed a name—Pastora, Fannia, Leda, Magdalen, Cecilia—must make us doubt. The "one Nymph" in the first line, which may be echoed in the last couplet of the paragraph with the singular "Charmer," seems to indicate that the diversities bracketed in this paragraph belong to some one name—to some one personal substance—or other. But the retrospective reach of "Charmer," whose actions are to "sinner it or saint it," is limited, covering only the preceding two cases, Magdalen and Cecilia. The four activities or "pictures" defined above simply elude this kind of Christian judgment. It would be difficult, indeed, to be sure whether a leering Fannia or a naked Leda conforms to sainthood. And what is the scope of "Fannia" anyway? Is it the actual name of a person (Fanny?) or, like Leda and Pastora (and Magdalen? and Cecilia?), just another pretty pose? Does it reach back to "Arcadia's Countess" in the couplet above, perhaps, and/or on to "Fair one" in that following? The parallel "Here . . . There" pattern, evident in the Fannia couplet and in that preceding it, seems to introduce separate cases, first the Countess who pretends to be Pastora and then Fannia who poses as Leda. But these two cases of discrepancy are similar,

similar in their discrepancy; and thus, possibly, one person in four pictures.

Pope's own use of "And" for "Is" in line six in early editions of the poem[13] enforces this possibility—but not decisively. And with the beautiful weeper in the next couplet he takes a new syntactic tack—as well as a new frame of reference (from Classical to Christian). Lines, couplets, and syntax all work, therefore, to undermine the definitive force of the verse paragraph and the "one Nymph" with which it opens. Each observation is "true" in itself, as meter, syntax, naming, and the separate descriptions all declare; but whether we should see here one wildly diverse tissue of views—as in the pictures of Atossa later—or a series of strictly individuated cases like that beginning with "Simo's Mate" is simply not determinable. And this uncertainty is perfectly appropriate, as the next paragraph about finding "a firm Cloud" and catching in it "the Cynthia of this minute" makes clear. Personal substance is so deeply undermined in this introductory passage that the separate names which do unquestionably serve as categorical headings to certain enclosed tangles of diversities—Silia, Narcissa and Cloe, for instance—are seriously compromised as signs of individual human substance even before they are produced.

The long address to the speaker's respondent, the lady, at the end of the poem (lines 249–292), although enormously different from this early material, intensifies the diversity within individual character. This lady, who can comprehend the general characterlessness of others, is, herself, a further case in point: she—and not Cloe, whom *she* brought forth as exceptional—is in fact the exception that establishes the rule. In the paragraph beginning with apparent resignation, "And yet, believe me," the poet describes heaven as shaking all the different human traits together and producing "You," as if this aspect of creation is both accidental—"shakes all together"—and—since "Heav'n" did the shaking—inarguable. This rough "blending" of antithetical tendencies has produced "at best a Contradiction still," a general situation about which the lady, to whom the poet has just given some suggestions about remaining "Mistress of herself," can apparently do nothing. Consider the climactic "You": it is either general—all you women—and thus decisively comprehensive; or particular—referring, that is, to the one person who might have maintained herself as an exception—and thus decisively comprehensive. This "You," therefore, despite its courteous equivocation, clinches the generality of the complaint: *all* women have no characters at all.

The many "pictures" by which Pope has illustrated this rule give it enormous weight and range. Each of these pictures is in fact an analysis, a disassemblage, demonstrating that, under any and every personal category, there is a tangle of diversities resistant to all attempts at synthesis. Consider, for instance, the case of Flavia:

> Flavia's a Wit, has too much sense to Pray,
> To Toast our wants and wishes, is her way;
> Nor asks of God, but of her Stars to give
> The mighty blessing, 'while we live, to live.'
> Then all for Death, that Opiate of the soul!   5
> Lucretia's dagger, Rosamonda's bowl.
> Say, what can cause such impotence of mind?
> A Spark too fickle, or a Spouse too kind.
> Wise Wretch! with Pleasures too refin'd to please,
> With too much Spirit to be e'er at ease,   10
> With too much Quickness ever to be taught,
> With too much Thinking to have common Thought:
> Who purchase Pain with all that Joy can give,
> And die of nothing but a Rage to live.

The first six lines reveal with considerable scope a primary diversity in Flavia's character between the intense desire to live and the desire to die intensely. Then after a suggested explanation, itself representing a radical contradiction in Flavia, follows a tissue of close-grained antitheses, by which the primary diversity—between contrary intensities of attitude—is extended and refined. Each of these, which come line-by-line, is both different from the others and itself an indication of diversity. To have too much spirit ever to be easy represents a restlessness in which two human goods, liveliness and comfort, are at odds; to be too intellectually penetrating to understand what ordinary folk know is a paradox; and to buy pain with gifts of joy, setting an obvious bad against a good, suggests a costly self-defeat. Thus Pope analyzes the varieties he finds attributable to one person, Flavia, describing contradiction within contradiction and concluding with an image of futile self-destruction. Pope has not constructed an inductive pyramid; rather, he has used the inductive procedures of synthesis and analysis to destroy a personal pyramid.

This analysis exemplifies one of the two competing foci of this tremendously rich and demanding poem, that is, the epistemological focus. It is also predominant in this picture of Silia.

> How soft is Silia! fearful to offend,
> The Frail one's advocate, the Weak one's friend:
> To her, Calista prov'd her conduct nice,
> And good Simplicius asks of her advice.
> Sudden, she storms! she raves! You tip the wink,   5
> But spare your censure; Silia does not drink.
> All eyes may see from what the change arose,
> All eyes may see—a Pimple on her nose.

There is no doubt an ethical element here—the possible condemnation for drunkenness, for one thing; and, indeed, the whole poem has a persistent ethical thread. But, unlike the prevailingly ethical analysis of Philomedé, the emphasis here is on seeing and understanding: the repeated term "see" in the last two lines has, indeed, first one and then the other of these meanings. So that the passage concludes by shifting, actually, from a possibly ethical attitude, that is, an attitude of judgment, to an epistemological one.

The whole poem reconciles or fails to reconcile moral judgment, with its often concomitant tone of personal involvement (anger, outrage, annoyance), and scientific understanding, or the awareness that understanding is not possible. Nowadays we are inclined to question and, indeed, to reject the judgment especially in its generality.[14] This is no doubt valid in so far as we find a distinction between male (reliable, good) and female (fickle, bad). I believe, however, that no one is able to resist the individual analyses, as individual, either as ethical or epistemological cases. But we have learned—if slowly—to deny their illustrative force or, rather, to deny the narrowness with which this force is brought to bear. What the many cases of feminine diversity illustrate, most people would surely accept, is this, that most people, male and female alike, have no characters at all. (Austen and Radcliffe would augment the same general conclusion by using male examples.) In making this suggestion, I no doubt de-emphasize Pope's ethics, at least as he tries to generalize that, and advocate his epistemology. In facing exceptions to his explicit argument, however, Pope has himself encouraged this as the primary value of his cases. The lady brings up one exception to this effort to generalize his understanding: "Yet Cloe sure was form'd without a spot," an exception to which Pope gives extensive experimental attention. And the ethically admirable lady, whom Pope attempted to conceive of as exceptional, provides the inductive clincher. Perhaps I may clarify the complexity of Pope's motives—

if not the fullest reach of his insight—by suggesting that the epistemology is general and discursive, the ethics singular and hortatory. Pope demonstrates that all the women of his and his friend's acquaintance lack integrity, that is to say, and urges her to strive for integrity in herself. Although the details of the integrity he proposes to her are questionable, the two expressive motives in general—that most people lack integrity and that each one should maintain his own—are surely subject to everybody's approval. Pope's failure we can thus reduce to an omission, a neglect. He has apparently failed to include men in developing either of his motives and thus allowed the inference of a qualitative difference between women and men.

To mitigate this failure, I note, first, that Pope has, even in this poem, suggested in males a similar diversity of individual being. Calypso, for example, men behold, or so it seems, with passion at one moment and with hate at another—or, perhaps, with a troublesome mixture of the two; Narcissa, again, inspires scorn sometimes and sometimes tolerance. Men are represented as enduring a range of feelings in confronting Atossa, repect, fear, gratitude, contempt, apprehension; the poet, himself, seems to have played host to such a parade of attitudes. Any man may be expected, then, to shift—if not so mysteriously as women—between such passions; and, since they are "shown . . . in Public," these shifts are no doubt observable. These incidental admissions of masculine shiftiness have been fully developed, moreover, in the epistle *To Cobham*, which, although, significantly, including several women, is focused on the characters of men.

In *To Cobham* Pope insists:

> That each from other differs, first confess,
> Next, that he varies from himself no less.

He provides many cases of individual males in "Passions' wild rotation tost":

> See the same man, in vigour, in the gout;
> Alone, in company; in place, or out;
> Early at Bus'ness, and at Hazard late;
> Mad at a Fox-chace, wise at a Debate;
> Drunk at a Borough, civil at a Ball,   5
> Friendly at Hackney, Faithless at Whitehall.

In this poem Pope is more emphatically concerned with epistemology—or rather, with its limits—than in the epistle *To a Lady:*

he is chiefly concerned, that is to say, not with the morality of individual men, but with the mistakes of inference and generalization we make in observing them. But he nevertheless defines cases which have ethical as well as epistemological implications:

> Catius is ever moral, ever grave,
> Thinks who endures a knave, is next a knave,
> Save just at dinner—then prefers, no doubt,
> A Rogue with Ven'son to a Saint without.

This is reminiscent in movement of the analysis of Silia. And Pope's general point about the difficulty of generalizing masculine psychology is, accordingly, essentially the same as that about choosing, in the pursuit of feminine psychology, "a firm cloud" in which to catch "the Cynthia of this minute:"

> Our depths who fathoms, or our shallows finds,
> Quick whirls, and shifting eddies, of our minds?
> Life's stream for Observation will not stay,
> It hurries all too fast to mark their way.
> In vain sedate reflections we would make,   5
> When half our knowledge we must snatch, not take.

Pope no doubt treats men, even here, with a trace of social respect: "we" have "depths" and "minds"; "we" reveal deep "whirls" as well as shallow "eddies." But considered as objects of understanding, masculine and feminine psychology present to Pope the same flickering tissue of experience and the same impossibility of generalization. When he narrows his focus to the point of death, the only point it seems, after all is said and done, where the "honesty" of nature is actually subject to human observation, he discovers both male and female examples, two women and five men.

The epistle *To Cobham*, then, both intensifies and extends Pope's grasp of human identity. And although the taint of a masculine prejudice remains, finally, I may nevertheless correct the most debilitating formulation (that only women lack integrity) and thus formulate Pope's principle: most people have no characters at all. This principle would seem to ruin any chance to reconcile the demands of particularity and generality, presenting a heap or bundle of hopelessly discrete human perceptions, from which no assurance of individual persons can emerge. But although the compositions Pope has organized in the *Epistle to a Lady* necessarily preserve this Humean understanding of particularity, Pope has nevertheless found ways—some of them the same that Hume advocates—to maintain an endurable social environment of men and women for men and women. He has also indicated not only the possibility of a practical integrity in certain individuals, more-over, but the possibility of a communion between them.

The individual pictures in the gallery of analyses, first of all, are always dynamic, never miscellaneous, meaning more as bun-dles than they would as mere lists.[15] In the case of the woman, for instance, that Pope catches

Now deep in Taylor and the Book of Martyrs,
Now drinking citron with his grace and Chartres,

two bibliographical companions are balanced against two drink-ing companions. And there is, moreover, a connection between the opposed activities since being "deep" in books is like "drink-ing citron," both being a kind of imbibing. "Simo's Mate" is also integrated as a plurality of impressions even as her individual discrepancy is enforced. If she can be thus represented, "No Ass so meek, no Ass so obstinate," then she is always an Ass. Cloe, again, whose character deviates from acceptable humanity, is al-ways like her self, always deficient. She "speaks, behaves and acts just as she ought"; and being too delicate to practice "Virtue," she is thus "content to dwell in decencies forever." Flavia, whose picture has already been examined, is a "wit" in both one extreme attitude and the other, first cleverly embracing life and then with equal cleverness, death, showing the same fine grasp of cultural properties in both and pursuing both with the same degree of dramatic intensity. The last thrust at her, moreover, "And die of nothing but a Rage to live," virtually recognizes these two ex-tremes, which are the very ones Pope started with, as one para-doxical state. Philomedé too is presented, for all her diversity, in bounds of a sort. For one thing, she is almost always lecherous; it is indeed in lechery that she is diverse. For another she is or may be a thoroughgoing hypocrite. She may thus really be com-mitted only to Charles and not to Charlemagne; or, at least, to the same lewd powers in each one. Her oscillations may conceal a relatively singular energy, that is to say, the energy Pope shows her honoring at the end of his analysis, turning from a pretended advocacy of romance to an abiding lust.

The possible imputation of hypocrisy, which complicates sev-eral of Pope's analyses, at the same time, unifies them. In the

epistle *To Cobham* Pope noticed that all human observation is
limited:

> . . . Grant that Actions best discover man;
> Take the most strong and sort them as you can.
> The few that glare each character must mark,
> You balance not the many in the dark.

In the epistle *To a Lady*, which recalls this point in making its
distinction between public and private life, Pope has often hinted
at "the dark," that realm of deep privacy, which may differ from
the glare of balls and masks and gossip, and which may be, unlike
some things that the glare reveals, truly pervasive. Since he cannot compel his subjects to strip, as Pope complains with mock
despair, he must both neglect the hidden evidence and yet somehow acknowledge it: behind or beneath the rage for life or the
laughter at hell may lie, Pope often suggests, persistent fears and
furies. Or beneath Cloe's personal deficiencies there may lie—as
a quite consistent personal fact—nothing at all. Papillia's diverse
feelings toward parks and trees seem to amount to a simple psychological twitch; but behind Flavia's diversities may lie a steady
feeling for a lover or for a husband. And although Atossa is described as "scarce once herself," a fury runs through Pope's picture of her—now mitigated, now released—that suggests that
even she, while obviously various in show and apparently sincere
in all her varieties, is or may be driven by one predominant
demon. Her shifting praise, love, hate, rage, admiration, and approval may thus seem like flickers of froth on one terrible, tumul-
tuous wave.

It is not certain whether these signs of integrity are attributable
to the figures Pope describes or to his powers of composition.
Since every thing is particular, of course, he has ultimate responsibility for all congeries. So we may best accept these signs of
individual integrity as Pope's own design. He is surely responsible for the inductive system in which he has placed them all.
For each one, at least in so far as we honor their flickering appearances, proves pertinent to Pope's argument; each one, as we observe her diversity of conduct, adds an atom of probability to the
general opinion that Pope has picked up from his friend and to
which they bend their joint attention. The lady raises Cloe explicitly to test the central principle; and the lady herself, as Pope
tests her integrity and acknowledges her diversity, represents a
final, decisive example. With the lady's claim, "Yet Cloe sure was

form'd without a spot," and the poet's acknowledgement of the challenge, Pope strongly implies that all earlier pictures have been addressed with this general question in mind and, indeed, as he analyzes Cloe's putative integrity, that this is the center of the present conversation. In proving to conform to the leading principle, moreover, she both strengthens it—transforming "most" to "almost all"—and establishes the intellectual procedure to which all Pope's pictures contribute. To summarize this aspect of Pope's procedure: either a particular picture acquires some implicit unity or it fails to do so and therefore supports the poem's general theme—contributing thus dynamically, as it reaches in either of the contrary directions, to a sense of poetic unity, pertinence and control.

In the passage immediately following the picture of Cloe, Pope attempts to augment, not only the unity of the discourse, but the unity of the subject: casting two or three generalities over it in the hopes of moderating the unmitigated diversity which he has— by confuting what looks like the only possible exception—just established. In courteously acknowledging the Queen as "the same forever!" and thus as an untouchable exception to the general situation, he discloses two limitations to its complete exposition: first, that women, especially the highly cultivated ones that concern him, cannot be required to expose themselves; and, second, that they are "seen . . . in Private life alone." These limitations to inductive observation, which Hume also recognizes, implicitly, in the Preface to the *Treatise*, are, on the one hand, useful in providing Pope with an almost scientific modesty and detachment; on the other hand, they seriously inhibit his conclusions. If women "hide . . . in Public," clothing their feelings in the same way that they clothe their bodies, and can be seen only in private—where (as in the dark) they can hardly be seen at all: the poet's purview is evidently a limited one. Against this we may put the pictures, already presented, that he has, despite such limits, actually shown, pictures he has been able to compose because of the connivance of the lady and, perhaps, of all society. Against this we may also tentatively put the brilliant general exposition about two ruling passions in all women that immediately follows. This may be seen, on the other hand, as the poet's desperate response to the acknowledged limitations of his observation. For this episode (lines 207–268) is not merely dogmatic as description; it is also dogmatically ethical, briefly abandoning the demanding epistemological concern with particular experience that otherwise characterizes this poem.

To recognize the extremity of this dogmatic move, notice that, for these few lines, Pope has turned from arguing no character for any woman to condemning one character in them all. This departure from an immediate dependence on particular observation is nevertheless built on the admission just above that men are observable in public, women only in private. Women, Pope suggests, are "almost" all divided between the love of pleasure, their private desire, and the love of sway, their public necessity: "They seek the second not to lose the first." Although "ev'ry Woman is at heart a Rake," (like Philomedé? Flavia?) each one must for the sake of her rakish pleasure (like Atossa? Cloe?) gain power in the world. This is a strategy, Pope explains, forced on them "by Man's oppression." Despite this mitigation, the moral judgment of women developed in the two paragraphs on power (lines 219–30) and pleasure (lines 231–42) and the severe summary, "Alive, ridiculous, and dead, forgot!" require some kind of rationalization. Pope condemns women in general, I would argue, because he has been unable to understand them in particular: this ethical episode thus strengthens, perhaps, the deepest point of epistemological awareness in the poem, that women altogether defeat male observation. This point, which especially informs the last paragraphs of the poem, radiates, moreover, in the still broader awareness of how skimpy, how fragmentary, and how unreliable is all human knowledge. If women necessarily project both real and apparent images, thus embedded by patriarchal society in necessary disguise, how do we understand, say, Rufa's contrary study of Locke (surely private) and her public flirtations; or Narcissa's shift from a private immersion in religious books to public dissipation; or Atossa's failed pleasure and notorious scandal? We must recognize not only a puzzling diversity of sincere and pretended attitudes in such cases, it seems, but acknowledge, further, that we cannot tell which is which. This episode in moral judgment, then, enriches the representation of individual feminine variety and validates the poet's return to his primary, his epistemological, concern.

My sense of an epistemological unity at this point of the epistle is, admittedly, a matter of inference. This ethical episode has a scope, an emphasis, and a brilliance that persist more vividly in the mind than any merely conceptual development such as I have described. However, this excursion in dogmatic certitude heightens—if only by contrast—the procedures of experimental induction to which, after its conclusion, Pope pointedly returns. And there are other cohesive forces at work in the poem as well. The chief of these is its prevailingly conversational method, that is, its persistent inclusion of the lady and of all society generally in the development and the verification of its argument.

The poem is throughout its course an exercise in discursive solicitation. All its statements, no matter how diverse in individual substance or in degree of generality, are alike in being supported at once, first, by the poet and his friend and, second, by all the ladies and gentlemen of society. The epistle *To a Lady* is an even more intense practice in public solicitation than the *Essay on Man*—even if it is a much stickier, a much more problematical, one.[16] The poet addresses the lady pointedly both at the very end of the poem, where he touches tactfully on, among other things, the detail of her age, and at its very beginning, where he courteously (cunningly) attributes to her their conversation's primary tenet. Throughout the poem he solicits her connivance and invites her participation. "Dear Madam" and "friend" he calls her at different points; he focusses requests and advice several times on "you"; and asks her variously to "see," to "turn . . . and look," to "grant," and to "believe me." These addresses are often subtle. In the little picture that begins "Or her, who laughs at Hell," the next expression, "like her Grace," recalls to the lady not one but a recurrent tissue of shared perceptions and—beyond this—a shared understanding: they both know what her Grace is like. Other expressions—"How soft is Silia!" "What then?" "we view," "we owe"—also imply a reliable community of observation and opinion that both includes the lady and reaches beyond her.

The lady herself speaks out at least once, suggesting Cloe as an exception to what the poet has quoted as her own general opinion. And she may be understood to participate in the discourse at other points as well. Immediately after the poet insists, "If Folly grows romantic, I must paint it," the poem proceeds:

> Come then, the colours and the ground prepare!
> Dip in the Rainbow, trick her off in Air,
> Chuse a firm Cloud, before it fall, and in it
> Catch, ere she change, the Cynthia of this minute.

The poet may have changed persons here and be addressing himself—as Alice does while she is falling down the rabbit hole; but, especially in so conversational an environment as Pope has inaugurated—"Nothing so true as what you once let fall"—it is easier and more natural to hear his friend encouraging him or, better perhaps, challenging him: you say you must paint such shifting images; now, let's see how well you can manage it. The question that interrupts the assertive description of Narcissa, "Why then declare Good-nature is her scorn?" also indicates a second, a different, intellectual presence. Pope has just acknowledged (with some sarcasm) Narcissa's "tolerably mild" character; and his friend, sensing self contradiction, breaks in to lodge a complaint. After Pope has displayed Flavia's shift from love of life to longing for death, she breaks in again to ask, "Say, what can cause such impotence of mind?" No matter how such breaks and shifts in the tone and slant of conversation are explained, they project a fluent discursive surface underlying which are different intellectual perspectives all attentive to the common topic.

Pope ends the poem by intensifying this conversational quality, distinguishing his friend from all other women of their joint acquaintance, not because of her unique integrity, but because of his unique admiration. He offers himself to her, indeed, in love, although in so subtle and oblique a way that she need not even acknowledge that he has done so. The closing couplet, in which Pope contrasts the special private gift of "a Poet" to her with the less respectable benefits enjoyed by other women—"the world shall know it"—thus acknowledges the broad social circle of discourse and a more intimate circle, and, just at this last moment, prefers the latter. The poet's unique offer of himself may be felt as merely a complimentary close, a graceful flourish actually taking place in society at large. The last couplet and the whole poem indeed allow this. The intimacy developed throughout the poem has been so rich and so reliable, however, that we may recognize this distinction as the distinction of love—especially strengthened as it is by a complimentary recognition of the lady's best feature ("those blue eyes") and the tactful neglect of her age. We may understand the poet to avow, then, that he loves her as a woman among women, as one who may not escape the prevailing human characterlessness any more than her sisters have; but as one who is different from them for all that. She is unique as the companion, the friend, with whom he can share even so divisive a social topic as this one which—if any could—is the most likely to divide a gentleman and a lady. Pope has thus reconciled the diversities of his subject and the complexities of his discourse.

*   *   *

Despite the integrity of this essay, however, both as an intellectual procedure and as an exercise in conversational companionship, and despite the subordinate integrity of the parts, in which

Pope has found a firm cloud in case after case and composed bundles of perceptual diversity into one picture after another, the diversities persist. Most people, including those we may love, have no characters at all.[17] Everything in the combined experience of the poet and his friend supports his helpless fascination before that contradictoriness of character that must finally be described even by a lover as a "shaking [of] all together and producing you." Pope has simply surrendered emotionally at the last to a most attractive example of this feminine—this human—characterlessness and with his eyes open. His friend may learn to obey or to command without seeming to; she may shine as serenely (and as steadily?) as the moon; and, although she shows traces of vanity, she may avoid "Pelf"; she may both understand the outrageous variousness of her sisters and mitigate it somewhat in herself. And yet believe me, "Woman's at best a Contradiction still."

When we consider individual people as they occur in our experience—in our acquaintance—and when we try, by sifting and packaging perceptions both diverse and fragmentary, to understand them, we find that we must love another before we can identify her—or so Pope implies. Indeed, we must resolve on this most ambitious exercise in identification knowing that identification will always escape us: the parts—that small selection that we can notice or discover—will never really add up to one personal substance, to one coherent category of being. At times a man will feel of any friend, no matter how beloved, that she is "Scarce once herself, by turns all Womankind." It is thus appropriate that the epistle *To a Lady*, which develops to the furthest reach of generality such an understanding, that this one of all Pope's poems should echo and reecho through *The Mysteries of Udolpho*, the most complete experiment British culture has produced in the analysis of individual human character. And if Radcliffe's skeptical gaze focuses chiefly on evidences of masculine character, Pope, as I hope I have established, has prepared for that too.

5

Radcliffe's Mysteries

Epistemology, the importance of which in eighteenth-century fiction Eric Rothstein has noted,[1] is even more evident in Ann Radcliffe's *Mysteries of Udolpho* than it is in the work of her great predecessors. It was at the center of British culture during this period, as Locke's and Berkeley's and Hume's avowed study of *Understanding* and *Knowledge* declares. I have located it, moreover, in the *Travels*, a primary purpose of which, as Swift explained, is to expose human kind individually as at best *animal rationis capax;* also in Pope's efforts to understand the traces of divinity evident in what we know from natural observation and the signs of personality evident from what we see in society. The epistemology developed in these literary exercises is, as I have shown, prevailingly perceptualist, representing the problems of sifting and organizing individual experience. The novels that preceded Radcliffe's *Mysteries* (1794), although most of these likewise represent a concern with perception, have also an external, materialistic component, presenting tissues of adventure in which concerns of the understanding and its processes are embedded. Tristram, for instance, endures serious physical harm as well as the chance for intellectual exercise; Joseph and Roderick, who are, of course, very tough specimens, take a lot of hard knocks. But Emily St. Aubert, who is Radcliffe's heroine, although she no doubt weathers a pretty threatening environment, is occupied almost exclusively with pertinent perceptions, with dubious inferences, and with eventual clarifications. She may fear murder, forced marriage and—to use a word Radcliffe avoids—rape; but in fact her foes hardly lay a finger on her. Emily never risks the bruises "poor Pamela" suffers in her attempted escape from Mr. B's Lincolnshire estate nor any such offense to her bosom as Pamela takes as a virtual matter of course. Tom Jones must act and react throughout his youthful adventures in order to learn the prudence that is necessary for a successful life; but Emily, who glides through her youthful travails almost without a scratch,[2] merely has to keep open her eyes and ears. Her reticence is a mantle, an impenetrable diving suit, honored by even the most ravenous of her male acquaintances, that allows Emily to navigate the murky pool into which her creator has plunged her attending with undivided intellectual alertness to "mysteries," that is, of course, to problems of perceptual experience.

Radcliffe's style of narration pervasively enforces this epistemological focus. Her many uses of the cant terms, "sublime" and "romantic," for instance, more often modify the response to some awesome or provocative scene than they describe its external substance. For every bona fide thug Emily encounters, she imagines a hundred banditti, populating bushes, rocks, and shadows with excitements that never actually emerge. The romance, that is to say, is mostly in the heroine's head. Radcliffe presents the reader, again, not nearly so often with "sublime objects" or "sublime spectacles" as with "sublime contemplation," "sublime pleasure," "sublime emotions," "sublime rapture," "sublime astonishment," "sublime complacency," and "sublime reflections." Sublimity, like romance, is less a state of nature than it is a state of consciousness. Even when Emily begins with an external awareness, Radcliffe immediately turns inward upon her quivering sensorium. "As [Emily's] eyes wandered along the boundless ether," the novelist reports on one occasion, "her thoughts rose . . . towards the sublimity of Deity and to the contemplation of futurity." The sublime, although attached externally to the divine that is evident in nature, thus begins in "thoughts" and ends in "contemplation." In a passage describing the Alps, "scenes" are immediately related to "mind"; and mind is represented as a series of actions, recollecting, imagining, and thinking. The term "sublimity" has been subordinated by the passage's conclusion to "those [thoughts]" which stirred her "mind" and "affections," dilating and elevating them. If consciousness is like a balloon—or a "bundle," as Hume would call it—it is more of an intellectual than an emotional balloon. It compares the remembered sublimity of the Pyrenees with present impressions; it imaginatively conceives the verbal responses of an absent friend; and, although "no colours" of language should "dare to paint" such scenery, it seriously attempts to absorb the colors that are perceived. The romantic was widely understood in Radcliffe's time, as J. M. S. Tompkins has noted, to provoke imaginative creativity, stirring intense psychological activity.[3] It is in observance of this usage that Radcliffe describes her three most romantic books each one explicitly as a "romance."

But in the *Mysteries*, even the sublime, which was normally understood to overwhelm and obliterate mental powers, arouses Emily's.

Radcliffe's characteristic use of the passive voice also enforces the focus on apprehension, virtually abstracting percepts from perception, and establishing them as pure objects of mental functioning. Consider, as an illustration of this effect, the rudely scribbled sign posted on the dashboard of a small-town limousine: "Tips will be appreciated." The sign does not say, "the driver [nor "I"] will appreciate tips." Rather, it pointedly excises the appreciative recipient, leaving the tip as an object of pure intellectual contemplation, that is, as a percept. The passive voice has the same effect in the *Mysteries*, isolating various sublime, romantic, or mysterious events for unhampered contemplation and reducing Emily—as Hume would have approved—to a collection of flickering impressions. (This is one reason she seems physically invulnerable as compared to her forebears in eighteenth-century fiction.) During the arduous trip Emily and her father took through the Pyrenees, to illustrate Radcliffe's practice, "the dashing murmurs [of a spring] were lost in the abyss"; "the eagle and the vulture . . . were seen towering round the beetling cliffs"; "the cheerful green of the beech and mountain-ash was sometimes seen . . . amidst the dark verdure of the forest"; "the village lights were seen to twinkle through the dusk"; and once, "as Emily looked back upon the road they had passed, [her lover] Valancourt was seen, at the door of the little inn." In the following sentence, Radcliffe's instinct for passive effects—if not, in this case, the passive voice—prompts her to endure what English teachers nowadays insist their students avoid, a dangling modifier: "On turning the angle of a mountain, a light appeared at a distance, that illumined the rocks and the horizon to a great extent." Actually, or so I take it, the travellers, on turning an angle, saw this light; but Radcliffe, at some grammatical cost, reduces them to secondary—indeed, to nonexistent—recipients of a powerful percept.

The first paragraph of the novel, which contains several passive constructions, establishes the appropriately epistemological atmosphere:

On the pleasant banks of the Garonne, in the province of Gascony, stood, in the year 1584, the chateau of Monsieur St. Aubert. From its windows were seen the pastoral landscapes of Guienne and Gascony stretching along the river, gay with luxuriant woods and vine, and plantations of olives. To the south, the view was bounded by the majestic Pyrenees, whose summits veiled in clouds, or exhibiting awful forms, seen, and lost again, as the partial vapours rolled along, were sometimes barren, and gleamed through the blue tinge of air, and sometimes frowned with forests of gloomy pine, that swept downward to their base. These tremendous precipices were contrasted by the soft green of the pastures and woods that hung upon their skirts; among whose flocks and herds and simple cottages, the eye, after having scaled the cliffs above, delighted to repose. To the north, and the east, the plains of Guienne and Languedoc were lost in the mist of distance: on the west, Gascony was bounded by the waters of Biscay.

The only person mentioned in this paragraph, Monsieur St. Aubert, appears only once, in the genitive case, and is immediately suppressed. (Emily, the heroine, is introduced unemphatically as "his daughter" in the middle of the sixth paragraph.) In this crucial paragraph, Radcliffe reports that the landscapes "were seen"; the precipices "were contrasted"; the plains "were lost." Since different kinds of agents, if we think of agents at all, must lie behind these different actions, the sense of agency is itself dissipated. The Creator may have done the contrasting; St. Aubert, the seeing; some other power or abnegation of power, the losing. Thus no single presence can be inferred, and we are left with a general sense of respondency and impressionability. It is "the [disembodied] eye, after having scaled the cliffs," that reposes in passive contemplation of landscape. And this is landscape with a vengeance: "the view was bounded" not only "to the south"; but to the north, east, and west as well, even if in the west it "was bounded" by conceivably boundless waters. This is not a merely natural scene, but an orderly catalogue (or a Humean collection) of natural data. One thinks of the well-attested influence, which I must eventually minimize, of Claude Lorrain and Salvatore Rosa. The view from the window of Emily's room, similarly, Radcliffe confines to the responsive "eye [which] was led between groves of almond, palm-trees, flowering-ash, and myrtle, to the distant landscape, where the Garonne wandered." "The eye" here is, once again, not a synecdoche, standing for Emily or for the reader: it is merely the visual conduit, the means by which "landscape" can be absorbed for use or storage.

Consider an even more apparent stylistic sign of Radcliffe's characteristic focus, her references to unsensed sensibilia. Again and again in the *Mysteries* she reports what a character did not in fact notice, but might have, thus providing perceptual data—

again in accordance with the teachings of Hume—strictly abstracted from any mental support. Had Emily raised her eyes at one point, the novelist reports, "she would have seen tears" in Valancourt's eyes. Thus his eyes and his tears exist—as visual properties—even when Emily's seeing eyes do not. Valancourt, on another occasion, failed, "because of the deep twilight," to see "the astonishment and doubting joy that fixed [Emily's] features." Neither Emily nor any one else observed the "hurried steps" of Valancourt as he wandered around the deserted gardens of Madame Montoni's estate in Toulouse; and this is a pity because, as Radcliffe asserts, they "would have discovered to a spectator the despair of his heart."[4] Whole tissues of such significant observanda, many of them explicitly reported, were missed because concerned observers were negligent or shy or simply out of place. Valancourt's persistent attendance on the remote tower at Chateau le Blanc, Du Pont's visits to the fishinghouse in La Vallee, and Madame Montoni's protracted presence in the remote turret at Udolpho, Radcliffe explains, Emily might have but did not in fact observe. Emily's own sobs and shrieks go often unheard, even when they are by report "distinctly audible"; and sometimes she scarcely hears "the whispering echoes of her own steps." The scenic frame of the *Mysteries* also sports a fringe of unperceived perceivables: seen waterfalls, for instance, because of their distance, are sometimes out of earshot, and heard falls are sometimes, contrariwise, "concealed from the eye." The *Mysteries* in general presents an enormous discrepancy between perceived and unperceived sensibilia, an explicit incongruency that dramatizes the central epistemological fact of the novel, that is, the recurrent presence of gaps between Emily's perceptions and her understanding. Radcliffe's primary novelistic purpose or, rather, the primary purpose of her heroine is to reconcile the perceptions and bridge the gaps.

*   *   *

In Emily St. Aubert, Radcliffe has created a heroine who is strictly appropriate to such a purpose. She is, in the first place, as her father recognized, a creature of intense sensibility, one, that is, who is especially responsive to every sense impression. Monsieur St. Aubert's primary use to the novelist is, quite simply, the making of this point. When Emily was young, Radcliffe reports, he attempted to modify this splendid but dangerous capacity, engaging his daughter in various intellectual gymnastics to toughen her up a little bit. He had "too much good sense" not to fortify her "too exquisite degree" of susceptibility:

> He endeavoured, therefore, to strengthen her mind; to inure her to habits of self-command; to teach her to reject the first impulse of her feelings, and to look with cool examination upon the disappointments he sometimes threw in her way. . . . He instructed her to resist first impressions, and to acquire that steady dignity of mind that can alone counterbalance the passions, and bear us, as far as is compatible with our nature, above the reach of circumstances.

St. Aubert not only stiffened Emily's quivering *tabula rasa;* he also provided her by the study of such subjects as Latin and English with "a well-informed mind," one "stored with ideas." He thus gave Emily a rich background of general understanding for her own particular experiences and prepared her to achieve the common sense that the eighteenth century advocated.

Emily's extreme sensitivity to experience was St. Aubert's chief concern even when he lay on his death bed. He did not wish, he eloquently gasped, to "teach her to become insensible," but she must govern her characteristic susceptibility, which "is continually alive to minute circumstances." (The term *circumstance,* by the way, is one of Radcliffe's favorites: she uses it almost technically to indicate a *pertinent percept*). In his dying words, St. Aubert echoed Hume's preference of taste to passion: "since in our passage through this world, painful circumstances occur more frequently than pleasing ones . . . those [like Emily] who really possess sensibility ought early to be taught that it is a dangerous quality, which is continually extracting the excess of misery or delight from every surrounding circumstance."[5] Radcliffe, who uses his death to emphasize this conception of her heroine, seems to judge that St. Aubert was in general successful at least in modifying Emily's practice: she did not impose "fierce and terrible passion" upon her experiences, twisting them—as Marianne Dashwood would do—into the shape her heart desired. Her heart was not driven, like Marianne's, by passion; or, better perhaps, she was not governed by her heart:

> Her sufferings, though deep, partook of the gentle character of her mind. Hers was a silent anguish, weeping yet enduring; not the wild energy of passion, inflaming imagination, bearing down the barriers of reason, and living in a world of its own.

Emily confronted the impressions that dashed against her awareness, as Elinor Dashwood would do, attempting to recognize and accept the sense of things that her understanding of nature and probability indicated.

There are "circumstances," her father had warned her, "of which your peace requires that you should rest in ignorance"; and she tried to apply this teaching: she burned unread, for example, the papers her father had asked her to destroy even after her eye had caught—by accident?—"a sentence of dreadful import." But she never in fact stops trying one way and another to discover the mystery ensconced in these papers. Emily's curiosity is, indeed, altogether commensurate with her sensibility. In the case of her father's papers, she overcame it although the desire to pry into them constituted a "temptation more forcible than any she [had] ever known." Usually she follows such a "thrilling curiosity" wherever it leads—even to a black veil, a frightening informant, or a blood-stained staircase. Emily's curiosity is seldom unalloyed. It is deflected at different times by "delicacy," "timidity," "tenderness," "surprise," and "terror"; but the desire to know eventually wins out. Her curiosity about the distant room in the Chateau le Blanc, for instance, in which the Marchioness de Villeroi died, was "not a common one," she assured the old housekeeper, Dorothee, who had the key; and, accompanied by that frail reed, she pursued it into apartments the threatening gloom of which would have scared away any but the stoutest heart—as Radcliffe acknowledges.

Emily has the other qualities that must support sensibility and curiosity in an adequate inductive intelligence, a sense of the probable (no doubt derived from her reading in English), an imagination both speculative and skeptical,[6] and rational energy. She spends her time reflecting upon available data, calculating resemblances and connections, and thus bringing the particular circumstances she has gotten hold of into accountable patterns. Passing through an unfamiliar corridor in Udolpho, for instance, she once "heard a voice." Although "terror" briefly "did not allow her to judge exactly whence it proceeded," she soon got command of her fears and traced it to a certain chamber. She attended it and identified it as "a voice of complaint," a judgment that was "soon confirmed by a low moaning sound." "It instantly occurred to her that Madame Montoni might be there confined"—a probable inference as circumstances would show; "but [she] was checked" from speaking through the door of the chamber by considering that she would thus expose herself to a stranger, who might discover her to Montoni; "for though this person, whoever it was, seemed to be in affliction, it did not follow that he was [like Madame Montoni, Emily's aunt] a prisoner." In this case, she soon recognized the voice of her maid, Annette, and this little essay in terror and detection comes to an end. It should be noticed that even when Emily's understanding gives way to terror—a normal dynamic in the *Mysteries*—Radcliffe keeps her focused on the facts. And she always bounces back quickly and begins to reflect.

When Emily first observed "the figure [that posted itself] opposite to her casement" in Udolpho and watched it "start away and glide down the rampart," she "scarcely [doubted] that she had witnessed a supernatural appearance." But "when her spirits recovered composure [and that doesn't take long]," she looked for some other explanation:

> Remembering what she had heard of the daring enterprises of Montoni, it occurred to her that she had just seen some unhappy person, who, having been plundered by his banditti, was brought hither a captive; and that the music she had formerly heard, came from him. Yet, if they had plundered him, it still appeared improbable that they should have brought him to the castle; and it was also more consistent with the manners of banditti to murder those they rob, than to make them prisoners. But what more than any other circumstance contradicted the supposition that it was a prisoner, was, that it wandered on the terrace without a guard; a consideration which made her dismiss immediately her first surmise.
>
> Afterwards she was inclined to believe that Count Morano had obtained admittance into the castle; but she soon recollected the difficulties and dangers that must have opposed such an enterprise, and that if he had so far succeeded, to come alone and in silence to her casement at midnight, was not the conduct he would have adopted, particularly since the private staircase communicating with her apartment was known to him; neither would he have uttered the dismal sounds she had heard.

This is part of an extended exercise, as the determination to watch on another night with which it concludes makes clear. For this moment, Emily's efforts ended in perplexity. But she reached such a state by engaging in extensive reflection. She surmised, perhaps a bit rashly, that "the music she had formerly heard" came from the same source: and thus that the invisible musician and the silently gliding figure were the same. But that seems, as she reflected, to rule out this figure's being an invader. She tentatively rejected his being a prisoner because of the infamous "manners of banditti"; and dismissed the identification with Count Morano on several grounds. Radcliffe thus represents Emily, in confronting the atoms of romantic probability, to have a remarkably clear and powerful intellect, an intellect sufficiently resistant to the terror implicit in each occurrence to sift it, to test it in connection with her accumulating sense of the probabilities, and to establish possible persons and relationships.

This quality is just as evident when she reflects, not on events external to her, but on her own future. While approaching Montoni's stronghold, for example, she was

> occupied by considering the probable events that awaited her in the scenes to which she was removing, and with conjectures concerning the motive of this sudden journey. It appeared, upon calmer consideration, that Montoni was removing her to his secluded castle, because he could there with more probability of success attempt to terrify her into obedience: or that, should its gloomy and sequestered scenes fail of this effect, her forced marriage with the count could there be solemnized with the secrecy which was necessary to the honour of Montoni.

The language here, as throughout the novel, is that of British philosophy: "probable," "conjectures," "consideration," "probability," "effect"; and it flavors the representation of Emily with a correspondent intelligence. She reflects upon past mysteries and future perils with an illuminated detachment that Newton and Boyle would have admired.

The characterization of Emily marks a fortuitous intersection in English literary history of two quite disparate cultural strains: the conventional social dogma that confined the human female to attention and response; and the developing philosophical understanding that confined all human intelligence in much the same way. Men, as Mr. Spectator complacently explained, should engage in purposive activity, in war or politics or courtship or commerce, following some kind of wide ranging business;[7] whereas women, whom Pope represented as "by man's oppression cursed," should stay at home, attentive and responsive to the impressions focused upon them individually by their men and chiefly, of course, their husbands. Pope once complained of women, "in public 'tis you hide," but this necessary response to social oppression he actually accepted, like his age generally, as the normal and appropriate state of things. The exemplary woman is

She, who ne'er answers till a Husband cools,
Or, if she rules him, never shows she rules;
Charms by accepting, by submitting sways,
Yet has her humour most, when she obeys.

A fine and tireless sensitivity to certain stimuli was, as both Pope and Addison saw it, a woman's chief function and glory.

Berkeley represented the function and the glory of all human intelligence in a closely analogous way: he acknowledged that the human mind could occasionally project a little idea—in the same way, Addison might have suggested, that a woman could affix a little patch—but it chiefly fulfilled itself in attending and responding to the imperative tissue of impressions focused upon it by God. The human mind in nature was thus analogous to the feminine mind in society: an unobtrusive awareness that chiefly realized itself in patient and humble attentiveness.[8] What Pope proclaimed about women, that they should be chiefly happy in obedience, Berkeley believed to be true of all Christian people. God plays the role in Berkeley's representation of nature, then, that man plays in Addison's view of society; and the Berkeleian mind, correspondingly, coheres with Addisonian woman.

Hume rejected Berkeley's inference of God as the necessary cause of the vast train of impressions entertained by individual intelligence, that train which both of them called "Nature": in the first place, it hardly displayed the "admirable connexion" it must to serve as the sign of a sufficiently admirable deity; in the second place, there simply was no reason to infer a cause of any kind for any or for any tangle of impressions. But Hume did recognize this natural train, this inconceivably rapid flux of impressions, as a recalcitrant, imperative concern of human awareness, and he represented awareness, therefore, in the same way as Berkeley represented the mind, in an attitude of attention and response.[9] When Hume deprives human consciousness of God, however, and leaves it all alone with its incredibly numerous, rapid, and disjointed collection of impressions, representing it as merely a bundle or a stage, he leaves woman—if we pursue the analogy— all alone as well, unprotected, or, to see it another way, unoppressed by a superior, an effective presence. And this is the situation of Emily St. Aubert especially in the gradually intensified isolation that Radcliffe represents. When Emily moves within the orbit of Montoni, attempting to divine his purposes from the appearances with which he encompasses her, she operates under the auspices of Berkeley; when she attends the disjunctive welter of sounds and sights in her own room at Udolpho, attempting to establish some accountable pattern or other, she is a disciple of Hume. She is always, whether attentive to the activities of a single power or adrift in a surge of impressions, both an extreme example of feminine gentility and, at the same time, a classic case of inductive intelligence. Although this intersection of Addison's conventional ethics and Hume's new metaphysics is briefly and erratically apparent in Adeline, the heroine of Radcliffe's *Romance of the Forest*, it reaches its only complete embodiment within her work in the conduct and the situation of Emily.[10]

Emily does lapse into terror from time to time when the circumstances confronting her seem particularly odd or disjointed. Sometimes—when she reflects on an early appearance of the strange apparition outside her casement, for example—she seems to fall victim to superstition:

> . . . She closed her casement, and retired to reflect upon the strange circumstance that had just occurred, connecting which with what had happened on former nights, she endeavoured to derive from the whole something more positive than conjecture. But her imagination was inflamed, while her judgment was not enlightened, and the terrors of superstition again pervaded her mind.

Here the practice of reflection has failed her: her efforts to reconcile the disparate circumstances of her experience and establish a "whole . . . more positive than conjecture" diverts her inflamed imagination into intellectually scandalous byways. There are many such points, especially in her Udolpho experience, when the circumstances Emily confronts prove too disjointed to support understanding. Once as she surveyed the two thugs, neither of them known to her, with whom Montoni had briefly sent her away from the castle, she was "seized [by] the most agonizing terror"; and "considerations" relevant to the probabilities of her situation "did not immediately occur" to her. She faced "so many circumstances [that] conspired to arouse terror," as Radcliffe reports, "that she had no power to oppose it, or inquire cooly into its grounds." By thus describing cool inquiry, however, Radcliffe both establishes that as the correct response to life's circumstances, even the most terrible ones, and suggests that Emily always or almost always achieves such an attitude. In this very case, although present circumstances appeared "so romantic and improbable . . . that there were moments when [Emily] could almost have believed herself the victim of frightful visions glaring upon a disordered fancy," she soon got a handle on things. Even in this representation of Emily's terror at its height, we should notice the terms "moments" and "almost" and recognize the persistence and the resurgence of her intelligence.

Consider Radcliffe's conduct on one of the few occasions in which she describes Emily as actually going awry, suffering a pure delusion—in this case the physical presence of her dead-and-buried father seated in his great chair. This episode occurred at La Vallee, when Emily had gone into her father's room to fulfill his dying instructions to find and destroy certain papers.

> There was a great chair in one corner of the closet, and opposite to it stood the table at which she had seen her father sit, on the evening that preceded his departure, looking over, with so much emotion, what she believed to be these very papers.
>
> The solitary life which Emily had led of late, and the melancholy subjects on which she had suffered her thoughts to dwell, had rendered her at times sensible to the "thick-coming fancies" of a mind greatly enervated. It was lamentable that her excellent understanding should have yielded, even for a moment to the reveries of superstition, or rather to those starts of imagination which deceive the senses into what can be called nothing less than momentary madness. Instances of this temporary failure of mind had more than once occurred since her return home—particularly when wandering through this lonely mansion in the evening twilight, she had been alarmed by appearances which would have been unseen in her more cheerful days. To this infirm state of her nerves may be attributed what she imagined when, her eyes glancing a second time on the armchair, which stood in an obscure part of the closet, the countenance of her dead father appeared there.
>
> Emily stood fixed for a moment to the floor, after which she left the closet. Her spirits, however, soon returned; she reproached herself with the weakness of thus suffering interruption in an act of serious importance, and again opened the door.

Radcliffe carefully preserves perceptual reality: "the countenance of [Emily's] dead father," she insists, only "appeared," and it did so because Emily was suffering one of those "lamentable . . . starts of imagination which deceive the senses," a state that "can be called nothing less than momentary madness." The novelist provides this virtually clinical exposition of Emily's "greatly enervated . . . mind," moreover, *before* describing the false apparition, so that we do not for a second participate in or connive at Emily's delusion. She recovered quickly, moreover, and reproached herself for her "weakness." We thus excuse Emily for one fully explained aberration from sense and reason and continue, except when given a similar indication that she has been briefly overcome, to trust her perceptions and rely on her intelligence.

The circumstances in the *Mysteries* being what they are, Emily remains almost constantly under great mental stress. She is required again and again to practice the Baconian alternation, descending to analysis, rising to demonstration, and then descending to analysis—or, at least, to the unmitigated involvement in experience—once again. This terrific demand of the circumstances and Emily's resilient sensitivity to them Radcliffe has often represented with oxymorons such as: "wild conjecture"; "superstitious meaning"; "ashamed of the weakness . . . she could not conquer." (Austen parodied this aspect of Radcliffe's art with Henry Tilney's phrase about Catherine's "surmounting your unconquerable horror.") These expressions, by which the novelist tests language to the breaking point, are required to encompass at once the enormity of the intellectual challenge to her heroine and the heroine's indomitable intellect. Emily's bouts of terror demonstrate the severity of the situations she confronts; and, as she recovers her composure, they actually enforce her intellectual sufficiency.

*   *   *

In the characterizations and narrative developments of the *Mysteries*, Radcliffe composed an epistemological challenge worthy of this heroine. To do so she carried to a greater length than any of her predecessors (except possibly for Swift and Hume) the vital concern she shared with them in the diverse impressions that nature presents to human awareness. Compared to Radcliffe these predecessors—philosophers, scientists, and novelists—often seem impatient and sometimes, indeed, slipshod. They pay a rather cursory attention to the actual particularity of the things in their experience and hazard general statements that they recognize—formally if not feelingly—to be only opinions and probabilities. We may recall Fielding's endorsement of prudence as advocated by Mr. Allworthy; Newton's eagerness to universalize the laws of gravity; and both Berkeley's apprehension of an "admirable connexion" and Pope's assurance of a "stupendous whole" uniting all the parts of nature. Laurence Sterne, similarly, reports with apparent approval the tendency of his idealized version of himself, Parson Yorick, to leap to general conclusions: if a man committed "a dirty action," Yorick would judge him "without more ado . . . a dirty fellow."[11] Radcliffe is far more conscientious than this and, indeed, than almost any of her great predecessors. In the *Mysteries*, especially, she takes strict note of the different bits and pieces of experience, describing perceptual things one at a time and holding all patterns, both those composed of resembling and those derived from contiguous impressions, in protracted abeyance. The perceptual bedrock or, rather, bedrocks of reality she invests with full dignity: each possibly pertinent sight and sound, each knock, melody, sigh, gleam, shape, groan, scratch, shadow, buzz, murmur and thump, is registered by itself, as itself. Its place in any complex of human or natural order is always subject to determination and—before Emily can determine—to mystery.

The problem of inductive reconciliation Radcliffe pointedly focuses on human identity. Can a certain figure or shadow be attributed to a certain general human category, "Valancourt," "Montoni," "Morano?" Again and again Emily faces the problem of attaching a certain percept, a voice, a footstep, a vibrating lute, or the turning of a lock, to some general human substance or other; and, more precisely, of fitting this percept with others that touch or resemble it and thus conceiving a single personal congeries. Once, for instance, as she was leaving Toulouse she looked out of her carriage and saw an "object," that is, as Radcliffe next informs us, "a person . . . with his hat, in which was a military feather"—that is, presumably, a soldier—who, on his turning "at the sound of wheels," as she finally reports, Emily identified as "Valancourt himself." Earlier at Toulouse, as she was crossing the hall in her aunt's mansion, Emily saw "a person" enter "whom, as her eyes hastily glanced that way, she imagined to be Montoni." She passed on rapidly then until "she heard the well-known voice of Valancourt."

Radcliffe is concerned, of course, with many resembling elements in experience: with two appearances of the same planet; with two renderings of the same melody; with two views of the same miniature; even with the same or similar degrees of sublimity. And she strongly endorses her century's self-conscious dedication to abstract generalization, that is, to the organizing of similar experiences into categories and the enunciation of categorical opinions. Emily's father was a strong advocate of certain ethical generalities especially of general controls on the sensibility; and Emily is described attempting to apply these controls— if with imperfect success—to the particular events in her own life. But the most important question of resemblance and generalization, as it should be in a novel, focuses on the combined creation-

and-apprehension of individual human character. Radcliffe explicitly brings Pope's doubts on this subject into her novel in the cynicism of Montoni, who speaks with dogmatic asperity of "female caprice." It is quite unreasonable, he insists, "to find sincerity and uniformity in one of [Emily's] sex." The contrary impressions one observes in any apparently individual woman—in church and at a ball, before and after the receipt of a certain gift, sober and drunk—simply do not cohere, as Montoni, following Pope, would insist. And what is true of individual women, as Pope could have informed Montoni, is equally true of men. In every human being we observe diverse modes of conduct; and it may be only by seeing a person at the point of death, as Pope once suggested, that we can generalize his character.

The problem of personal identification Radcliffe has made much more difficult for Emily, if that is imaginable, than Pope indicated. And much more important, since Emily's personal compositions, her judgments of personal character and her response to personal evidence are matters of life and death. She is usually denied, moreover, Pope's access to conversation. We may suggest two reasons for this: the conversational inhibition, which I have recently noticed, that society imposed on women; the dwindling reliance on other minds, on minds separate from one's own, which is, as Hume's skepticism of personal identities may illustrate, evident in British culture. Emily must pretty much go it alone, at any rate, with little chance to augment or to test her own experience. She must observe her acquaintance for herself; she must catch them by fits and starts; and she must operate under the most trying circumstances, often with one or another of them apparently attempting to hide or to deceive. In confronting Montoni on one occasion, Emily entertains an altogether unlikely wish: "Oh, could I know . . . what passes in that mind; could I know the thoughts that are known there, I should no longer be condemned to this torturing suspense." But she never can, and she never, in fact, establishes anything like a character of Montoni: she never even discovers for sure whether to apply the term "banditti" to him and his frightening companions. Montoni presents to Emily, finally, only a puzzling collection of threats, scowls, cajolery, false promises and formidable posturing.

Certain characters Radcliffe no doubt defines quite adequately: Monsieur Bonnac is a worthy man oppressed by vicissitudes; Monsieur Quesnel is a crass, self-deceived snob. But even so reliable a personal focus as St. Aubert or as the Count de Villefort presents Emily serious problems in character. Emily never actually doubts the virtuous integrity of her father: the original judgment in his favor, which Radcliffe represents as the accumulation of many years of paternal duty and care, the loving daughter refuses to relinquish. But she must absorb several very disquieting impressions. She accidentally saw him one dark night weeping over the picture of a woman whom she did not recognize. Curiosity and tenderness had led her to his room where she observed him, after looking over some letters that she surmised to be from her mother, kneeling in prayer.

> When he rose, a ghastly paleness was on his countenance. Emily was hastily retiring; but she saw him turn again to the papers, and she stopped. He took from among them a small case, and from thence a miniature picture. The rays of light fell strongly upon it, and she perceived it to be that of a lady but not of her mother.
>
> St. Aubert gazed earnestly and tenderly upon this portrait, put it to his lips, and then to his heart, and sighed with a convulsive force.
>
> Emily could scarcely believe what she saw to be real. She never knew till now that he had a picture of any other lady than her mother, much less that he had one which he evidently valued so highly; but having looked repeatedly, to be certain that it was not the resemblance of Madame St. Aubert, she became entirely convinced that it was designed for that of some other person.
>
> At length St. Aubert returned the picture to its case; and Emily recollecting that she was intruding upon his private sorrows, softly withdrew from the chamber.

This suspicious conduct of her father plus something in these papers "of dreadful note," which she saw later when, at his dying direction, she was burning them, forced Emily for some time to entertain the surmise that he had had a mistress, who (if facial resemblances, still later recognized, mean anything) might, indeed, be her real mother! She steadily resists this complex revision of her familial situation and, finally, with vindication: the picture was that of St. Aubert's unacknowledged sister, the unlucky Marchioness de Villeroi. But St. Aubert's character throughout much of the book is thus constituted of apparently irreconcilable atoms of evidence.

Emily's attention is chiefly focused, as Addison would have approved, on Valancourt, whose identity or, better, whose identification is given a tremendously vexed rendering. He presents, first of all, the conventional novelistic problem of constancy, the problem Austen would focus on such characters as Willoughby early in her career and Wentworth near its close. When Emily saw Valancourt after their year-long separation, during which she had been immersed in Udolpho and he had been enthralled by Paris, she detected "with some regret that [his countenance] was not the same as when she last saw it"—although he "perceived [on the other hand] the same goodness and beautiful simplicity [in her] that had charmed him on their first acquaintance." True, "the bloom of her countenance was somewhat faded"—everything flickers in Radcliffe's world. But the resemblance is sufficient to support Valancourt's judgment of "the same" Emily. His countenance, however, had lost so much of its former "simplicity" and "open benevolence" as to throw particular resemblance and general identification in doubt. Valancourt's face, after a year of debauchery in Paris, was hardly "the same" as that of the young hunter Emily had grown to love in the Pyrenees.

The judgment of the honorable Count de Villefort, who had observed Valancourt's conduct in Paris, confirms Emily's perception: he is indeed different from the youth who, as St. Aubert observed in the Pyrenees, "had never been to Paris." She may be to him "still my own Emily," as Valancourt puts it; but he is, as he himself admits, crucially different. "I ask you," Emily says quite pointedly, "whether you are conscious of being the same estimable Valancourt—whom I once loved?" To which he responds, "the same—the same!" Notice how Radcliffe emphasizes the point. Then, after pausing to consider, he adds, "in a voice at once solemn and defeated, 'No—I am not the same.'" And, after some cross-examination, Emily must agree: "'You are no longer the Valancourt I have been accustomed to love.'"

During the rest of the novel, hard, circumstantial evidence accumulates to prove, contrariwise, that the post-Paris Valancourt is sufficiently similar to the earlier Valancourt to deserve this customary love: evidence that the Count had misapprehended Valancourt in Paris and, more positively, that he is just as benevolent and almost as simple as he ever was. He supports Emily's old maid, Theresa, even in his own straitened circumstances; and, although he has recently returned to gambling, he did so to rescue the estimable Monsieur Bonnac from prison. For some time, however, Emily, who is appropriately skeptical, enjoys the melancholy assurance that her lover is "no longer the same Valancourt" and that his "beloved idea . . . was an illusion of her own creation." She is sickened "at the blank that remained in her consciousness" once "Valancourt seemed [thus] to be annihilated." In taking this line, she is prosecuting personal relations in precisely the way Locke and Berkeley and Hume have described them: constructing from the available experiential bits and pieces a whole person, if she can. Emily feels at this point in her apprehension of "Valancourt"—with some sense—that the pieces simply cannot be reconciled; there is no tissue of resemblance, with which to support the proper category, "Valancourt": hence her sense of a "blank." She seems merely to confront a few perceptions of simplicity and a few of corruption and thus, as Pope might say, no character at all.

The accumulation of evidence, however, finally allows her to reinstate "Valancourt" in her affection. "Many minute circumstances"—or "atoms of probability," as Johnson might call them—come together to form a sufficiently resembling tissue, bringing to a happy conclusion the kind of "painful conjectures" that such a one as Radcliffe's heroine is always in danger of. The new circumstances, that is, are found sufficiently similar to the old ones to fill the blank in Emily's consciousness with the single beloved category of being. His conduct, she discovers, had been "cruelly . . . misrepresented"; and this had degraded him in her "opinion." Once she understands this—and it happens only in the last pages of the novel—she acknowledges his beloved sameness and they live happily ever after. But such a difficulty in the establishment of a character who is, in the first place, intensely beloved and, in the second, actually integral, forcefully indicates the problem of establishing human character in general. If Valancourt was just barely able to maintain himself in Emily's regard, how confused and accidental must the relevant perceptions of most of one's acquaintance seem.

Radcliffe focuses on Valancourt an even more basic problem in general identification, not only that of personal substance—a normal stock in trade of the novel—but the more radical problem of physical being as well. At one point in Udolpho, Emily must try, not for the sophisticated apprehension of Valancourt's character, but merely for an assurance of his presence. Radcliffe provides her heroine almost as much immediate evidence of Valancourt's presence in Udolpho—to work out this experiment in physical identification—as Austen was to provide Elinor on the engagement of Edward Ferrars to Lucy Steele. There is, first, the mysterious music that Emily, who carries a pertinent musical memory from La Vallee, hears for herself over and over again. (She was merely to gather second-hand reports on Valancourt's Parisian corruption.) This recurrent musical evidence is, in the first place, French, as Emily comes to recognize. It is sometimes, moreover, "the same [French] melody" she had heard emanating invisibly from the fishinghouse back home; and, or so Emily perceives, exactly "the same" rendering of this melody. Eventually the singer, who seems to be located in a cell below her chamber and thus to be a prisoner, works her name into the lyrics of his song— as the unknown poet had formerly worked her name into the lines Emily found scratched in the wainscot of the fishinghouse.

There is a collection of purely visual impressions to go along with these purely audial ones. Emily sees a strange figure on several different nights on the ramparts below her chamber. This figure, whose actual existence Emily doubts for a while, posts itself immediately before her casement; and it once waves to her "with what seemed to be its arm" before being startled by the guard and gliding away (with no sound of footsteps) down the rampart. This figure, although it once makes "a faint groan," never sings; but Emily gradually comes to connect it (correctly, as it turns out) with the invisible music and to compose in her imagination a musical French prisoner who cares for her. Finally, there is some startling ocular evidence, the very miniature of herself—passed to her from the prisoner by way of the trusty servant, Ludovico—that was stolen months before from the fishinghouse. This confirms the identification she made when the singer, who had responded to Annette's call with silence, "answered . . . her voice alone." She recalls other "circumstances" during this desperate exercise in induction that point strongly toward Valancourt, chiefly this: "he had more than once said [during their actual companionship] that the fishinghouse, where she had formerly listened to this voice and air, and where she had seen pencilled sonnets addressed to herself [notice how carefully Radcliffe crosses the t's and dots the i's of her evidence] had been his favorite haunt before he had been made known to her." There is also a piece of negative evidence—Emily "did not recollect to have ever heard [Valancourt] sing"—but unfortunately she neglects it. Nevertheless, the evidence, strengthened by the anonymous prisoner's professions of affection for Emily—professions that Ludovico reports back to her—clearly supports the identification of this disparate bundle of things with Valancourt.

That Emily is wrong in making and acting upon this identification and thus one dark night in Udolpho, "advanced to meet Valancourt" only to sink "in the arms of a stranger" wonderfully enforces the problem of personal induction which, as I have been suggesting, stands at the heart of Radcliffe's fiction. In retrospect, to drive her point home, Radcliffe makes us reconsider the evidence. Emily never saw the figure on the ramparts closely enough to detect its physiognomy—although she had once judged that it was the wrong shape to be one of the castle guard; and she had never seen the fishinghouse artist at all: thus any connection between him and Valancourt has to be perilous. And although Valancourt has a fine feeling for literature—underlining passages in books of poetry that he especially wants Emily to notice—he had never showed any creative skill, either as a singer (as Emily once recalls) or as a poet. And he never mentioned the poem scratched on the wainscot of the fishinghouse nor claimed to have done any singing there. There is in short no tissue of images in Emily's awareness that really validates her effort to reconcile this Udolphean set of impressions—neither the visual nor the audial—with the recollected set she can surely attribute to Valancourt. When DuPont, the "stranger," explains his own conduct, which had long kept him at the very edge of Emily's experiential field—a subject (never recognized) only to the most ambitious metonymic inferences—the failures of resemblance and contiguity and the consequent failure of generalization become clear.

In the *Mysteries* Radcliffe bases, not only the sense of other people, but the understanding of all nature on the particulars of experience, taking more seriously—or more radically, at least—than any of her colleagues the principle that each thing exists in particular. In the first place, she faces it in its purest and strongest sense, pointedly defining particular percepts, particular sense data. In the second place, she reduces these percepts to atomic singularity, forcing her heroine to assemble reality in its entirety from originally miscellaneous bits and pieces of sensation. Emily's first view of Udolpho, appropriately, presents this task with the fullest possible effect, providing her a nice exercise in the intellectual activity which will soon become a matter of life and death. In Valancourt Radcliffe shows that even the most reliable acquaintance can be disassembled by the vagaries of circumstance into virtually irreconcilable constituents. In Udolpho, despite the confident introduction of Montoni, she shows that the most solid edifice has the same susceptibility:

> The sun had just sunk below the top of the mountains [Emily] was descending, whose long shadow stretched athwart the valley; but his sloping rays, shooting through an opening of the cliffs, touched with a yellow gleam the summits of the forest that hung upon the opposite steeps, and streamed in full splendour upon the towers and battlements of a castle that spread its extensive ramparts along the brow

of a precipice above. The splendour of these illumined objects was heightened by the contrasted shade which involved the valley below.

"There," said Montoni, speaking for the first time in several hours, "is Udolpho."

Emily gazed with melancholy awe upon the castle, which she understood to be Montoni's; for, though it was now lighted up by the setting sun, the Gothic greatness of its features, and its mouldering walls of dark grey stone, rendered it a gloomy and sublime object. As she gazed, the light died away on its walls, leaving a melancholy purple tint, which spread deeper and deeper as the thin vapour crept up the mountain, while the battlements above were still tipped with splendour. From those, too, the rays soon faded, and the whole edifice was invested with the solemn duskiness of evening. Silent, lonely, and sublime, it seemed to stand the sovereign of the scene, and to frown defiance on all who dared to invade its solitary reign. As the twilight deepened, its features became more awful in obscurity; and Emily continued to gaze, till its clustering towers were alone seen rising over the tops of the woods, beneath whose thick shade the carriages soon after began to ascend.

The extent and darkness of these tall woods awakened terrific images in her mind, and she almost expected to see banditti start up from under the trees. At length the carriages emerged upon a heathy rock, and soon after reached the castle gates, where the deep tone of the portal bell, which was struck upon to give notice of their arrival, increased the fearful emotions that had assailed Emily. While they waited till the servant within should come to open the gates, she anxiously surveyed the edifice: but the gloom that overspread it allowed her to distinguish little more than a part of its outline, with the massy walls of the ramparts, and to know that it was vast, ancient, and dreary. From the parts she saw, she judged of the heavy strength and extent of the whole. The gateway before her, leading into the courts, was of gigantic size, and was defended by two round towers crowned by overhanging turrets embattled, where, instead of banners, now waved long grass and wild plants that had taken root among the mouldering stones, and which seemed to sigh, as the breeze rolled past, over the desolation around them. The towers were united by a curtain pierced and embattled also, below which appeared the pointed arch of a huge portcullis surmounting the gates: from these the walls of the ramparts extended to other towers overlooking the precipice, whose shattered outline, appearing on a gleam that lingered in the west, told of the ravages of war. Beyond these all was lost in the obscurity of evening.

Everything is in flux in this most ambitiously solid and stable of images. Light shifts and fades; vapor creeps and mounts; viewers change their point of vantage; and the breeze stirs the fringes of things, deconstructing Udolpho, reducing it from a single substance into a kaleidoscope of images. The battlements may be "still"—that is, briefly—"tipped with splendor"; but the walls are always changing as evening gloom overspreads them. The years are evident as well, although they leave enough to allow Emily imaginatively to create from actual appearances a former shape of things, "from the parts . . . the whole." Her thoughts reach into the future, imagining "banditti," and into the past, conceiving "the ravages of war." Udolpho thus provides the proper scene for the challenge to Emily's sense and her imagination that awaits her once she has passed its shadowy gates.

Throughout the *Mysteries*, although most forcefully within Udolpho's walls, Radcliffe separates perception from judgment and percept from percept. In this narrative passage from Emily's brief return to La Vallee after her father's death, for instance, Radcliffe meticulously isolates from one another several striking sense impressions:

> She cast an anxious eye around [the dark garden, painfully conscious that she might catch a last glimpse of Valancourt] and often stopped for a moment to examine the shadowy scene before she ventured to proceed: but she passed on without perceiving any person, till, having reached a clump of almond-trees, not far from the house, she rested to take a retrospect of the garden, and to sigh forth another adieu:—as her eyes wandered over the landscape, she thought she perceived a person emerge from the groves, and pass slowly along a moonlight alley that led between them; but the distance, and the imperfect light, would not suffer her to judge with any degree of certainty whether this was fancy or reality. She continued to gaze for some time on the spot; till on the dead stillness of the air she heard a sudden sound, and in the next instant fancied she distinguished footsteps near her. Wasting not another moment in conjecture, she hurried to the chateau, and, having reached it, retired to her chamber, where as she closed her window she looked upon the garden, and then again thought that she distinguished a figure gliding between the almond-trees she had just left.

Here Radcliffe has rendered several percepts separately: "a person" (seen); "a sudden sound"; "footsteps" (more sound); "a figure gliding" (seen, that is, but not heard). At no point do these impressions cohere. Their effect throughout, as Radcliffe insists, is to deny any inference of a substantial support: Emily could "not . . . judge with any degree of certainty whether this was fancy or reality." The final "figure" she "thought that she distinguished," by "gliding" away, fails to give that confirmation of one sense (sight) by another (sound) from which we customarily derive our confidence in physical reality. Emily would like to reconcile these diverse impressions and infer the presence of her lover, but, as she recognizes, they will not allow it.

In Udolpho she endures many such problems. One night in her chamber, for instance, "she was awakened by a noise." Radcliffe thus stimulates at first just one sense and does so with a vague, strictly unidentifiable impression. Time passes and then, "A return of the noise again disturbed her." This mere doubling of sound, between which stretches a strongly felt gap, sets Emily to work: she recalls pertinent impressions from the past, primarily "the odd circumstance of the [stairway] door having been fastened [from outside] during the preceding night." The noise continued and, as she attended it, "it seemed like that made by the drawing of rusty bolts." And Emily begins to infer a "hand [that seemed to] fear . . . discovery" and tentatively conceives an intruder. She can do so because she has gradually located and identified the noise. So far it has been all sound, but now follows an essay in sight:

> While Emily kept her eyes fixed on the spot, she saw the door move, and then slowly open, and perceived something enter the room, but the extreme duskiness prevented her distinguishing what it was. Almost fainting with terror, she had yet sufficient command over herself to check the shriek that was escaping from her lips, and letting the curtain drop from her hand, continued to observe in silence the motions of the mysterious form she saw. It seemed to glide along the remote obscurity of the apartment, then paused, and, as it approached the hearth, she perceived, in a stronger light, what appeared to be a human figure. Certain remembrances now stuck upon her heart, and almost subdued the feeble remains of her spirit; she continued, however, to watch the figure, which remained for some time motionless; but then, advancing slowly towards the bed, stood silently at the feet where the curtains being a little open, allowed her still to see it; terror, however, had now deprived her of the power of discrimination, as well as of that of utterance.
>
> Having continued there a moment, the form retreated towards the hearth, when it took the lamp, surveyed the chamber for a few moments, and then again advanced towards the bed.

In sharply separated instants, she "saw the door move," "perceived something enter," and, getting command of her faculties, observed a "mysterious form." "It seemed to glide"—still soundless; and only when it finally got into better light, could she confirm the earlier implication of "hand" and actually ascertain "a human figure." Emily has watched and remembered pertinent images from the past and, despite fits of mind-destroying terror, works to construct a coherent human purpose. It is, however, several percepts later before she can fill the frightening void with a general understanding of things—that is, with her suitor, Morano, on an errand of rape.

Radcliffe separates not only percept from percept in presenting pertinent experience to her heroine but, as has already emerged, sense from sense, thus intensifying in strict accord with the tenet of particularity the challenge to this highly sensitive intelligence. Emily once "heard footsteps approaching and then the door of the pavilion open and, on turning, she saw—Valancourt." On another occasion, "a hasty footstep approached [Emily] from behind the plane-tree and, turning her eyes, [she] saw Madame Montoni." At Udolpho this disturbing separation of sound and sight is virtually the rule. Emily and Annette once, for instance, "heard a key turn in the lock of the gate near them, and presently saw a man advancing. It was Barnardine." Notice the step-by-step progression and the suspense of the human identification: first Radcliffe presents the vague impression, "man," and only in the next sentence his identity. In her chamber, again, Emily once "thought she heard a voice; and raising herself to listen, saw the chamber door open, and Annette enter." Soon afterwards, "as she sat musing, a peal of laughter rose from the terrace, and going to the casement, she saw, with inexpressible surprise, three ladies dressed in the gala habit of Venice, walking with several gentlemen below." The laughter rises, strictly removed from any apparent cause, and reverberates quite disembodied for quite long enough to preserve the Humean skepticism of necessary connection and, beyond this, of physical being, so that discovering the cause itself constitutes a surprise. Consider this case: "She heard a footstep approach her chamber; and opening the door saw not Annette, but old Carlo!" For just a phrase in Radcliffean narrative, it seems as if Emily did not have any visual confirmation of the audial impression and, once again, the necessary myth of human substance is held in terrifying abeyance. Old Carlo is, of course, something of a surprise; but he is, after all, a well established servant, a kindly one at that, who has always had the run of the place. The terror is not in seeing him, but in the gap, here extended by the novelist, between hearing the footstep and seeing anything at all.

Emily is confronted with such basic problems of inductive rec-onciliation, that is, the establishment of substantial identities from resembling percepts and the apprehension of causal tissues among contiguous ones, throughout the *Mysteries*. Looking down from a position of knowledge upon the mysteries that had trou-bled her in the Castle of Udolpho, for example,

> Emily could not forbear smiling at . . . the deception which had given her so much superstitious terror, and was surprised that she could have suffered herself to be thus alarmed, till she considered that, when the mind has once begun to yield to the weakness of supersti-tion, trifles impress it with the force of conviction. Still, however, she remembered with awe the mysterious music which had been heard at midnight near Chateau le Blanc, and she asked Ludovico if he could give any explanation of it; but he could not.

She is thus plunged in a second from the elevation of amused understanding to the depth of bemused awe. And so it goes throughout the novel as Emily ascends to new vistas of certainty and descends into new valleys of doubt; and so it is, *The Mysteries of Udolpho* implies, for human intelligence in all its epistemologi-cal adventures.

*   *   *

Radcliffe has used the conventions of romance to illuminate the realm of sensible nature that British philosophers, scientists, and authors had been considering for two centuries. Within her *Mys-teries* she has presented the ultimate fictional version of their teaching that every perception, every sense datum, is different from every other, that each one exists in particular. This means, as Radcliffe forces her readers to recognize, that all general notions whatever, including those to which we give proper names, are intellectual constructs, inductive tissues, created and maintained by individual human consciousness. *The Mysteries of Udolpho* con-stitutes, in its own oblique way, an analysis of the same human myths, those of natural constancy among like images and natural coherence among unlike ones, that Hume had both explained and punctured—although with disappointingly negative public effect—in his *Treatise*. Like Hume, Radcliffe understood that ordi-nary human kind—"the vulgar," Hume called us—must embrace these myths of constancy and coherence simply to carry on our lives. We must believe that the individual members of our ac-quaintance may remain "the same" over time and that the surge of events in which we are immersed may be comprehended as tissues of probability. Probability is as important to Radcliffe as it is to Hume. If one reduces human experience to its unquestionable components strictly observing their particularity, as both Radcliffe and Hume have demonstrated, human life becomes impossible. But although both the bold thinker and the shy novelist recognized the human need—the irremediable human limitation—both obviously believed, nevertheless, that an occasional—as it were, an experimental—observance of reality might be useful. Radcliffe's unique genius was this, that she also found a way to make it entertaining.

She enjoyed and enjoys this remarkable success because she is such a compassionate—such a tactful—guide through these terrors of reality. The fortuitous intersection of entrenched ethics and revolutionary metaphysics I must invoke again here to explain, not the admirable character of Emily, but the successful style of her creator. Radcliffe's narrative conduct transforms the oppressed female into an omniscient narrator. She never commands her readers to acknowledge a resemblance between Emily's extraordinary experiences and their own; she merely offers them the opportunity. If she rules us, as Pope might say, she never shows that she rules. She has given signs, however, that the actual twitches and discomfort we suffer in following Emily through corridors none of us would enter are in fact representative of the natural environment in which we all must live. The mysteries, which receive an intense exposition at Udolpho, actually pervade the whole novel, in the south of France—when Emily is at home in La Vallee or visiting relations at Chateau le Blanc—as well as in the remoteness of the Apennines.

The end of the *Mysteries* is thus expressively similar to the end of *Rasselas*. In Johnson's work, Abyssinia was originally presented as remote from the real world, as a setting for fantasy. But the return at the end of Johnson's tale is, to the contrary, an acceptance of everyday life. The prince and his companions "deliberated a while what was to be done [and having recognized that] . . . none of [their] wishes . . . could be obtained . . . [they resolved] . . . to return to Abyssinia." Their experiences have deflated—or redeemed—the fabulous; and, enlightened with new or enhanced understanding, they take the place in their world that is appropriate to them, a place now seen as common reality. In *The Mysteries of Udolpho*, Radcliffe has, in the same way, removed her tale from the orderly society of eighteenth-century England to the sixteenth-century south of France. She continues throughout half the novel indeed to withdraw further and further into this fantastic realm, depriving her heroine of mother, father, relatives, and protectors and plunging her deeper and deeper into what shockingly turns out to be reality. This may explain the loss of Emily's fortune, which her father reveals before he dies; the apparent loss of her home, which she suffers in Venice; the death of her aunt; and her forfeiture of the aunt's property. In the course of these deprivations, Emily has been meticulously divested of all social support, that is, of all social insulation. In her remote room at Udolpho, virtually every percept is naked, particular, different; and no connection of either resemblance or causation is reliable. Every pattern must be constructed; all must be held with cautionary skepticism; and none is safe from new evidence. Udolpho thus represents the realm that, according to Hume, philosophers occasionally behold, a realm in which constancy, coherence, and the external existence of things that they seem to support are all recognized as mythical—necessary to human life but unconvincing to the human mind.

When Emily returns from Udolpho, however, she does not simply leave this terrifying realm behind. Consider, for example, this episode, which Emily endured at Chateau le Blanc, an episode that apparently occurred to Jane Austen at a crucial moment in the composition of *Northanger Abbey*:

> A step disturbed her, and, as she paused to listen, she heard it ascending the stair-case of the tower. The gloom of the hour, perhaps, made her sensible to some degree of fear, which she might not otherwise have felt. . . . The steps were quick and bounding, and, in the next moment, the door of the chamber opened, and a person entered, whose features were veiled in the obscurity of twilight, but his voice could not be concealed, for it was the voice of Valancourt! At the sound, never heard by Emily without emotion, she started in terror, astonishment and doubtful pleasure.

Wonders can be, if not totally explained, as this one finally is, somewhat mitigated; some of the pieces, if not all, can be reconciled; and patterns of events can thus be composed without the supernatural glue that Emily always keeps (unopened) at her elbow. But the tardiness of explanation, the necessity of imaginative patching, the threat of present terror and future mistake are not and cannot be corrected or outrun. Like Rasselas, Emily carries the new understanding back home, thus generalizing, not the vanity of human wishes, however, but the particularity of human experience.

This understanding of reality is normally smoothed over or ground down, as Gay demonstrated in *The Beggar's Opera*, by marriage, money and the other customary institutions of society, the comforts of which Radcliffe has emphatically endorsed in closing up her novel. But, as her account of the heroine's return home implies, the severe demands of experience persist even there, whispering, rattling, scraping, stirring, threatening, just behind the most commodious structures society can erect. This may explain why Radcliffe's reality, with its relentless challenges and perils, becomes Austen's too in the specious renovations of *Northanger Abbey*, where she explicitly denies it, and throughout her novels.

6

Austen's Acknowledgments

Charlotte Smith's novelistic career spans that of Ann Radcliffe;[1] but she is not for all that the last student of differences in eighteenth-century English literature. Smith is, indeed, hostile to the perceptual particularities from which Radcliffe composed the *Mysteries*, devoting her work, rather, to representations of generalized human individuals and a generally firm social structure. Those great pillars, constancy of character and coherence of society, undergird Smith's novels, despite their incidental romantic trappings, with formally decisive adequacy.

It is easy enough, no doubt, to discover in these works the properties of terror and suspense—the secret passages, dark tapestries, striking resemblances, shabby structures, flickering lights, gliding figures, and distant footsteps—that both she and Jane Austen explicitly deplored. But they do not play the part in her plots or in her effects that they do in the *Mysteries*. For one thing, these odd bits and pieces of romance are quite sparse in Smith's novels: one can read for many pages together in *Celestina* or *Emmeline* without detecting the shadow of such shadows. But more important is Smith's handling of this stuff. She presents elements of it, not as points of mystery, but as objects of exposition, describing them, not from the viewpoint of entranced observation that one finds in the *Mysteries*, that is to say, but from the vantage of rational action. The glidings, whisperings, and hauntings that Radcliffe's Emily perceives Smith's Monimia performs. The similarity of the settings and of the names of the heroines between Smith's *Emmeline, the Orphan of the Castle* (1788) and Radcliffe's *The Mysteries of Udolpho, A Romance* (1794) is surely no accident; but the similarity ends there. As the very titles of the two novels indicate, the one is interested in one person, a single, identifiable character, the other in the emergence of certain puzzling percepts.

When Emmeline, Smith's orphan, races through a castle's dark corridors, fleeing a masculine threat—an early event in Smith's novel—she is engaged in an activity specifically appropriate to the whole novelistic design. This castle has been Emmeline's home, not her prison, from infancy: she thus knows exactly where she is and where she is going. She also knows her pursuer, young Delamere, and understands (as we do) that his conduct, although no doubt impulsive (like everything he does), poses her no real threat: he wishes only to court Emmeline, and, as things develop, to marry her. Here, as throughout much of the novel, which takes place mostly in settings that Austen would approve, Emmeline faces, somewhat like Elizabeth Bennet in *Pride and Prejudice,* a broad social and personal decision, that is, whether she wishes to favor this pursuer and to accept him as a husband. No doubt the castle through which Delamere pursues her differs from the Collins's cottage, in which Darcy brings the first stage in his pursuit of Elizabeth to an equally premature climax; but these heroines confront the same general problem, whether to engage in a perilous marriage with a wealthy but difficult man or to continue single in relative poverty. Despite the shadowy setting, oddly enough, Emmeline is much more truly aware of her suitor than the Elizabeth who rejects Darcy as the last man in the world she would marry is of hers. Elizabeth must make a radical change in her opinion of Darcy, analyzing past conduct and future prospects bit by bit, as she painfully discovers; but Emmeline sees Delamere here and always for what, here and always, he is.

The difference between Emmeline's situation and Emily's, when Radcliffe's heroine flees through the corridors of Udolpho, despite the similarity in setting and activity, is enormous. In a relatively brief episode, Emmeline goes directly to a person, Delamere's father, who will, as she well knows, free her of his son's attention; she rouses him, after first mistakenly knocking at the door of another guest, and receives the relief she is seeking. Emily's flight, which has no destination, is much more protracted and eventful. She climbs in doubt and terror up unfamiliar stairs as "an odd sound" strikes her and flees from "increasing voices." The sound of not one but two pursuers, both undesirable, both arguing seemingly about her, makes her tremble so that she "with difficulty supported herself"; and "when she hears the sound of their steps," she runs down a dark gallery. One of them falls and drops the light, Emily recognizes, but the other, Verezzi, a very scary guy, comes on as she reaches the corridor that leads to her room. A different light, glimmering mysteriously under the door opposite it, and the fear of Verezzi's continuing pursuit drive Emily on. She evades him in the darkness when he presses down the corridor where she is resting; and she determines finally "to trust . . . to chance" and darts down the next hall she can find. Much of this time Emily does not know where she is or where she should run. She seems hemmed in by unaccountable impressions—sudden sounds and sights of several kinds—and is chased by pursuers whose identities change and whose intentions—although she is no doubt wise to fear the worst—she does not know. Even when thus uncharacteristically plunged in action, then, Emily's problem is chiefly epistemological, a problem, that is, of knowledge and understanding: what light? what sound? what man? what intention? which hall? Emmeline must merely settle her own general feelings, determining whether she can love this flashy but unstable suitor enough to encourage and eventually to marry him; but Emily, whose emotions are quite clear, has other problems: here as always, she must sift the disjointed bits and pieces of her experience and establish, if possible, reliable personal identities and coherent orders of events. Even in this apparently active sequence, therefore, Radcliffe continues as the radical student of differences, confronting the unmitigated particularity of sensation and the challenge this presents for human intelligence. Smith, on the other hand, has embraced without question the customary myths of human identity and natural design: these are givens in her work. Society is sufficiently orderly and personal identity is sufficiently firm, even in the dark hall of Mowbray Castle, to allow the most unprotected young woman to judge her surroundings and to choose her companions. Truly, there are poisonous spiders—rakes and lawyers—weaving away in the corners of the social structure, but these are quite recognizable and eventually subject to the general conditions that govern all civilized life.

Even when Emmeline must, now and then, endure the kind of situation that pervades Udolpho, observing particular "circumstances" and fitting them together, she still enjoys Smith's prevailing novelistic security. One balmy night from an upstairs window of her comfortable bedroom, for instance, Emmeline observes "the figure of a man, tall and thin," lurking outside the front gate of her house, an ordinary eighteenth-century domicile on the Isle of Wight. Notice, at this first, most potentially mysterious moment, that she can be sure of a flesh-and-blood human being and begin to make a precise identification: this is a tall, thin, masculine person. As Emmeline watches him, she hears his footsteps and his breathing and, thus supported by contiguous impressions of sight and hearing, concludes confidently that this is not a "phantom" but a "gentleman." Only one possible identification occurs to her, a tall, thin gentleman of her acquaintance, Fitz-Edward, who is, as Emmeline knows, the repentant lover of a fellow inhabitant of this very house. Although she judges this identification "improbable," it is because of strictly personal, strictly natural, considerations; and a page or two later—the next day, as it were—this identification proves to be in fact correct. The difference between this little exercise and Emily's protracted effort to identify the gliding will-o-the-wisp that haunts the platform below her window at Udolpho is clear enough.

Or consider Smith's handling of a secret passage in *The Old Manor House*, which the heroine, Monimia, could use to reach the library and join her lover, Orlando, for a series of sentimental but seemly tutorials. In the first place, the reader is situated inside the mystery, closely attending the lovers as they make use of this convenience. It is thus no mystery at all except to the other dwellers in the house, the minor characters, that is, in Smith's fiction. We watch the tender heroine and the kind lover, who has shown the passage to her, make their candle-lit way night after night to their accustomed rendezvous. The library is thus almost a home. One day when Orlando accidentally strikes something on the floor there with his foot, he immediately supposes it to be— not a rusty dagger—but "what was indeed the truth," one of Monimia's books. There is, as things develop, a fellow frequenter of the library unknown to these studious lovers and hence to Smith's readers, a small-time smuggler who has been working out of the old manor house basement. Orlando and Monimia discover him, moreover, in a radically perceptual way: they hear "a noise," see a lock move, detect a footstep, and see a human face—disjunctive impressions striking first one sense and then another. But Orlando, a stout-hearted young man, takes immediate action: having resolutely but cautiously "glided" after the intruder, he quickly apprehends, subdues, and identifies him as a local rascal. End of excitement. Orlando is ashamed, moreover, of the mystery he and his beloved are perpetrating and wishes only, as we always understand, to declare his love of Monimia, marry her, and settle down. And that is what, after much ado, Smith describes. She almost never suspends her reader in mystery, then, even when, with a change in viewpoint or in the mode of exposition, she might well do so. She seems actually to invoke the properties of romantic suspense to denigrate and indeed to annul them.

Toward the end of *Celestina*, which takes place chiefly in the central part of England, Smith draws her hero, young Willoughby, to the Pyrenees. Here once again, she introduces the materials of romance—"sublimely beautiful" scenery, the lonely izard, ruins, convent bells, courteous peasants, and fears of both ghosts and bandits—stuff that Radcliffe no doubt borrowed for the early chapters of *Mysteries* and employed to inspire terror and imagination. But Smith rejects this line of development, accounting for the connections between things before mystery can emerge. The ghosts, for example, are actually the hero and his chum, as we are informed well before the scary rumors start; and they merely move around through an uninhabited section of the local castle with prudent circumspection so that they can remain secretly near a certain maltreated maiden—whom they immediately inform of their presence—and eventually rescue her. Like Orlando gliding around the old manor house, these young fellows "glide" about their business, scaring the credulous locals. As such incidental effects show, Smith recognized the mystery in an unmitigated experiential environment; but that is not an important novelistic concern for her. Actually, she raises such effects to oppose them, enforcing, with the contrast they provide, the activities of generally substantial humanity in a generally accountable situation. Willoughby, she once records, "fancied himself a knight of romance"; but no one else entertains such a fancy. Willoughby is a well-bred Englishman in straitened circumstances, engaging in actions—despite their occasionally exaggerated nobility—altogether appropriate to the domestic, social and economic concerns that face him in a time strictly contemporary with that in which the novel was composed and published.

There are in Smith's plots mysteries of a romantic cast, usually concerned with parentage and inheritance. But she does not emphasize these elements in the development of her stories. Celestina turns out at the end of *Celestina*, for example, to have rich and noble connections, and this allows her to marry the financially struggling Willoughby. But everyone, readers and characters alike, discover this all at once, hardly considering the mystery of her birth until being presented with its solution. Until this very late point in the novel, Celestina is treated by all as a mere dependent, albeit a highly attractive one. True, she is a foundling, adopted in infancy by Willoughby's mother, so that the eventual discovery—unlike the slapstick denouement of *Joseph Andrews*—is fully prepared for; but the adoption, which lacked romantic accoutrements—casket, letter, birthmark—is quite straightforward; Celestina accepts without question the humble place she has fallen into; and, except for its conclusion, the novel describes in rigorously accountable ways the familial, social, and economic forces that keep her and Willoughby apart. Orlando's beloved, Monimia, does not seem to have any fancy connections either, and, indeed, she does not: Orlando simply becomes able through the normal but vexed processes of inheritance to afford marriage with the lovely pauper.

None of Smith's heroines is influenced in the choice of life or mate, moreover, by circumstances. True, Celestina must wait for her inheritance to unite her with Willoughby—sometimes thinking him too poor to take her and sometimes supposing him already married to an heiress. Emmeline and Monimia must also endure a tough set of deprivations and delays. But their choices are firm and right all along: they need no new perceptions to influence them and are indeed impervious to all impressions whatever. These heroines never vary in themselves nor face the danger of variance in their lovers;[2] each one, when the skies clear, settles down with the only man of her choice. No disappointments such as those faced by Emily in *Mysteries* or Marianne in *Sense and Sensibility* ever threaten their feelings or their destiny. Thus neither Smith's heroines nor her heroes, all of whom are perfect both in their feelings and—allowing for certain tough emergencies—in their conduct, could serve in a Radcliffe or in an Austen novel. The constancy of Smith's characters—whether described as romantic or not—strictly cancels the mystery Emily must face and the disillusion endured by Marianne and Elizabeth. The questions Austen's and Radcliffe's heroines must contemplate—is Wickham (St. Aubert) a rascal? is Wentworth (Valancourt) the same? is Montoni (Mr. Crawford) a reliable protector?— Smith's heroines are almost entirely spared. Once hero and heroine have become aware of one another in a Smith novel, the need and the use of further experience is over.

Smith avoids—rejects—Radcliffe's two primary narrative commitments: that to the radical fragmentariness of natural circumstances and that to the disparate evidences of human character. Events occur in Smith's novels—even those that might look in isolation like romantic or mysterious obtrusions—in immediately explicable sequences; and characters, no matter how trying these events may be, preserve, without question or doubt, their individual integrities. That, in fact, is what Smith's novels, as a survey of her landscapes will confirm, are all about. She is thus—although different understandings and uses of the term *romantic* may blur this—almost as different from Radcliffe as she could possibly be.

*   *   *

Radcliffe, Smith, and Austen all establish landscapes that are relevant to their general designs; but each of them both describes and uses landscape differently from the others. It will be useful, especially in turning toward the works of Austen, to distinguish them from one another in this respect.

Like Radcliffe, whose scenery I have already discussed, Smith gives a great deal of descriptive attention to the out-of-doors. She sends her characters on even longer and more demanding journeys, not only to Italy and France, where they spend quite a lot of time, actually; she also ships them off to the tempestuous Hebrides and the tropical wilds of New York. She represents the uncontrollable dangers of these situations, if not with perfect accuracy, at some length. The word "sublime" is not common in Smith, but scenery that will raise feelings of sublimity in Radcliffe's Emily provide an impressive and sometimes frightening backdrop to her actions. Her central characters do not actually derive their destinies from storms at sea, blizzards, or pathless wilds, but they do endure threats from such natural conditions. The mere distances represented by the Hebrides, the Pyrenees and the American colonies constitute danger to one lover and incertitude to his-or-her respondent. Celestina recognizes and takes precautions against some mean weather on the isle of Skye; and Orlando is shown—unlike Austen's sailors—facing dreadful perils on the stormy Atlantic. Even in England, Orlando travels through "frost [that] now set in with great severity," picking his way over a rugged road that "hardly allowed a footing to his horse," and crossing "a sheet of ice, on which his horse was every moment in danger of falling." The out-of-doors, in short, is not symbolical in Smith's novels, as it is in Radcliffe's; it provides, rather, a concrete intensification of the many-sided difficulty Smith raises against the natures and hopes of her central figures. The splendor of the scenery, which she acknowledges, is incidental to her novelistic designs; but the incipient threat, on which she insists, strengthens the dangerous conditions faced by her characters and thus eventually enforces her representation of their individual resistance and integrity.

Radcliffe's representation of external nature is altogether different in quality and value, providing not a narrative but a symbolical intensification of her work. The elements do not really threaten in *Mysteries:* Emily emerges unscathed from the worst that sea and forest and mountain can do. Her only real danger, from a storm at sea, Radcliffe describes, significantly, from the view point of a different person, Lady Blanche de Villefort, who views Emily's beleaguered boat from cozy quarters on land. The novelist reveals that this bark has held such a passenger as Emily, moreover, only after she and her companions are, not only safe on land, but comfortably accommodated by Lady Blanche's father at their chateau. Emily, before embarking on this voyage, wrote a poem, "The Mariner," in which all hands were described as lost in a storm; and other poems of hers also describe violent death in the hostilities of the external world; but Radcliffe keeps her heroine from suffering even the shadow of such a fate, leaving her comfortably ashore in Leghorn and picking her up again only when she has safely disembarked in France.

Unlike Smith, who represents the elements inhibiting and endangering the very lives of her characters, Radcliffe emphasizes their effects on her characters'—especially Emily's—thoughts and feelings: not human involvement but human responsiveness is her interest—quite appropriately, of course, given Radcliffe's primary design. Emily's insouciant responsiveness to landscape, which was documented in the last chapter, projects her upon Radcliffe's reader as a perfect example of the Humean sensorium, that theater of impressions and ideas or—in Hume's words—that "bundle or collection of different perceptions, which succeed each other with an inconceivable rapidity, and are in a perpetual flux and movement." The interpenetration of human and natural impressions that Radcliffe characteristically indicates—Hannibal in the Alps, the recurring confusion of wind and music, weeds growing in ruined walls—enforces the situation Emily faces, on the one hand, undermining all assurance that any one percept— a banging door, a creaking tree limb, a flickering light—is or is not a sign of humanity; on the other, establishing all perceptions, human and natural alike, as part of the perpetually shifting surge of experience. Scenery, whether mingled with traces of humanity or not, thus enforces the mysteries confronted by Radcliffe's heroine, presenting her a relentless experiential flux and a corresponding epistemological challenge.

Austen's much more limited scenery, which is as steady almost as a picture and as orderly as hands could make it, has a strikingly different effect. It not only frames and delimits the world of her interest, the world of strictly human events; but it also seems to indicate that this realm is quite manageable, that it is, if not strictly stable, surely subject to human designs of stability. The orderliness of her landscapes implies a tendency toward order, that is to say, in human affairs. The out-of-doors in her novels is all "English verdure," as Emma suggests, a scene in which every tree, every stone, and every blade of grass has been organized for human purposes in accordance with human intelligence.[3] Elizabeth Bennet may imagine collecting a few petrified spars somewhere in Derbyshire, which is as far north as she ever goes, but Darcy's estate there is a "park," which has been tastefully improved. It is large, no doubt, but its extent is totally accessible to a pony-driven phaeton which, as Mrs. Gardiner, no outdoors person, suggests, will draw her and her niece all round it. The stream running through this park, although "of some natural importance," has been "swelled [by human contrivance] into greater." If it produces "some curious water plant," this is or seems to be for human "inspection"; and its trout are strictly available to Darcy and his sporting guests. Rushworth's big estate, Sotherton, is similarly subject to human improvement or, at least, human manipulation.[4] Its "wilderness" is "a planted wood of about two acres," which chiefly provides visitors with comfortable shade. And surrounding this little retreat, once again, is a "park." Sotherton's plants and animals are the product of cultivation and breeding, so that Aunt Norris can sponge a little heath from the gardener and four fertilized eggs from the housekeeper to provide her some amusement, she says, in the lonely hours at her own home.

Not that there are many lonely hours in which Austen's characters pay attention even to the gardens and barnyards outside their homes. Inhabiting "the midland counties of England," as Austen explicitly defines the realm that interests her, they are almost always, in larger-or-smaller social groups, walking about or sitting about as comfortably outdoors as in, enjoying gardens and shrubbery that they seldom visit—and never need to visit—except when it is mild and dry.[5] No doubt Fanny Price's brother and Anne Elliot's lover have been to sea and have faced, as the sailing contingent in *Persuasion* acknowledges, some pretty tough weather. But this lies outside the realm in which Austen's stories take place, and most of her characters stay right at home. Frank Churchill, rich and indolent, talks about going abroad, but he only ranges in fact from Weymouth to York and appears only in the cozy purlieus of Highbury—and never in bad weather. There is a snow storm of sorts in *Emma* before Frank comes on the scene, which threatens to trap Mr. Woodhouse in the home of Frank's father a good mile from Hartfield, presenting, as Mr. Wood-house's splenetic son-in-law suggests to him, "a spirited begin-ning" of this feeble valetudinarian's "winter engagements." But, as the sensible Mr. Knightley assures everyone, it actually pre-sents "not the smallest bit of difficulty in their getting home," the snow being "nowhere above half-an-inch deep."

Fanny Price once gazes from a window of the great house in *Mansfield Park* upon a "scene without," in which "the deep shade of the woods" was nicely contrasted with "the brilliancy of an unclouded night," and speaks of the ethical benefits humankind might enjoy "if the sublimity of Nature were more attended to"; but this is both a brief and a carefully moderated incident. The wildest word Austen uses with any emphasis to describe condi-tions out-of-doors in the world she defines for herself is "pictur-esque"—subject, that is, to being made into a picture.[6] And even this word seems out of bounds to the sensible Edward Ferrars, who, in *Sense and Sensibility*, admits to no knowledge and no taste for it. He apologizes to Marianne:

> "You must not inquire too far, Marianne—remember I have no knowl-edge in the picturesque, and I shall offend you by my ignorance and want of taste if we come to particulars. I shall call hills steep, which ought to be bold; surfaces strange and uncouth, which ought to be irregular and rugged; and distant objects out of sight, which ought only to be indistinct through the soft medium of a hazy atmosphere. You must be satisfied with such admiration as I can honestly give. I call it [the Dashwood situation in Devonshire] a very fine country—the hills are steep, the woods seem full of fine timber, and the valley looks comfortable and snug—with rich meadows and several neat farm houses here and there. It exactly answers my idea of a fine country, because it unites beauty with utility—and I dare say it is a picturesque one too, because you admire it; I can easily believe it to be full of rocks and promontories, grey moss and brush wood, but these are all lost on me. I know nothing of the picturesque."
>
> ....
>
> "I am convinced," said Edward, "that you really feel all the delight in a fine prospect which you profess to feel. But, in return, your sister [Elinor, who has questioned Edward's sincerity] must allow me to feel no more than I profess. I like a fine prospect, but not on picturesque principles. I do not like crooked, twisted, blasted trees. I admire them much more if they are tall, straight and flourishing. I do not like ruined, tattered cottages. I am not fond of nettles, or thistles, or heath blossoms. I have more pleasure in a snug farm-house than a watch-tower—and a troop of tidy, happy villagers please me better than the finest banditti in the world."

And, of course, he is right at home in Austen's bandit-free England.

With such landscape, which she refers to with meticulous economy, Austen focuses her reader's attention, not only on humanity, but on the social actions of humanity: murder, torture, war and all physical violence have thus been cancelled from her world. To this extent her landscape is symbolically reliable. But the lives that stir in the homes and villages and estates thus indicated, are not as orderly, as well controlled, or as well known as the environment in which they transpire suggests that they might be. As far as Austen's scenery reaches in its implications, actually, it deceives, providing an ironic foil to the disjunctiveness of human evidence and the uncertainty of human knowledge. Austen's narratives, although occurring within comfortable houses, cottages and parks, illustrate Hume's atomistic description of human experience in as profound, if not in as showy, a way as Radcliffe's. The elements do not distort the evidence Austen's heroines must confront; but neither, when all was said and done, did they significantly intensify the mysteries Emily faced. In comfort and security, Elinor and Fanny face epistemological problems that are quite as challenging—if not quite as terrifying—as those confronted by Emily.[7] And they are precisely the same kind of problems as well: the uncertain constancy of persons; the undiscovered coherence of events.

Austen's neat English scenery no doubt lulls readers and characters alike, confounding even such intelligent observers as Henry Tilney and Emma Woodhouse. Consider Emma's response, for example, to this view of Donwell Abbey and its surroundings:

> She felt all the honest pride and complacency which her alliance with the present and future proprietor could fairly warrant, as she viewed the respectable size and style of the building, its suitable, becoming, characteristic situation, low and sheltered—its ample gardens stretching down to meadows washed by a stream, of which the Abbey, with all the old neglect of prospect, had scarcely a sight—and its abundance of timber in rows and avenues, which neither fashion nor extravagance had rooted up.
>
> ....
>
> The considerable slope, at nearly the foot of which the Abbey stood, gradually acquired a steeper form beyond its grounds; and at a half a mile distant was a bank of considerable abruptness and grandeur, well clothed with wood;—and at the bottom of this bank, favourably placed and sheltered, rose the Abbey-Mill Farm, with meadows in front, and the river making a close and handsome curve around it.

One notes in this harmonious blend of the human and the natural that the bank is "well clothed"—as a gentleman should be—and that the stream, like a dutiful, unobtrusive servant, washes the meadows and arranges things in "a close and handsome curve." The scene is fine but neat, grand but orderly. And it is interwoven in Emma's mind with similar thoughts about the Knightleys, chiefly Mr. George Knightley, who had no faults of temper like his brother but was even gracious enough—"she was glad to see it"—to engage her little friend Harriet "in pleasant conversation." Mr. Knightley shows the same generous concern for Harriet, to enunciate the implications here, that he has shown for his estate.

But an apparent difference between Mr. Knightley's estate and his conduct will soon strike Emma, forcing her to recognize with horror a possible split, because of sexual lust or romantic credulity, between the farmer and the man. In her anguished fancy, a fancy well supplied with supportive evidence, she beholds Mr. Knightley as the lover of Harriet Smith. Although the coherence between landscape and humanity is preserved in this case when Mr. Knightley proves to love only the strictly suitable woman, Emma's fears dramatically reveal that the world of human affairs, unlike its natural environment, may present shocking disparities and contingencies.

*   *   *

The crucial moment in defining the relationship in Austen's novels between the English environment and English society and, in the same stroke, between her work and Radcliffe's occurs, quite obviously, in *Northanger Abbey* with Henry Tilney's discovery and reproof of Catherine Morland's full-blown Radcliffean conduct. Henry's dogmatic confidence about life in England's green and pleasant land "where roads and newspapers lay everything open" and the impressive rhetoric with which he dissolves all human mystery seem to settle the matter.

> "If I understand you rightly, you had formed a surmise [that his father had murdered his mother] of such horror as I have hardly words to— Dear Miss Morland, consider the dreadful nature of the suspicions you have entertained. What have you been judging from? Remember the country and the age in which we live. Remember that we are English, that we are Christians. Consult your own understanding, your own sense of the probable, your own observation of what is passing around you—Does our education prepare us for such atrocities? Do our laws connive at them? Could they be perpetrated without being known, in a country like this, where social and literary inter-

course is on such a footing; where every man is surrounded by a neighbourhood of voluntary spies, and where roads and newspapers lay every thing open? Dearest Miss Morland, what ideas have you been admitting?"

In a well-ordered country like this there is no reason, Henry avers, for well-bred people to entertain Radcliffean inferences. This society, every event of which is subject to illumination and every member of which is subject to scrutiny, is as neat as the natural environment in which it transpires: it allows no odd gaps in experience, no hidden corners of human activity, and thus denies all shocking emergencies. "The liberty which [Catherine's] imagination had taken," "the absurdity of her curiosity and fears," these had led to strictly "causeless terror," a "self-created delusion" of fear and alarm. The need, the appropriateness, of Emily's curiosity and imagination has thus been cancelled.[8]

Apparently projecting her own opinion through the painfully enlightened understanding of her heroine, Austen pontificates: it is not in "Mrs. Radcliffe's works . . . charming as [they] all were that human nature . . . was to be looked for [not, at all events, as it can be found] in the central part of England." Here Austen recognizes both her chief concern, "human nature," and its external milieu, "central . . . England": within the orderly boundaries of the one she will develop an orderly exposition of the other. In such an environment, if any place, she insists, human actions are observable and human motives, accountable. In this enamelled countryside, she assures us, at least here, as her irony extends the focus, humanity can be freed from the mysteries that Radcliffe described.

An experience Catherine endured just before Henry discovered and reproved her confirms Austen's assurances. The fledgling romantic had been visiting the late Mrs. Tilney's room, driven by the curiosity and imagination that her reading of *Mysteries* prompted her to practice; and she had found it, to her "astonishment," to be an ordinary neat, sunlit, altogether English bedroom, totally unsuitable for the play of her horrid fancies. Its details are metaphorically reconcilable with those apparent in the rest of the modernized Abbey and in the well-kept grounds around it; they also fit metonymically with the devotion to neatness that General Tilney, the focus of Catherine's Radcliffean inferences, had always projected in public. This room, which is thus romantically sterile, provides a preliminary illustration, therefore, of Henry's lecture. And Catherine vividly recognizes this. She has suddenly no desire to look beyond the closet doors, the Radcliffean analogues to which revealed to Emily in Chateau le Blanc the long-dead Countess de Villeroi's Bible opened to the last page she had read before her death and the decomposing black veil she had worn on the day she died. "Would the veil in which Mrs. Tilney had last walked, or the volume in which she had last read, remain to tell what nothing else was allowed to whisper? No." And thus point by point does the disillusioned Catherine reject Radcliffe's authority.

But on her way back to her own room, between the time of this disillusionment and the confrontation with Henry, something very odd occurs:

> The sound of footsteps, she could hardly tell where, made her pause and tremble. To be found there, even by a servant, would be unpleasant; but by the General, (and he seemed always at hand when least wanted,) much worse!—She listened—the sound had ceased; and resolving not to lose a moment, she passed through and closed the door. At that instant a door underneath was hastily opened; some one seemed with swift steps to ascend the stairs, by the head of which she had yet to pass before she could gain the gallery. She had no power to move. With a feeling of terror not very definable, she fixed her eyes on the staircase, and in a few moments it gave Henry to her view. "Mr. Tilney!" she exclaimed in a voice of more than common astonishment. He looked astonished too.

Astonishment upon astonishment! Terror upon terror! for both Catherine, who is just awakening from dreams of terror and astonishment, and for Henry, who is always superior to such emotions.

Apparently returning from the world of Ann Radcliffe, Catherine hears "the sound of footsteps, she could hardly tell where"; and trembling, she imagines "the General [who] seemed always at hand when least wanted." After an unmistakably Radcliffean gap of silence, she hears a new sound: "a door underneath was hastily opened [and] some one seemed with swift steps to ascend the stairs." (We may recall the "bounding steps" Emily heard, very near the end of *Mysteries*, in the apparent security of Chateau le Blanc.) Then follows a suspense of visual awareness during which Catherine fixes "her eyes on the staircase"; after a pause, "it gave Henry to her view." Each one of them suffers astonishment at the "extraordinary" appearance of the other—so unexpected and, in both cases, so strange. She is out of her place; he is out of his time: and the romance, which Radcliffe confined to southern Europe of the sixteenth century, has broken into the central part of England. It has broken in, more strangely still, just in time to be contemptuously denied. Did Austen recognize this? Had she in fact learned more from Radcliffe's romances than Henry Tilney? In absorbing them "all" so fully that she could parody them precisely on immediate recall, had she come to see the truth, the reality, lurking behind their conciliating facade? Not Henry: his "sense of the probable" (a favorite concern, of course, of Radcliffe) does not tolerate the extraordinary disjunctiveness of human experience, an illustration of which he himself has just now both witnessed and provided. Such astonishment as he has suffered and as Catherine also endured simply does not exist in the central part of England. But the reality of this disjunctiveness in experience—all experience, even the most firmly governed and closely observed—Austen has dramatically, if implicitly, acknowledged.

Later in *Northanger Abbey* there is, moreover, another example of it. When the fancies and follies of romance have been explicitly replaced by "the anxieties of common life," and the two girls, Catherine and Eleanor, from whom Henry has briefly departed, are one night on their way to bed, they are interrupted, "as far as the thickness of the walls would allow them to judge [by the sound of] a carriage." Austen seemingly transcends Radcliffe's Humean skepticism, actually asserting the substance, "a carriage," without question and thus buying into the myth of external reality that all of us—in what Hume would call our "vulgar" understanding—accept. But "the [muffling] thickness of the walls" reverberates strangely. And the episode proceeds with unmistakable Udolphean traces. After "the first perturbation of surprise," Eleanor hurries down to meet her elder brother, Captain Tilney, as she imagines, while Catherine retires to her own chamber. Almost half-an-hour of suspenseful neglect follows, during which Catherine considers the awkwardness of meeting the Captain, whose appearance she also expects; and then she begins to wonder.

> At that moment Catherine thought she heard [Eleanor's] step in the gallery, and listened for its continuance; but all was silent. Scarcely, however, had she convicted her fancy of error, when the noise of something moving close to her door made her start; it seemed as if some one was touching the very doorway—and in another moment a slight motion of the lock proved that some hand must be on it. She trembled a little at the idea of any one's approaching so cautiously.

Here, once again, just as in a remote castle in the Apennines, natural experience, in its radical disjunctiveness, emerges. Catherine endures a "step"—a possible "step"; a pause that "fancy" necessarily attempts to fill; "something moving close to her door"; and, in another pause, with sound still deprived of any confirming sight, the inference of "some one" lurking just outside; then a slight motion of the lock—a visual percept, at last, if a disembodied one—and the inference of an invisible "hand" on the other side. At this moment, although "she trembled a little," Catherine applies the lesson—the necessary obtuseness of awareness—she has learned from Henry. But the reality of perceptual particularity remains persistently present behind the very doorway of everyday life. In this case it will again emerge, if in a slightly different form, almost immediately. For here follows the reversal in the General's conduct, his cruel dismissal of Catherine, and her solitary trip through central England—a reflection, not quite a parody, of Adeline's scary trip through strange French terrain in Radcliffe's *Romance of the Forest*. Radcliffe's disturbing vision of the human situation, despite Henry Tilney's powerful rhetoric, simply will not go away.

Austen also accepts, again without seeming to admit it, Radcliffe's atomistic understanding of individual human character. The reversal of General Tilney just described or, rather, the reversal in Catherine's understanding of him makes an obvious example. Austen, as this case suggests, composes her fictions, both in their representation of the human world and in their exposition of human character, as a confirmed, if reluctant, disciple of Radcliffe.

Charlotte Smith, as I have argued, represented characters of rigid integrity—men and women, virtuous and vicious—herself completely embracing the myth of human identity, which she found in earlier fiction and in Christian teaching: it is, of course, a myth that civilized human kind generally embrace—and embrace without question. Both Orlando and Monimia, both Celestina and Willoughby are strictly constant, always the same; they are individually, as Celestina must explain again-and-again to counselors and suitors, impervious to circumstances. For her, no matter what happens, it is Willoughby or no one, until death if she should die first and after death if he does. There are a few changes in human nature on the outskirts of Smith's fictions, a little room for the maneuvers of repentant rakes. But secondary figures like Vavasour, Delamere, and young Thorold are strictly consistent in one situation and in one exercise after another. And, once again, the central characters are, for all their travels and all their vicissitudes, immovable. In *Mysteries*, however, Radcliffe, as I showed in the last chapter, situates the question of individual human integrity at the heart of the heroine's experience, that is, at the heart of the novel, practicing even upon its hero the skepticism that necessarily follows the tenet of particularity. Emily, Radcliffe's observer of human and natural events, must entertain serious exceptions to her father's character and serious doubts about her lover's.

Austen presents all her heroines—not just Catherine Morland—with the same kind of problem, formally speaking, that Emily faces, the problem, that is, of reconciling the atoms of their experience and creating from these, if it is possible, coherent sequences of events and individually integral acquaintances. Even in *Northanger Abbey*, where the awakened Catherine explicitly rejects both the natural reality that Radcliffe represents and what she takes as Radcliffean characterization, she in fact accepts both.

> Among the Alps and Pyrenees, perhaps, there were no mixed characters. There, such as were not as spotless as an angel, might have the dispositions of a fiend. But in England it was not so; among the English, she believed, in their hearts and habits, there was a general though unequal mixture of good and bad. Upon this conviction, she would not be surprised if even in Henry and Eleanor Tilney, some slight imperfection might hereafter appear; and upon this conviction she need not fear to acknowledge some actual specks in the character of their father, who, though cleared from the grossly injurious suspicions which she must ever blush to have entertained, she did believe, upon serious consideration, to be not perfectly amiable.

This admission of the "unequal mixture" of individual character, such as we have seen in Valancourt and St. Aubert, despite Austen's inadequate acknowledgment of her "charming" predecessor, determines her throughout her novelistic career.[9] She no doubt hankers for the kind of strict integrity that Smith described. In this quotation, for example, while admitting the possibility of "some slight imperfection" in the characters of Henry and Eleanor, Catherine strongly suggests the happy hope that there may not be any. But Eleanor herself fears that some of her brother's odd jokes will strike Catherine as "intolerably rude"; and, in her first encounter with him, she does indeed find him "strange" and fears that he indulges himself "a little too much with the foibles of others." As Catherine travels home from Northanger, moreover, after a long aquaintance, she speculates on Henry's response to her treatment, sometimes imagining him calmly acquiescent, at others, seriously resentful. His actual response obviously takes her, moreover, by complete surprise. And there is, finally, the broadly drawn character of Isabella, who is transformed in Catherine's understanding, as evidence accumulates, from the dearest of friends to "a vain coquette."

Elizabeth Bennet, in her early vanity, can speak of "making out a character," seeming to believe that one "illustration" might allow her to establish an enduring generalization. But even at such a confident moment, she is aware, as well she might be, that a premature judgment, one based on an insufficient body of data, may be mistaken. The development of Darcy as a topic of her own understanding—and of Wickham, too, for that matter—dramatically illustrates the point. Mr. Elliot in *Persuasion* Austen presents almost entirely as a problem in the creation of character, requiring Anne Elliot to reconcile the mixed evidence from her senses and from report in order gradually to realize how wrong Lady Russell is in recommending him as her husband. And although Henry Crawford finally justifies Fanny's judgment of him as totally selfish and vain, there was the very live possibility of a different judgment, a different character.

* * *

Austen devoted her whole novelistic career to absorbing and refining the understanding of life and nature that she found in Radcliffe. In the late novel, *Mansfield Park*, for example, one can readily detect the recalcitrant presence of this disowned predecessor.

The very title, which, like that of the *Mysteries*, puts the primary emphasis on a certain place, suggests the connection. Admittedly, Radcliffe's place name and even its syllabic constituents are unfamiliar, foreign, giving no sign, except for its Italic flavor, of the experiences the heroine must face there. The term and its syllables—by obvious design—provide almost no preliminary associations (except for a vague exoticism) to which Radcliffe's heroine—or her reader—can anchor new perceptions. Both the prefix—if it is a prefix—and the suffix are obviously foreign. And the root, *dolph* or *udolph*, leaves English sensibilities in the lurch. The possible name, unlike the familiar Germanic *Rudolph*, gives no intellectual comfort. The nice French (*echt* English) girl and the nice English reader—Eleanor or Catherine or Henry—must be ready to endure mysteries in such a place, as Radcliffe redundantly insists. Austen's title, both as a whole and in its parts, is quite another thing. *Man, field,* and *park* are not only good, plain English words, but words that enforce one another and suggest a certain, well-ordered landscape. They present a fabric, both metonymic (*man-field, man-park*) and metaphoric (*field-park*), of impressive assurance: this novel describes a realm in which things fit together in sensible and accountable ways. The situation, evident in both *park* and *field*, is an enclosed one, like that indicated by Austen's scenery, an area the various segments of which are arranged, cultivated, both by and for humankind. If "the proper study of Mankind is Man," Austen's novel, we may be sure, constitutes a chapter in this study. This fictional situation, moreover, will be, not only ghost-free, but, like the rows in a field or the planting in a park, strictly comprehensible especially, once again, to English understandings. However, despite these crucial differences between them, the titles of these two novels imply that their readers will cope with them similarly, understanding or trying to understand in each case a vitally important place.

The similarity in form and point of view between *The Mysteries of Udolpho* and *Mansfield Park* is actually closer than this similarity of titles suggests, quite a lot closer. The Mansfield environment is, at the beginning of the novel, almost as formidable a situation as Udolpho, the comfortable civility implicit in the title being actually long deferred. In Austen's novel, as in Radcliffe's, an apparently portionless young female both sensitive and helpless—her sensitivity being in fact underscored by her vulnerability—is tucked away upstairs in a strange, large building firmly in the control of an uncle by marriage, a figure whose countenance presents a forbidding mask and whose motives are a mystery to his solitary ward, from whose vantage and in whose understanding the story chiefly develops. Montoni presents a countenance that is "dark and stern" in Emily's first interview with him after they reach Udolpho; Sir Thomas, in his first meeting with Fanny at Mansfield, projects "a most untoward gravity of deportment." There is in each case a dreadfully unsympathetic aunt and a gradually emergent young champion of the opposite sex if not, as it may be, a romantically appropriate champion. *Mansfield Park* also describes, as does *The Mysteries of Udolpho*, a retreat from this demanding situation, a return home to straitened circumstances and an apparent attenuation of hope followed by the surprising appearance there of a determined but possibly unacceptable lover.

The differences in detail between these parallel developments are, of course, great. Indeed, by observing them one may usefully emphasize the quality of each novel. When Emily returns home to La Vallee, for example, she finds exactly what she expects and, except for deficiencies in fortune and companionship, exactly what her heart desires. She seems simply to have made a circle, returning to the same place she left and with exactly the same notions of life; and one may wonder how she has benefitted, what she has learned, by enduring and resolving the terrible mysteries of Udolpho. Fanny's sentimental return has a shocking, a shockingly different, effect. In her stay at Mansfield Park Fanny has received an understanding of civilized life, a system of social principles, that makes her parental home quite unacceptable; Mansfield, she recognizes, has become her "home." Imagine Emily saying such a thing about Udolpho! Strange as it may seem, *Mansfield Park* presents a shocking denouement, therefore, and the *Mysteries* a cozy, comfortable one. Nevertheless, each of these novels is focused on a youthful female intelligence both impressionable and powerful, which must endure and understand an alien environment and then, enlightened by what she has learned, return to her childhood home.

The central intelligences are also quite similar in the two cases. Austen originally confers on Fanny a radical impressionability by simply making her ten years old, and, as it seems, backward and timid even for this age. She preserves Fanny's special sensitivity by making her extremely delicate, susceptible to almost any external impulse, heat, damp, motion or cold: walking for even short distances and bending down to cut roses half-a-dozen times or so—if the sun is shining—pretty nearly wipe Fanny out. Emily's extreme sensitivity, as I argued in the last chapter, Radcliffe establishes by making her father warn her against it with his dying breath. She enforces it by stripping her of friends, society and all familiar objects and submitting her virtually naked intelligence to the alien environment of Udolpho. Emily's sole companion there, the silly maid, Annette, helps Radcliffe underline this situation. But Fanny is, if anything, even more isolated than Emily:[10] she is quite without confidential companionship, her passion for Edmund, ironically, separating her from her only possible friend. Each heroine thus confronts the challenge presented by an alien environment virtually alone, each one being forced to make sense of things strictly with her own powers of observation and reflection.

The trains of impressions endured by the two heroines are no doubt different. That which Fanny faces is, nevertheless, although its elements are completely domestic, similarly fragmentary and at least as vivid. From a vantage as isolated in its way as Emily's, Fanny absorbs significant sights, sounds, conversations, and countenances, from all of which she assembles general notions of character and coherent tissues of events, identifying Henry Crawford, Maria Bertram, and the development of their affair, for example, in quite the same way that Emily determines the natures and the intentions of her aunt, Montoni, and Morano. Fanny's shy efforts to influence the actions of characters like Maria—"you will tear your dress"—are quite as ineffective as Emily's suggestions to Annette or to her aunt. Fanny's final removal from the center of significant activity to Portsmouth, where she frantically awaits letters or carriage wheels, enforces her profoundly responsive, epistemological role, a role, once again, very similar to that played by the equally curious and equally inactive Emily.

Fanny's efforts at understanding are more successful, more immediately successful, at any rate. At Udolpho Emily believes for some time that her aunt has been murdered: the disappearance, the bloody steps, the failure of a response to her call, and Montoni's cruel demeanor lead her to this false conclusion. Similarly mistaking the pertinent atoms of evidence, she believes that Montoni has brought her to Udolpho to marry her off to Morano; later that he has removed her into the Tuscan woods to have her murdered; finally, that his French prisoner is Valancourt. Fanny has problems too, however: she takes almost the whole novel, for instance, to detect Sir Thomas's benevolence; that puts her just a little ahead of Emily, who never penetrates the character of Montoni. Fanny also responds inadequately, despite a little hedging by her creator, to Henry Crawford. She recognizes his powers and his attentions to herself at Mansfield, but, in an error Elinor Dashwood detected in her sister and Willoughby, she lumps these attentions with those she has observed earlier when he was flirting with Maria and judges, first, that these mean no more than those and generalizes, second, that Crawford is through-and-through a vain and selfish man. She is thus struck with "astonishment and confusion" by his proposal of marriage and remains dogmatically determined never to accept him—a judgment his generous aid to her brother William, his generous visit to Portsmouth, and the signs he gives there of a better nature do little or nothing to change. But Fanny, who is of course painfully involved in this identification—as Emily was with the double identification of Valancourt—can no doubt be forgiven—especially after Crawford elopes with Maria and thus justifies her general assessment of him.

Usually she sifts the evidence impeccably. She sees Tom, Edmund, and Mary, for example, despite her secret rivalry with Mary, for exactly what they are; and follows Edmund's infatuation with painful accuracy. She perfectly understands Maria, Julia, Rushworth and Crawford as that early quadrangle develops and notes with geometrical precision both the course of Crawford's and Maria's flirtation and the different feelings for one another of the two participants. Thus their later elopement, although it emerges as a terrible shock, providing the kind of Radcliffean climax that occurs in every one of Austen's novels, she can reconcile with the categories of character and action that she has been constructing of what—especially toward the end—are sparse and disjunctive bits and pieces indeed. The elopement gives the confirming illustration of both Maria and Crawford and allows the final flattening of Crawford into the vain, selfish person Fanny has, despite several contrary impressions, long concluded him to be. The intellectual processes of Fanny and Emily, whose father is epistemologically similar to Crawford, are, therefore, strictly analogous: each heroine must gather fragmentary items of evidence, sifting each and all the impressions she has and attempting to establish the best sense of things, the most probable opinion of people and activities, that she can.

Austen's central characters are struck throughout her career from this Radcliffean mold. In *Sense and Sensibility*, Elinor Dashwood works out the question of Willoughby's relationship with her sister and of Edward's with Lucy Steele, general questions of engagement in both cases, with scientific rigor: reconciling particular items of evidence with impressive if not perfect detachment.[11] In the second case, for example, she calculates "probabilities and proofs," "the picture, the letter, the ring," and draws the conclusion that all these particulars support and that no evidence can overturn. Elinor has a somewhat subtler but hardly less voracious curiosity than Emily and an equal determination to analyze her impressions and to compose the general understanding of things that they indicate. In the case of Willoughby and Marianne, for example, she has closely followed Hume's prescribed method: "we must . . . glean up our experiments in this science [that is, the study of human nature] from a cautious observation of human life, and take them as they appear in the common course of the world, by men's behavior in company, in affairs, and in their pleasures." Elinor, accordingly, is "resolved," Austen tells us, "not only upon gaining every new light as to [Willoughby's] character which her own observation or the intelligence of others can give her, but likewise upon watching his behavior to her sister with such zealous attention, as to ascertain what he was and what he meant." Elinor, like all of Austen's heroines—and like Emily before them—has some useful support in this enterprise from sensible witnesses like Colonel Brandon and from fools like Anne Steele. An early conversation between Elinor and her intelligent, if romantically credulous, mother is a model of common sense in action. But Elinor, like Emily, is usually forced to work by herself toward an adequate general sense of people and situations. In London, especially, which is Elinor's Udolpho, she feels quite alone in her resolve to understand both her own and her sister's affairs.

Although each Austen heroine has special qualities, every one is an intense student of experience. Elizabeth Bennet, for example, whose early view of things is, as the novel's title suggests, prejudiced, is abruptly required, by Darcy's peremptory letter, to clarify her understanding and reconsider the particular circumstances underlying her judgment of Wickham, Darcy and even her own family, circumstances she has thought she perfectly understood.[12] As she reviews her experience, both prodded and enlightened by Darcy's letter, Elizabeth finds that she must virtually reverse her general opinions of her competing Valancourts. She must also face her family's general deficiencies, seeing beneath her father's unfailing wit, for example, a cold-hearted detachment hardly becoming in the father even of quite silly daughters. "You have delighted us long enough," as the reader no doubt joins Elizabeth in her review, is transformed, perhaps, from an appropriately dismissive reproof to a case of paternal devastation: we may recall that its object, "Mary, though pretending not to hear, was somewhat disconcerted." The little pun on the last word now fails to amuse, as Mary's embarrassment and her father's cruelty emerge. Jane's apparent diffidence too, which led Darcy to make an error of judgment, Elizabeth must reconsider, especially since both the attitude and the misunderstanding have been confirmed by the intelligent Charlotte Lucas. Elizabeth, then, because of the involvement Austen has described, achieves at first a less adequate awareness than that evident in the prevailingly clear-sighted Elinor. Both characters, however, play the same epistemological role and demonstrate at last the same particular responsiveness that Radcliffe created in Emily.

The removal of her heroine from the scene of action and information near the end of *Pride and Prejudice*, a narrative procedure Austen, again following Radcliffe, practiced in every one of her novels, intensifies her representation of Elizabeth as an inductive intelligence. As Elinor went home from London, Elizabeth goes home from Derbyshire. Lydia, who has been at the center of events, lets it fall that Darcy was present at her wedding, a circumstance with possibly wonderful implications, but just one little circumstance. And Elizabeth, who is frantic with curiosity, writes her Aunt Gardiner in London insisting on a report by which she can satisfy herself. Elinor similarly received the single item of news about "Mrs. Ferrars," we may recall, and also suffered from the need of more information. And Fanny Price, although too timid to make demands for information, endures the same painful narrowing of the evidence in Portsmouth. By all such blank periods, in which the access to particular circumstances is cut off, Austen dramatizes her epistemological conception of her heroines and the atomistic particularity of her narratives. Each of her novels in short is a bundle of mysteries, a fragmentary tissue of impressions, the illuminated exposition of which she accomplishes by describing their shift and flux in the understanding of an intellectually responsive heroine.

The "clever" Emma Woodhouse, who suffers a shorter if not less anguished period of intellectual suspense than Austen's other heroines, attempts to break out of the purely responsive mold, at least to some extent, believing that she can effectively engage in actions: she is not the mere Humean or feminine intelligence that endures and reflects; she can accomplish changes, influence the course of events. At the opening of the novel, Emma congratulates herself on making the recently formalized match between Miss Taylor, her former governess, and Mr. Weston. She brags to Mr. Knightley about "this matter of joy." "I made the match myself. I made the match, you know, four years ago." And despite the fact that Mr. Knightley denies that he knows any such thing, Emma persists in self-congratulation. Mr. Knightley describes what Emma calls her "success" and her "triumph" as "a lucky guess," reducing it to an inference and reducing Emma—at best, since a "guess" is a rather humble form of inference—to the responsive intelligence from which Austen always creates her heroines. Emma continues to insist, however, not only on the cleverness of her observation, but also on the effectiveness of her activity: she claims that there is "a something between the do-nothing and the do-all," and sets herself firmly to the task of doing something for her little friend, Harriet Smith. Elizabeth's intelligence is complicated by prejudice; Emma's, by ambition. And *Emma*, like *Pride and Prejudice*, is crucially devoted to curing the heroine's complication, reducing her to the virtually pure bundle of impressions and ideas that Austen was able to develop in Elinor.

This novel describes three possible consequences of Emma's ambition, that is, three matches for Harriet: Mr. Elton, Frank Churchill, and Mr. Knightley. Each of them is a more outrageous mate for Harriet than the last; but Emma conceives of each in its turn as a real probability and as a probability, moreover, to which she has actively contributed. Emma confronts the three probabilities, of course, with strikingly different attitudes: she pushes the Elton match hard; approves the Churchill match, but restrains her hand; and views with horror Harriet's match with Mr. Knightley. But she feels as strongly effectual in the influence of events in this last, most outrageous case, which she abhors, as in any other. "She had not quite done nothing," Emma believes:

> for she had done mischief. She had brought evil on Harriet, on her-self, and she too much feared, on Mr. Knightley.—Were this most unequal of all connexions to take place, on her must rest all the re-proach of having given it a beginning; for his attachment, she must believe to be produced only by a consciousness of Harriet's;—and even were this not the case, he would never have known Harriet at all but for her folly.

On her must rest all the credit—"all the reproach"—for this suc-cess. But, in fact, everything works out to deny Emma any credit at all for her activity; all marriages, her own included, fall into place quite by other means. And she is reduced, like Elizabeth before her, to the condition of sense, that is, to the condition of Emily.

Never does Emma more purely fulfill this proper constituent of her nature—which is always evident, of course—than in contemplating Harriet's claims of Mr. Knightley's regard and her hopes of being his choice. Emma listens, trembling, to Harriet's confused but compelling exposition of the "evidence." Many "cir-cumstances" that Harriet recalls have been—as in the *Mysteries*— "unnoticed . . . by Emma"; "but the two latest occurrences to be mentioned, the two of strongest promise to Harriet, were not without some degree of witness from Emma herself." Thus here after it seems that her actions have ended in tragedy, Austen's heroine plays the responsive role that British philosophy and En-glish custom dictated. Here when it seems, to her at least, to be too late, Emma both plays the Radcliffean role and wishes that she had always confined herself to it. She reflects on the two crucial "circumstances," his walking apart with Harriet at Donwell and his having sat talking to her for half an hour in Emma's absence before leaving for London. The first Emma questions: might Mr. Knightley not have had Mr. Martin in mind when he spoke with Harriet at Donwell? But the sum of Harriet's particulars has "a substance to sink her spirit—especially with the corroborating circumstances, which her own memory brought in favor of Mr. Knightley's most improved opinion of Harriet." This success, however galling to her hopes, would vindicate Emma's ambition: here she could say, as formerly, "I made the match." But for Emma happiness and failure come together; and the failure is essentially her reduction to the Humean intelligence that Radcliffe's genius had equated with the socially oppressed feminine mind.

This failure of judgment is actually one more example of Emma's persistent failure to comprehend the circumstances that she has faced all along, that is, her continuing lack of success in the tasks of observation and reflection. For clever as she is—and it is Austen's genius to have preserved that trait throughout one intellectual embarrassment after another—she has often misinterpreted the evidence:

> She was bewildered amidst the confusion of all that had rushed on her within the last few hours. Every moment had brought a fresh surprise; and every surprise must be matter of humiliation to her.— How to understand it all! How to understand the deceptions she had been thus practising on herself and living under!—The blunders, the blindness of her own head and heart!—she sat still, she walked about, she tried her own room, she tried the shrubbery—in every place, every posture, she perceived that she had acted most weakly; that she had been imposed on by others in a most mortifying degree; that she had been imposing on herself in a degree yet more mortifying.

Mr. John Knightley had tried to urge a more adequate sense of Mr. Elton's gallantry; and Mr. George Knightley had suggested a better understanding of Frank Churchill's conduct: but Emma confidently rejected these expert witnesses, although she knew how perceptive and observant they were.

However, although her neglect of others' testimony is a bad error in the induction of character, she handles her own impressions at least in the right way. She notes the circumstances around her, sifts and collects and composes them, reaching through them to general conclusions. From Mr. Elton's conundrum, his enthusiasm for Harriet's portrait, his concern over Harriet's illness (infectious?), and his congratulations on Harriet's improvement—

"skillful has been the hand": Emma infers the courtship she has been promoting. Even when her own schemes are not involved, Emma has been an eager respondent to her experiences, finding in Jane Fairfax's conduct, for instance, the signs of a secret relationship with the husband of Jane's dearest friend. And, despite her serious errors in inference, her observations are keen and her conclusions are close to the mark: Mr. Elton is engaged in courtship; Jane Fairfax does have a secret relationship. Emma's errors—personal involvement, the neglect of others' testimony, and excessive haste in jumping to conclusions—are classic errors in procedure. And the novel makes its readers variously aware of them even when Emma is not.[13] Throughout its course, then, *Emma*, formally speaking, presents an imperfect exercise in induction comprehended by a perfect inductive intelligence.

It is necessary, however, to emphasize the heroine's persistent cleverness. She is strictly right about some things: the implausibility of Jane's reasons for staying in Highbury; Mr. Knightley's indifference to Jane; the fact that the mysterious piano is a gift of love, and, more generally, that Jane is involved in a secret affair. She misses the identity of Jane's lover truly, although he is right before her eyes; but many real perceptions support the general notion that he is her own lover and blind her. Emma thus misses the full meaning of Frank Churchill's sly comment in the Bates's front room, although she observes the whole situation closely. When Frank recalls that a certain tune Jane has just played on the new piano "was danced at Weymouth" (a lovely use of passive voice), and Jane has just "looked up at him . . . [and] coloured deeply," Emma can only imagine, as the lover she rightly infers, Mr. Dixon. Frank's racing away to fetch Jane for her ideas about the ball Emma plausibly reconciles with the generally indiscriminate Weston sociability. She is wrong, again, in identifying Harriet as the object of Mr. Elton's conundrum; but she correctly attributes the inconsistency of a "ready wit" (which is not true of Harriet) and a "soft eye" (which is) to Mr. Elton's stupidity. Again and again, in short, even when Emma errs, she has followed the inductive method of reasoning toward general opinions from particular circumstances.

The variety within the separate characters that Emma and other of Austen's heroines confront is best explained, accordingly, not in the terms of psychological development, but in those of perceptual particularity: her characters, that is to say, are, like Radcliffe's and Pope's, mixtures of disparate perceptions, mixtures that Austen largely (but not entirely) focuses, like Radcliffe before her, in the responsive sensibility of a heroine. When she is trying to marry Mr. Elton to Harriet, Emma conceives him as competitive in personal excellence with Mr. Knightley; when she considers him as the husband of Mrs. Elton later in the novel, she finds him quite intolerable; and yet he seems hardly to have changed. Elinor, similarly, sees Willoughby at first as an admirable person— if not quite the determined fiancé of her sister; later, as new evidence emerges, she judges him a cold-hearted rake. Wickham and Mr. Elliot present the same shifting mixture of impressions, at first being perceived by Elizabeth and Anne, respectively, quite positively and afterwards, as reports and circumstances accumulate, quite negatively. The changes occur almost entirely, although Mr. Elliot's selfishness has taken an apparently new turn, in the judgments of the responsive beholders. Both Darcy and Wentworth deny any change in themselves: "unjust I may have been," Wentworth insists, "but never inconstant." But these characters also shift—if not with inconceivable rapidity—in the perceptions and judgments of the women who observe them. Even Mr. Knightley, despite the generally firm uprightness of character which his name implies, presents a mixture of different attitudes and feelings as Emma beholds him in the shifting flux of events. One day when he is passing the Bates home, for instance, he agrees, on hearing that "Miss Woodhouse and Miss Smith" are present, to pause "for five minutes, perhaps"; and then, when Miss Bates mentions that Frank Churchill is also there, he responds, "No, not now . . . your room is full enough." The enormous varieties of character observable everywhere in Austen, then, are not cases of organic development—although her people are by no means set in Platonic concrete as those of Smith seem often to be—but shifting mixtures of perceptions and consequent shifts in judgment usually attributed to the gradually enriched understandings of her heroines. Catherine Morland's recognition of "a general though unequal mixture of good and bad" among the population of Austen's world and her willingness to perceive "some slight imperfection" even in Henry and Eleanor Tilney introduce the narrative mode and the conception of character that Austen developed throughout her career. It is, once again, for all its range and variety, closely analogous to the characterization in *The Mysteries of Udolpho*.

Austen never completely neglected even the most radical trace of Radcliffe's art, that is, the shifting particularity of perception, a couple of cases of which we noticed in *Northanger Abbey*. Every Austen novel has a few slamming doors, strange footsteps, vague human figures, or invisible carriage wheels. *Mansfield Park*, in which we have described special formal affinities with the *Mysteries*, has quite a few of these traces, quite a few reminders, I would argue, that all human understanding, however confident, is based on shifting perceptual circumstances. Seated alone in the Sotherton "wilderness," Fanny endures with an anxiety approaching Emily's a whole series of disjunctive impressions: "voices and feet approaching" (made by the wrong party, as it turns out); "sudden footsteps" (and another disappointing emergence); and, finally, after a string of sudden arrivals and departures, "the voice and laugh of Miss Crawford once more caught her ear." In the isolation of her little white attic, Fanny is similarly troubled on occasion by surprising noises: "a tap at the door" is followed by "the appearance of one"—finally explained as "the sight of Edmund"; on a different occasion, "a gentle tap at the door . . . [is] followed by the entrance of Miss Crawford," and, then, soon afterwards, "a tap at the door [brings] a pause [in the two women's rehearsal], and the entrance of Edmund." Such isolated sensations create incidents of momentary suspense and suggest still more disquieting reverberations in every one of Austen's major novels.

Austen's organization of such events in *Sense and Sensibility* is instructive. When Marianne and Elinor arrive at Mrs. Jennings's house in London, to begin with a dramatic example, this sequence occurs:

> The tea things were brought in, and already had Marianne been disappointed more than once by a rap at a neighbouring door, when a loud one was suddenly heard which could not be mistaken for one at any other house. Elinor felt secure of its announcing Willoughby's approach, and Marianne starting up moved towards the door. Every thing was silent; this could not be borne many seconds, she opened the door, advanced a few steps towards the stairs, and after listening half a minute, returned into the room in all the agitation which a conviction of having heard him would naturally produce; in the extasy of her feelings at that instant she could not help exclaiming, "Oh! Elinor, it is Willoughby, indeed it is!" and seemed almost ready to throw herself into his arms, when Colonel Brandon appeared.

Shades of Udolpho and Emily's mistaken embrace of Dupont! Marianne's Radcliffean "shock" here is reflected in Colonel Brandon with Radcliffean "astonishment." Beforehand, moreover, come a couple of disjunctive audial impressions, suspense, interpretation, and surprise—the whole Radcliffean practice in miniature. A few days later, however, when Willoughby's inconstancy has emerged, Austen describes a significantly different analogue to this scene. Elinor and Marianne are once again alone in the same room as before,

> when Marianne, whose nerves could not then bear any sudden noise, was startled by a rap at the door.
>
> "Who can this be?" cried Elinor. "So early too! I thought we *had* been safe."
>
> Marianne moved to the window—
>
> "It *is* Colonel Brandon!" said she, with vexation. "We are never safe from *him*."
>
> "He will not come in, as Mrs. Jennings is from home."
>
> "I will not trust to *that*," retreating to her own room. "A man who has nothing to do with his own time has no conscience in his intrusion on that of others."
>
> The event proved her conjecture right, though it was founded on injustice and error; for Colonel Brandon *did* come in; and Elinor, who was convinced that solicitude for Marianne brought him thither, and who saw *that* solicitude in his disturbed and melancholy look, and in his anxious though brief inquiry after her, could not forgive her sister for esteeming him so lightly.

Marianne's correct generalization, that they are never safe from Colonel Brandon, asserts the analogy. But in this case "shock" has been replaced with "vexation" and "astonishment" with "solicitude." The moment of suspense has been curtailed and all misidentification, cancelled: "'It *is* Colonel Brandon,'" as Marianne, who has moved immediately to the window for a view of the intruder, reports. Same man; different effect.

This revision is strictly appropriate to the changed situation in the novel, underscoring the fact that Marianne has now no hope of Willoughby's addresses and suggesting further that she had better begin consoling herself with Colonel Brandon's steadier if less glamorous attentions. But the pattern of two analogous moments of Radcliffean suspense, the second of which sharply reduces the effect of the first, is a recurring element in *Sense and Sensibility*. Early on, for instance, "a man on horseback" (a visual percept) appears to Elinor and Marianne when they are on a walk. Marianne, after seeing that he is "a gentleman," identifies him as Willoughby although, as the keen-sighted Elinor notes, "the person is not tall enough and has not his air." Elinor walks on rapidly "to screen Marianne from particularity"; Marianne then sees—if still vaguely—that this "gentleman" is not Willoughby;

she turns around in disappointment, only to be summoned by "voices [unidentified audial percepts, one of which is] almost as well known" as Willoughby's; she then turns back around "with surprise to see and welcome Edward Ferrars." Again, in this relatively early scene, Austen preserves Radcliffean suspense, describing a development from vague to clear apprehension such as was often practiced in the *Mysteries*, separating visual and audial impressions and postponing identification with the machinery of narration. The reader is enlightened here, as often by Radcliffe, after the confused character is. Toward the end of the novel, Elinor, trusting to sight alone, suffers a strikingly similar event in which, however, suspense and shock have been attenuated. Again, she sees "a man on horseback," in whom, as before, she recognizes "a gentleman." She misidentifies him as Colonel Brandon, whom she was just expecting; but this gentleman, like the one Marianne mistook, "had neither his air nor his height": the echoes here are many. And, once again, it turns out to be Edward. This analogue, as in the case of the second rap at the door of Mrs. Jennings's house, provides much less Radcliffean excitement, being narrated more quickly, developed without audial complication, and resolved for the reader exactly when the heroine gets it right.

To test this pairing of greater-and-less Udolphean analogues as an element in Austen's novel, consider Edward's two surprise visits to Mrs. Jennings's house, only the first of which is presented primarily as a surprise. In this case, Lucy and Elinor are discussing Edward when Elinor is "prevented from making any reply . . . by the door's being thrown open, the servant's announcing Mr. Ferrars, and Edward's immediately walking in." This presents, clearly enough, the shocking emergence of exactly the worst possible caller, a shock Austen makes a part of her narrative. The second time Edward calls on Elinor, also at a most inopportune time, when Elinor has just sat down to write him about the living Colonel Brandon wishes to give him, Austen cancels the shock effects, emphasizing instead the social awkwardness of the encounter, and presents it with some pains, not as an object of terrific involvement, but as one of detached, almost comical observation. Elinor, Austen tells us, contemplated the letter with some anxiety, equally fearing to say too much or too little, "deliberating over her paper, with the pen in her hand, till broken in on by the entrance of Edward himself." But then she goes on:

He had met Mrs. Jennings at the door in her way to the carriage, as he came to leave his farewell card; and she, after apologizing for not

returning herself, had obliged him to enter, by saying that Miss Dashwood was above, and wanted to speak with him on very particular
business.

Elinor had just been congratulating herself, in the midst of her
perplexity that however difficult it might be to express herself properly by letter, it was at least preferable to giving the information by
word of mouth when her visitor entered, to force her upon this greatest exertion of all. Her astonishment and confusion were very great
on his so sudden appearance.

Elinor suffered the "astonishment" of a "sudden appearance";
but we, who have had everything recounted and explained, behold the distress and embarrassment of these lovers with amused
diffidence, which, Austen might explain, perfectly suits life and
society in the central counties of England.

The most striking pair of Udolphean analogues occurs, however, near the end of the novel with two contrasting cases of
carriage wheels. In the first case, Elinor has just left the room
where Marianne, finally recovering from a protracted bout with
pneumonia, is peacefully asleep. Elinor expects their mother, for
whom Colonel Brandon was sent when it looked like Marianne's
disease might be fatal. The night is cold and stormy; wind roars
round the house; rain beats against the windows: providing such
preliminary impressions of audial turbulence as Radcliffe loved.

The clock struck eight. Had it been ten, Elinor would have been con-
vinced that at that moment she heard a carriage driving up to the
house; and so strong was the persuasion that she *did*, in spite of the
almost impossibility of their being already come, that she moved into
the adjoining dressing-closet and opened a window-shutter, to be
satisfied of the truth. She instantly saw that her ears had not deceived
her. The flaring lamps of a carriage were immediately in view. By
their uncertain light she thought she could discern it to be drawn by
four horses; and this, while it told the excess of her poor mother's
alarm, gave some explanation to such unexpected rapidity.

Never in her life had Elinor found it so difficult to be calm, as at
that moment. The knowledge of what her mother must be feeling as
the carriage stopt at the door,—of her doubt—her dread—perhaps
her despair!—and of what *she* had to tell!—with such knowledge it
was impossible to be calm. All that remained to be done, was to be
speedy; and therefore staying only till she could leave Mrs. Jennings's
maid with her sister, she hurried down stairs.

The bustle in the vestibule, as she passed along an inner lobby,
assured her that they were already in the house. She rushed forwards

towards the drawing-room,—she entered it,—and saw only Willoughby.

Here, quite near the end of the novel, Austen presents another full-scale episode of Radcliffean romance: first a sound, interrupting the sounds of the storm, and an appropriately tentative inference. Then a sight, which Austen, who never simply gives in to Radcliffe, represents as confirming the former sound: flaring lights prove that Elinor has heard a carriage. Another flickering impression of four horses confirms a further inference, one that will, of course, prove mistaken. Then, driven by this erroneous identification of her mother, Elinor races toward the door where she endures, first, another vague sound, that of "bustle in the vestibule," and, finally, the shocking visual emergence of the last person she or Austen's reader would expect to see. (Notice the wonderfully misleading "they" in the last paragraph.) At this singular appearance, Elinor suffers feelings common to Emily, first "horror," then "amazement," and then a feeling even more central to Emily's nature, "curiosity."

Immediately after the scene of Willoughby's explanation, confession, and departure, a scene that somewhat resembles Valancourt's meeting of explanation and contrition with Emily in Chateau le Blanc, comes "the sound of another carriage." No stormy sounds precede this impression; the sound, the object, and its occupants are all certain in Elinor's mind this time and are all correct.

> Eager to save her mother from every unnecessary moment's horrible suspense, she ran immediately into the hall, and reached the outward door just in time to receive and support her as she entered it.

No mysterious impressions, no doubtful inferences, no false conclusions, and no shock disturb Elinor on this second, this revised, trip downstairs, through the hall, and to the door: her concern to reduce her mother's "suspense" effectively quells the impression that she is suffering any suspense herself. And Mrs. Dashwood's relief is described before her entrance into "the drawing-room"—the same room in which a few minutes before Elinor was amazed by Willoughby—is even announced. Once again Austen has endured and then revised a Radcliffean moment, submitting her story to the disjunctiveness of experience, with its shocks, mysteries and terrors, and then, the second time around, rescuing it from them.

With these recurrent pairs of Udolphean material, Austen seems to be wrenching her own work from her predecessor's powerful grasp, insisting—not on Radcliffe's error, by no means, for the traces of Radcliffe's understanding haunt the pages of this novel—but on her own different sense of subject. Austen has pointedly acknowledged the disjunctiveness of human experience that Radcliffe described and reaped Radcliffe's affective benefits. But as her systematic revisions of Radcliffean material imply, this is not her chosen concern as a novelist. The remainder *is:* Marianne's anguish, Edward's embarrassment, the pleasure of social exchange, and the joy of family life. And within this realm of concerns, Austen's revisionary practices in *Sense and Sensibility* further imply, men and women can both understand and organize their own affairs. Within a house, a park, a town, that is, within the purlieus of English society, she assures us, although the world may occasionally distract with its rapid flux of events, human beings can carry out orderly, elegant lives, variously correcting the problems of human difference, vagary, and mobility and establishing systems that are attributable to human agents and conformable to human laws.

There persist, however, traces of Radcliffe's genius in every one of Austen's six major novels. Every novel has a shifty natural underpinning that obtrudes now and again—more in the early novels, no doubt, than the later ones. And every novel has at least one shocking revelation. More important than this, in every novel one attends the challenge particular circumstances present to human understanding, enduring these sympathetically through a highly wrought feminine intelligence. Every event in Austen's stories, whether it shocks or confirms, trails a wake of evidence in perception and report that reveals the Radcliffean discipleship. Every event emerges as an object of intelligence, a point of immediate and an element in wider knowledge. Anne Elliot, seated alone under a hedge near Winthrop or feeling herself to be alone at a concert in Bath, endures the same kind of perceptual challenges and carries out the same kind of epistemological tasks as those that Catherine Morland faced at Northanger Abbey. All six of her major novels indeed declare Austen to be the last student of differences in eighteenth-century English literature.

*   *   *

She is also the most philosophically compelling, whether she wanted to be or not. Her observance of the confluence between oppression and experience, which she found in *The Mysteries of Udolpho*, gives her work, like Radcliffe's, a special resonance. Each of Austen's novels is by virtue of this observance essentially more than a genteel account of elegant young women enduring a few stresses and strains during the transition from one stage of oppression to another. Each of her novels, by virtue of her grudging but profound assimilation of this intersection between ethical conservatism and philosophical revolution, acknowledges the human intellect's contact with the natural world that all of us—male and female, privileged and neglected, young and old—must endure from the beginning of life to the end.

Nor is this the sum of her fiction's philosophical force. Like her great predecessors in the literature of particularity, Austen gravitated to the exceptional case, the extreme case, that, in proving to be no exception, proved the rule. Her novels are literally composed of superlatives: the last, the most, the least likely, the best. Edward shows up twice when he is least wanted, when he would be most embarrassed and most embarrassing. Darcy is "the last man in the world" Elizabeth would ever wish to marry; whereas Wickham is Mr. Bennet's most favorite son-in-law. Colonel Brandon is the man Willoughby can least bear as Marianne's husband—and something like the man Marianne can least bear as well; Benwick is the last man both to make a quick engagement and to become attached to Louisa Musgrove. Emma, although preeminently clever, can give herself credit for nothing but "blunders [and] blindness." Mr. Knightley, although "the last man in the world" to misrepresent his feelings to someone like Harriet, has done just that; and a marriage between these two—the least elevated woman and the most elevated man in the Highbury hierarchy—although it would "distance every wonder of the kind," both Emma, who hates it more than anyone else, and Harriet, who most desires it, expect to come about. It should not be surprising then that, in the selection of her general literary subject matter, Austen has, as persistently as in her particular literary expositions, grasped an extreme case, a case once again that, in proving to be no exception, proves a rule.

Austen assures us that in her world, in her representation of the central part of England—*if any place*—human kind can escape the miscellaneous particularity of human experience. Here—*if any place*—where the very landscape has been composed in accordance with general human understanding and common human desires, we can expect a realm of order and clarity. In this comfortable countryside, infused with social proprieties, guided by religious teaching, and illuminated by civilized discourse, human beings can reconcile the shifting circumstances with which they are confronted, organizing the disparate bits and pieces, the atomic flux, that threatens to confound them—to confound us all. And at the end of every Austen novel her heroines, at least, are represented as successful in this enterprise. Although Emma realizes that "complete truth . . . seldom [belongs] to any human disclosure," she and Mr. Knightley satisfy the confidence of their true friends "in the perfect happiness of [their] union." Elizabeth and Georgiana—not to speak of Elizabeth and Darcy—"were able to love each other, even as well as they intended"—which was "exactly what Darcy had hoped to see." As Mr. Elton would say, "exactly so."

But within the novels themselves, as I have tried to suggest, the challenge of experience is relentless, every heroine facing throughout her career—*even here*—a variety of events she can almost never control and often not understand. And the fact that Austen's heroines are, in every case but one, themselves extreme cases, each one having the most powerful, responsive intelligence imaginable, intensifies the point. If the most perceptive person cannot or can hardly comprehend the most civilized train of experiences, the general human situation is surely a demanding one. This acknowledgment, which lurks just beyond the deliverance that every Austen heroine is finally assured and just behind the very doorway of the world in which all must conduct their lives, infuses her novels with a subversive energy that makes them among the most dynamic compositions in English literature.

7

Conclusion

The developing understanding of things that has emerged in the preceding chapters can be described as a turn from what Samuel Johnson might have called the atoms of matter to what he did call the atoms of probability. The literary response to the first kind of atoms I have chiefly illustrated with Swift's *Tale* of 1704; to the second, most emphatically with Radcliffe's *Mysteries* of 1794.

These two kinds of atoms, however, despite their philosophical opposition to one another, were always mixed to some extent both in British sensibilities and in British discourse. For one thing, they met—if not comfortably—in substances. A man, for example, although a system of constantly fleeting material particles, as Locke taught, might also be an identifiable train of perceptions, that is, as Locke taught, a person. At least his acquaintance, especially as Austen represented them, assumed and hoped so. Her young women were always concerned, indeed, with both the personal and the material qualities of their lovers. We may also recall Fielding's discrimination between Tom Jones's appropriately complex love of Sophia Western and Blifil's inadequate desire to possess her. Although Elizabeth Bennet was determined, like Tom, to enjoy a marriage of true minds, she fully recognized, also like Tom, the necessity of a fortune, as her sensible Aunt Gardiner represented this to her; and she managed, finally, to reconcile the two requirements.[1] Elinor Dashwood, likewise, although she considered the mere competence of a thousand pounds a year to be material fortune enough, hardly considered setting up housekeeping with the person of her choice on much less than that. The most materialistic figures, on the other hand, take notice of experiential particularity as circumstances variously allow or demand. Moll Flanders normally reduced her different belongings admittedly to what she called stock, that is, to strictly material wealth: she cut up ninety pounds worth of fine holland, for instance, and made a clean hundred pounds of it; and when she could not thus reduce an acquisition to stock—as in the case of the horse she once got hold of outside a bar—she considered the matter a failure. However, Moll almost always had to engage in different modes of conduct to steal different things. She was able to respond abstractly to the opportunity presented once by a fire and simply attached herself to the bundle that fell, as an Epicurean accident, into her hands; but to get possession of another person's watch, trunk, or bolt of cloth, she had in every case to calculate her action with scientific discrimination. In getting her hooks on men, of course, she was not so careful.

Some mixture of the two opposing notions of things can be found everywhere in eighteenth-century English literature. The narrator of *Tom Jones*, for instance, normally presents his story as "a great creation of our own." He produces the separate elements and the different actions, regardless of the reptilian critics lurking here and there in his garden; he analyzes both characters and events according to the principles of human nature that his learning and experience have furnished him; and, thus assured, he composes his own story in his own way, attempting, as Berkeley would advise, to arouse in his audience individually trains of images analogous to those he has aroused in himself. While he is weeping, he formulates the language that will also make his reader weep. And yet this narrator often takes refuge, like Defoe, in claims of external reality. It is "with sorrow we relate" Tom's sexual indulgence with Molly, he complains; but, alas! "the fact is true." "It surprises us and so, perhaps, it may the reader," he suggests on another occasion, that the virtuous lieutenant was more concerned to secure the man who had attacked Tom than to attend the wounds of the victim. "We have taken uncommon pains," he asserts, likewise, in explaining the questionable appearance of Mrs. Waters, "to inform ourselves of the real fact"— as if such facts exist all by themselves out there in material nature whether the narrator has drawn them into his awareness or not. The situation of Mr. Allworthy's house, moreover, the inn at Gloucester, which the narrator recommends "to every reader who shall visit this ancient city," the intrusions of the Stuart invasion of 1745, and the whole tangle of roads that lead the hero and heroine to London: all this provides a material environment to which the narrator's imaginative fiction is related. Tristram Shandy too has the self-willed Jenny, the persistent gentleman in black, the pesky critics, and Mr. Pitt, who may take this book into the country with him, to indicate a world elsewhere although the setting, the characters and the events of Tristram's story have been almost completely reduced—or, perhaps, exalted—to items of recollection and conversation. When Tristram says that his life is over, all but the telling of it, Sterne is bragging a little about the virtually pure fictionality, the purely perceptual existence, of his narrative. Within the story, however, Tristram's father—significantly unlike his uncle—lives in and contends with a recalcitrant realm of material circumstances.

The most incorrigible advocate of matter in this literature, however—except possibly for Swift's inflatable evangelist—is John Dashwood, who inhabits one of the most pointedly perceptualist works, *Sense and Sensibility*, that I have considered. "It would give me great pleasure to call Colonel Brandon brother," he once says to his sister, Elinor, who he hopes will "secure" this materially weighty gentleman: "His property here, his place, his house, everything in such respectable and excellent condition!—and his woods!" That's what makes Colonel Brandon worthy of the name *brother*. When, on another occasion, Elinor and John consider which of the two Ferrars brothers will marry Miss Morton and her thirty thousand pounds, Elinor asks him, with an edge of irony, if it is "the same to Miss Morton whether she marry Edward or Robert." John answers comfortably: "Certainly there can be no difference, for Robert will now to all intents and purposes be considered the eldest son [that is, he will come into the money];—and as to anything else, they are both very agreeable young men, I do not know that one is superior to the other." Elinor, of course, has a strong sense of Edward's personal superiority; but for John, the adhering particles of wealth define the man. He once thought that Marianne would marry "better" than her sister, he confides to Elinor during another of their chats; but since Marianne has lost her bloom, "I question whether [she] . . . will marry a man worth more than five or six hundred a-year, at the utmost, and I am very much deceived if *you* do not do better"—if, that is, Elinor does not marry a man he might be pleased to call *brother*.[2] Doing *well* or *better* in life means nothing more to John Dashwood than acquiring a big or a bigger fortune; that is, in the words of Moll Flanders, who seldom had any more interest than he does in "the mere vice" of personal relationships, "the main thing."

This mingling of material and perceptual understandings of things is evident not only in the individual works of this period but, on a larger scale, throughout its history. *Moll Flanders*, which was produced at very nearly the same time as *Gulliver's Travels* (and a decade after Berkeley's *Principles*) is, as I have suggested, an intensely materialistic work. So is *Pamela*, which appeared at almost the same time as Hume's *Treatise*. Consider, for example, Pamela's effort to decide which of "three parcels" of clothing she can properly attach to herself. The contents of the third parcel, the pieces of which she has bought with her own money, she particularizes at considerable length: "There is a quilted cala-manco coat, and a pair of stockings I bought of the pedlar, and my straw-hat with blue strings . . . a remnant of Scots cloth, which will make two shirts and two shifts . . . [and] a cotton handkerchief I bought of the pedlar"—among other things. This parcel she hugs to herself, symbolically enacting the materialistic linkage of one body with another. The other two parcels, although Pamela reports that she particularized these for Mrs. Jervis's benefit, she does not in fact analyze in her letter. The first, which contains things given her by her lady that are too fine for Pamela to wear, that is, to attach to her body, in the humble place into which her evil fortune is about to cast her, she properly relin-quishes: "so much for the first parcel." The second, containing the gifts of her lecherous master, she is "as brisk and as pert as could be" in dismissing. These two parcels she might reduce, like Moll Flanders before her, into financial stock, as she says; but it is only the contents of the third parcel that she can wear—or turn into wearable garments for her dad. These and these alone, therefore, become included in the realm of her experience: their shape, color, texture and use are made part of the perceptual environment that Pamela expects to inhabit, whereas the other parcels are just two characterless bodies drifting back into the void. Throughout Richardson's novel, Pamela inhabits two dis-tinct circles, a narrow circle of distinguishable experiences and a vast, mysterious circle cast about her by Mr. B's material wealth. Unlike Moll Flanders, however, who always reduces things to stock, Pamela gradually extends the realm of experience, breaking finally into an existence that Elizabeth Bennet would at least have recognized.[3]

If a serious concern with matter persists in English literature right through the eighteenth century, a self-conscious reliance on experience is evident from very early on. It actually emerges be-fore or near the time in 1710 when Berkeley first distinguished formally between the two. We may recollect Swift's London poems of around 1710, Pope's vividly imagined "Epistle to Miss Blount" of 1714, and many of Mr. Spectator's catalogues—his list of outrageous tragic effects, for example. Consider, finally,

Millamant's plea to her betrothed, Mirabell, in Congreve's *Way of the World* of around 1700:

> Good Mirabell, don't let us be familiar or fond, nor kiss before folks, like my Lady Fadler and Sir Francis; nor go to Hyde Park together the first Sunday in a new chariot, to provoke eyes and whispers; and then never be seen there together again, as if we were proud of one another the first week, and ashamed of one another ever after. Let us never visit together, nor go to a play together, but let us be very strange and well bred; let us be as strange as if we had been married a great while; and as well bred as if we were not married at all.

Millamant has observed the conduct of couples in her acquaintance with a sharp eye and she clearly dislikes what she has seen. She calculates accordingly what she wants others to see of her and Mirabell, arranging what Swift's Author might have called the superficies of things. Her plea to Mirabell, however, is strictly analogous to Pope's exhortation to the lady: each speaker urges a beloved acquaintance to calculate and project an integral tissue of widely visible perceptions; each proposes to a friend the case-by-case erection of a coherent public character, being confident that, in the world of social attention and conversation, *percipi* is *esse*.

While recognizing the interconnectedness between the material and the perceptual apprehensions of things in both the texture and the structure of eighteenth-century English literature, I must nevertheless conclude by emphasizing the development away from the corporeal bodies of Hobbes toward Hume's rapid train of ideas. The examples discussed in earlier chapters of this book not only indicate such a development; they also represent a few of its major pivots. Chief among these are Swift's change from the *Tale* to the *Travels*; Pope's change from the first epistle of the *Essay on Man* to the epistles *To Cobham* and *To a Lady*; and the change evident between these highly sociable works and Radcliffe's *Mysteries*.

In my chapter on Swift, I have attempted to elucidate the striking change from the *Tale*'s primarily material understanding of things, that is, its concern with bodies and institutions existing in an external environment, to a pointed emphasis in the *Travels* on mental properties and mental states. In the decades before the *Tale*, to augment my account, English literature has a strong material flavor, which is especially evident in works by Wycherly and Rochester and Dryden. Dryden's *MacFlecknoe*, for example, is a satiric reduction of a certain poetic exercise from the imaginative or, speaking with more precision, the aesthetic to the corporeal or, speaking with more precision, the excretory. When Dryden opens the poem, "All human things are subject to decay," he exactly indicates this effect, not only in the reference to the processes of corporeal corruption, but in the expression "human things": "human," with its proud implications of awareness and rationality, is reduced to an adjective, modifying the abstract "things"; whereas "things," in contrast with this ennobling modification, retains a lumpish characterlessness. The second line, "And when fate summons monarchs must obey," spans the natural requirement of death, that tragic moment in which the intellectually illuminated body finally falls, and nature's call to the privy, with its diurnal detachment of another human body. Dryden privileges experience, no doubt: he prefers a poem the imaginative force of which is worthy of intellectual attention to any "toast" at all. But the material world continually encroaches, presenting, not only a metaphor with which he can belabor his fellows, but a force that threatens himself, his work, his country, and all human things. Nature, conceived in this way, has mellowed what he has long labored to perfect, Dryden once complains, to the dull sweets of rhyme, gradually reducing his own best poetic conceptions to rot.

Swift, who began his career with a similar sense of human things, turned, in the years after Berkeley split mind and matter asunder, to the remote, recollected account of that *splendide mendax*, Lemuel Gulliver, presenting, not a laughable collection of public machines, but a vexatious intellectual exercise. I do not mean that Swift simply applied Berkeley's teaching and thus focused his satire away from the external world onto the percipient mind; but rather that British culture, of which the works of Swift and Berkeley are major ornaments, was in general making this kind of a turn. Swift's poetry, his "Baucis and Philemon," for example, showed this tendency before Berkeley's work appeared. The *Principles* and *Travels* are merely two great manifestations—two of the greatest manifestations—of this broad cultural movement.

In the late Pope, to acknowledge a second major pivot in the eighteenth-century understanding of things, there is a new and shocking awareness of the separability of percepts from substances and of percept from percept:

> That each from other differs, first confess;
> Next, that he varies from himself no less.

Even as Pope used the notation of human substance—"each . . . other . . . he . . . himself"—it crumbled in his hands. Instead of being able to represent all coquetry in general in the figure of one pure coquette, he found every character different both from every other and—in the experience of one minute and the next—from itself. He saw the basic referents of particularity—*each, one, this*—lose their contact with such substances as *he* and *she*; and he ended by describing to a dissolving person of his acquaintance the dissolution of all personal substance: "believe me . . . Woman's at best a contradiction still." And, as he made painfully evident, this means "You." What Pope enacted in his analytical essays on the characters of men and women, in short, was a crucial instance of the perceptual atomism Hume was describing at very nearly the same time in the world at large, the world Pope had formerly composed with confident eloquence into "one stupendous whole."

Radcliffe, finally, located in strict isolation both the different percepts from which, as Pope showed, human substances must be creatively inferred and the different perceivers too. Pope, who had shared his painful sense of particularity with Lord Cobham, Mrs. Blount, and all society, held the separate perceptions and the inference from these of substantial characters as a common property, a socially shared enterprise. But in her *Mysteries of Udolpho*, Radcliffe reduced the traces of humanity to the barest minima—to even less than a foot print in the sand—and focused the challenge each and all present upon one, unassisted mind. Oddly enough, Addison in 1710 had indicated something like the same intellectual attitude—if not something like the same situation—in describing Mr. Spectator. Mr. Spectator never meddled in the active part of life, he himself insisted, but always took the part of a looker-on. He overheard from the vantage of a cozy invisibility all the conversations in the public rooms he visited, never opening his own lips but attending in silence to every conversation around him—practicing himself, that is to say, the attitude he advocated for the fine women of his acquaintance.[4] The challenge of perceptual experience, to which Mr. Spectator thus responded, was reinforced in the creative consciousness of Radcliffe and Austen, as I have suggested, by social oppression. They represented it accordingly in an especially compelling form: projecting it with their narratives and resolving it with the activity of their heroines. Radcliffe disclosed the severity of this challenge; Austen acknowledged its universality.

Notes

Chapter 1. Introduction

1. Although by no means universally received in Western culture as a whole, the principle can be traced through the Middle Ages and back to antiquity. See, for example, Etienne Gilson, *History of Christian Philosophy in the Middle Ages* (New York: Random House, 1955), who describes its espousal by Roscelin, 154, Abelard, 155–60, and Occam, 489–97. The eighteenth century, taking Bacon as its prophet, gave the principle not only a wider range of acceptance but a more rigorous meaning and a more extended application.

2. In *Some Versions of Pastoral* (London: Chatto and Windus, 1935), 35.

3. The self-consciousness British philosophers brought to the definition of *thing* is evident in an exchange in Berkeley's *Three Dialogues*, during which Hylas accuses Philonous of transforming "things into ideas" and Philonous counters by insisting that he wishes, rather, to transform "ideas into things." The term *thing* was widely encountered by Augustan literature, sometimes with bawdy consequences; *Tristram Shandy* being, perhaps, the most obvious instance.

4. Hoyt Trowbridge, "Scattered Atoms of Probability," *ECS* 5 (1971), 1–38, has made Johnson's expression the focus of an excellent exposition of eighteenth-century sensibility.

5. The different congeries that Pamela creates in organizing her clothing into separate piles and that Moll creates in calculating her "stock" are, to the contrary, material compositions, jumbles of externally existing possessions which, as these heroines well know, can become attached to others as well as themselves and of which they can thus be deprived. We may distinguish between the novels of Richardson and Defoe, on the one hand, and those of Radcliffe and Austen, on the other, by recognizing that the former represent the ambition to organize bodies into larger and larger material systems and that the latter represent the effort to organize percepts into firmer and firmer opinions. On the construction of substances from impressions see Gabriele Barnhard Jackson, "From Essence to Accident," *Crit* 29 (1987), 27–66.

6. See George Williamson, "The Rhetorical Pattern of Neo-Classical Wit," *MP* 33 (1935), esp. 62–65 and 75–81, for an impressive demonstration of the prompting toward antithesis in the closed heroic couplet.

7. See Donald Davidson, *Inquiries into Truth and Interpretation* (Oxford: Clarendon, 1984). Davidson actually says, 257, "all similes are true and most metaphors are false." It is his awareness, not that everything is like everything else in trivial ways, but that two things linked in resemblance—"my uncle is a pig"—always tolerate difference that enhances my argument.

8. See John Richetti, *Philosophical Writing* (Cambridge: Harvard, 1983), 48–116, for an illuminating description of Locke's philosophical style.

9. Anyone using figurative terminology nowadays owes more debts than he can acknowledge: those of which I am chiefly aware, besides the common debt to antiquity, are to Jakobson, Culler, Todorov, Davidson, Burke, Beardsley, and White.

10. Ronald Paulson, *Breaking and Remaking* (New Brunswick: Rutgers, 1989), 55–58, illustrates one limit of resemblance, adynaton, or "impossibility," from the poetry of Pope.

11. This is not a new idea, merely a normal consequence. Roland Barthes, for example, in "Introduction to Structural Analysis," *Image, Mosaic, Text* (New York: Hill and Wang, 1977), has made an assertion, albeit modifying that with a dash of equivocation, to much the same effect. See for the classic discussion of this matter: Ian Watt, *The Rise of the Novel* (Berkeley: California, 1957).

12. See especially H. H. Price, *Hume's Theory of the External World* (Oxford: Oxford, 1940), for a full exposition of this element in Hume's philosophy.

13. See, for example, Richard E. Grandy, "The Physical Reality of Colors," *Mind, Value, and Culture*, ed. David Weissbord (Atascadero: Ridgeview, 1989), 229–45.

14. My quotation comes from a paper composed by Steele; but that Addison was also well acquainted with this body of philosophy *Spectator* No. 413 declares; in which piece, moreover, Addison supposes it to be "universally acknowledged."

15. *The Structure of Scientific Revolutions* (Chicago: Chicago, rev. ed. 1970). My debt to this book, especially in this section on "Perceptions," is greater than I have been able to acknowledge.

16. Gilson, 74. See also Roger D. Lund, "Martinus Scriblerus and the Search for the Soul," *PLL* 25 (1989), 150, for an Augustan response to the effort by Hobbes to describe and locate a material soul.

17. Gilson, 495–97, explains that Occam preserved certainty "of an immaterial soul . . . on the strength of faith."

Chapter 2. Swift's Satires

1. See J. A. Downie, "The Political Significance of *Gulliver's Travels*," *Swift and his Contexts*, eds. John Irwin Fischer, Hermann J. Real, and James Woley (New York: AMS, 1989), 1–19, for a balanced and compendious exposition of the protracted scholarly effort to detect "parallel history" in the *Travels*; also Simon Varey, "Exemplary History and the Political Satire of *Gulliver's Travels*," *The Genres of "Gulliver's Travels*," ed. Frederik Smith (Newark: Delaware, 1990), 39–55, who acknowledges—although himself a partisan—"consistent identifications . . . are simply not to be found." Irvin Ehrenpreis, *Swift*, III (Cambridge: Harvard, 1983), 454 asserts with well-deserved finality: "The most profound and essential ingredients in the fantasy detach themselves from time and place, and point at the various definitions of our nature which men of various cultures have accepted." It is these definitions and the particulars in which Swift has embedded them that I wish to examine.

2. Veronica Kelly, "Following the Stage Itinerant," *Studies in Eighteenth-Century Culture*, 17 (1987), 239–58, distinguishes between two concepts of "person," Hobbes's theatrical (or external) concept and Locke's psychological (or internal) concept and explains how Swift manipulates the two in the *Tale*.

3. Ronald Paulson, *Breaking and Remaking* (New Brunswick: Rutgers, 1989), 5, remarks that, like other authors of his time, Swift was deeply influenced in his literary aims and practices by his awareness of the civil war.

4. Phillip Harth, *Swift and Anglican Rationalism* (Chicago: Chicago, 1961), 77, asserts that "the literal antithesis of religion is materialism"; and, 77–95, provides a valuable description of the English effort (prior to George Berkeley) to distinguish, not only religion, but experimental science from materialism. Ann Cline Kelly, *Swift and the English Language* (Philadelphia: Pennsylvania, 1988), 83, recognizes, on the other hand, "the atomistic world Swift depicts in *A Tale of a Tub.*" Everett Zimmerman, *Swift's Narrative Satires* (Ithaca: Cornell, 1983), 102, suggests something like the resolution of this apparent contradiction that I am developing: "The narrator [of the *Tale*] adopts an Epicurean view of his physical world [and] reduces all to material . . . purpose." I am further indebted to Zimmerman for explaining, 90–110, Swift's sympathy with Bacon and for emphasizing his awareness of Lucretius.

5. For convenience I use the Loeb edition of *De Rerum Natura*, eds. W. D. Rouse and Martin Ferguson Smith (Cambridge: Harvard, 1975); I have drawn my translations from this work.

6. In *Swift and Anglican Rationalism*, 91–92, Harth describes Robert Boyle's attack on materialistic metaphysics, that is, on the view that the universe is nothing but a fortuitous jumble of atoms.

7. Swift practices a strict analogy here between the relation of atoms to sensible matter and the relation of letters to meaningful discourse: just as atoms are too small to be perceivable, letters are too small to be meaningful. See Zimmerman, who remarks, 48, that "literalization . . . returns the book to its status as a physical object."

8. Clive Probyn, "Haranguing upon Texts," *Proceedings of the First Munster Symposium on Jonathan Swift* (1985), 187–97, has described with what I believe to be too solemn an emphasis the transience and the vulnerability of text as represented in and by the *Tale.* See for a useful corrective, Marcus Walsh, "Text, 'Text,' and Swift's *Tale of a Tub,*" *MLR*, 85 (1990), 290–303.

9. In "Text, 'Text,' and Swift's *Tale,*" Walsh also presents Swift, although from quite a different perspective, as a defender of the Anglican establishment.

10. Ronald Paulson, "The Parody of Eccentricity," *Jonathan Swift*, ed. Harold Bloom (New York: Chelsea House, 1986), 49, notes quite truly, I believe, that the religious theme (which is developed alongside the intellectual theme in Section IX) is "crucial."

11. J. A. Downie, *Jonathan Swift* (London: Routledge and Kegan Paul, 1984), 97, identifies the father as Christ. Since Christianity emerged from Christ's death, this is clearly defensible. But the term "Father" and this father's pronouncement of both instructions and penalties allows another, more troublesome identification as well.

12. G. Douglas Atkins, "Interpretation and Meaning in *A Tale of a Tub,*" *EL*, 8 (1981), 233–39, sees in the explicit, if brief, acknowledgment of common sense, as I do, the announcement of the "Swiftian standard."

13. See Frederik Smith, *Language and Reality in Swift's "A Tale of a Tub"* (Columbus: Ohio State, 1979), esp. 27–69, for a cluster of illuminations.

14. See Harth, *Swift and Anglican Rationalism*, 113–14, for a different explanation of imperial madness.

15. The Author apprehends the surface of things equivocally (not altogether surprising in a disciple of Lucretius). Consider his explanation that the senses,

which are concerned with surfaces, examine only what "dwell or are drawn by art upon the Outward of bodies."

16. Anne Steele in *Sense and Sensibility* (written about the turn of the century) embarrasses her sister Lucy by speaking about "smart beaux."

17. Locke, we may recall, defines "person" psychologically as a persisting consciousness; "man" (and presumably "woman") materially as an animal of a certain shape and mass.

18. "Nature" has an unstable meaning even within the few pages of the Digression: it is equated at different points with the plain outside of things; with the vulnerable cover for internal flaws and imperfections; and with the enhanced outside that projects sparkling films and images. This instability intensifies the shiftiness of meaning that I am here describing.

19. This is Berkeley, parodying Locke's illustration of an abstract idea—in the Introduction to his *Principles*.

20. This is Gay's phrase; for which see Ehrenpreis, *Swift*, III, 507.

21. Again I recall Ehrenpreis, *Swift*, III, 454, who suggests that the *Travels* constitutes a challenge to "both reader and author [that is, Gulliver] by the situations presented."

22. Frank Brady, "Vexations and Diversions," *MP*, 75 (1978), 346–67, has provided an excellent example of the flexibility of apprehension that, as I am arguing, Swift's devotion to things in particular requires.

23. Peter Steele, "Terminal Days among the Houyhnhnms," in Bloom, 113, warns that houyhnhnms and yahoos are unimportant except as "rhetorical entities" that furnish opportunities for illuminating encounters. I think this overstates the case since the question of the general substance of *houyhnhnm* and of *yahoo*—even if these are strictly mental entities—is often at issue. But the final focus on human experience of nature, which I take to be the real force of this warning, I strongly endorse. In studying yahoos and houyhnhnms we exercise our capacity to cope with problems of general substance in fictional experience and, by doing so, improve our capacity—when we turn back to natural experience—to cope with the problems of substance and generality presented by that.

24. Patrick Reilly, *The Literature of Guilt* (Iowa City: Iowa, 1988), 29–30, has also pointed out this "series of parallels and contrasts"; but he has a somewhat different sense of it from me.

25. Gulliver shifts between two terms in describing houyhnhnm vehicles, "carriage" and "sledge," thus allowing us at some moments, it seems, to infer the existence of wheels in Houyhnhnmland.

26. "The Distorted Image," *PLL*, 15 (1979), 320–32.

27. I suppose every one notices the resemblance in sound between *houyhnhnm* and *human*.

28. The two physical qualities on which the houyhnhnms chiefly pride themselves, "strength and agility," are also those by reference to which they prefer yahoos to Gulliver. Pursuing this a little further, I question the houyhnhnms' agility: the image of young horses leaping "over head and ears into a pond" gives me a lot of trouble. Boys and girls, yes, but horses?

29. A number of scholars have explained the self-conscious subordination of reason to sense in the inductive procedures advocated by the British Augustans. See esp. Harold Kelling, "Reason in Madness," *PMLA*, 64 (1954), 198–222.

30. Even critics who swallow the houyhnhnms' intellectual claims usually choke a little. F.R. Leavis, in his essay on Swift in *Common Pursuit* (New York: New York, 1952), 84, says with revealing equivocation, for example, "Swift did his best for the houyhnhnms, and they may have all the reason."

31. Clive Probyn, *The Art of Jonathan Swift* (New York: Barnes and Noble, 1978), 7–12, recognizes the error a reader makes who thinks "that he alone is comfortably above and beyond implication" in the toils of the *Travels*.

Chapter 3. Gay's Jests

1. See Frederik Smith, "Swift's Descriptions," *Teaching Eighteenth-Century poetry*, ed. Christopher Fox (New York: AMS, 1990), 187–96, for a fine explication of the London poems.
2. Wallace Cable Brown, "Gay's Mastery of the Heroic Couplet," *PMLA*, LXI (1946), 121, aptly compares Gay with Mr. Spectator.
3. In his classic essay, "*The Beggar's Opera*: Mock-Pastoral as the Cult of Independence," *Some Versions of Pastoral* (London: Chatto and Windus, 1935), 35. I will rely on Empson's searching study at several points in this chapter.
4. See Howard Erskine-Hill, "The Significance of Gay's Drama," *English Drama*, eds. Marie Axton and Raymond Williams (Cambridge: Cambridge, 1977), 156–59, for a good description of clashing contiguities in the *Opera*.
5. Maynard Mack, in his Introduction to *The Augustans*, second ed. English Masterpieces series (Englewood Cliffs: Prentice Hall, 1961), 17–18, describes in the *Opera* "satire of a world where everything is for sale."
6. *John Gay* (New York: Twayne, 1965), 151–54.

Chapter 4. Pope's Essays

1. Pat Rogers, *An Introduction to Pope* (London: Methuen, 1975), 9, notes that "Pope is always discriminating"; and G. Douglas Atkins, *Quests of Difference* (Lexington: Kentucky, 1986), 67, sees "the relationship of parts to parts and parts to whole" as a leading concern of Pope's poetry. I am attempting to document and to extend these insights.
2. For an explicit dedication to this kind of exercise see *Three Dialogues between Hylas and Philonous* by Pope's friend, George Berkeley, the explicit design of which "Is plainly to demonstrate the Reality and Perfection of Humane Knowledge, the Incorporeal Nature of the Soul, and the Immediate Providence of a *Deity*"; see also my essay, "Common Sense as a Basis of Literary Style," *TSLL*, 19 (1977), 624–41.
3. In the Twickenham Edition of Pope's *Epistles to Several persons* (London: Methuen, 1961), xlviii, the editor, F. W. Bateson, quotes this statement from Pope's letter to Arbuthnot of 2 August 1734.
4. Leopold Damrosch, Jr., *The Imaginative World of Alexander Pope* (Berkeley: California, 1987), 215, proclaims, in Pope's behalf, "The more you see of the complexity of things, the more you are able to recognize the common patterns that recur."
5. This is the implicit force of *Dunciad IV*, the epic utterance of which strictly denies the interposition of society and projects a discourse—as Milton put it in *Paradise Lost*—that is properly the concern of "fit audience . . . though few."
6. See Spence's *Observations, Anecdotes and Characters*, ed. James M. Osborn (Oxford: Clarendon, 1966), I, 135–36. I will refer to the substance of this passage, the importance of which Osborn has emphasized, two or three times in this chapter.

7. These are Pope's own words in "The Design" he prefixed to the *Essay.* See the Twickenham Edition, ed. Maynard Mack (London: Methuen, 1970), 7–8.

8. In *The Imaginative World,* 266, Damrosch reminds us that "Original Sin is absent in the *Essay.*"

9. See Mack's note, 41–42 of the Twickenham Edition.

10. A. D. Nuttal, *Pope's Essay on Man* (London: Allen and Unwin, 1984), 113, has demonstrated the argumentative failure of Pope's narrative procedure in the third epistle.

11. Others have preceded me in the study of feminine integrity in this poem: Douglas Lane Patey, "Art and Integrity," *MP,* 83 (1986), 364–78; and Frederic V. Bogel, *Acts of Knowledge* (Lewisburg: Bucknell, 1981), esp. 80–107—among others.

12. See, for instance, Raymond Smith, "The 'Character' of Lemuel Gulliver," *Tennessee Studies in Literature,* 10 (1965), 133–39.

13. See Bateson's textual note to the Twickenham Edition of *Epistles,* 49.

14. For one among many responses to Pope's misogyny see Ellen Pollak, *The Poetics of Sexual Myth* (Chicago: Chicago, 1985). For a discussion of it as it occurs precisely in the epistles *To Cobham* and *To a Lady* see Carol Virginia Pohli, "The Point where Sense and Dulness Meet," *ECS,* 19 (1985–86), 206–34.

15. For a pointedly unorganized list of feminine traits, see Swift's "Furniture of a Woman's Mind"—a fascinating contrast to Pope's pictures. C. N. Manlove, "Swift's Structures," *SEL,* 29 (1989), 471, notes that Swift's prevailing structural "mode is . . . the atomistic list."

16. In his *Traditions of Formal Verse Satire* (Princeton: Princeton, 1992), 190, Weinbrot recognizes that Pope engages the lady in dialogue and suggests that "hostility is reduced in the amiable example of the lady herself."

17. On the erosion of personal identity throughout the century, a concern that is centrally evident in Radcliffe and Austen, see Christopher Fox, "Locke and the Scriblerians," *ECS,* 16 (1982), 1–25. Locke's equation of personal identity with consciousness, as Fox explains, deeply undermined personal substance, which was "central to Christian belief," and with which until the eighteenth century Christianity had confidently endowed each and every one of the faithful. See also *The Imaginative World,* 140, in which Damrosch describes Locke's teaching as "a time bomb." Preliminary explosions are evident, as I have tried to show, in *Trivia* and the *Travels.*

Chapter 5. Radcliffe's Mysteries

1. *Systems of Order and Inquiry in Later Eighteenth-Century Fiction* (Berkeley: California, 1975), 244–45. I use *epistemology* throughout this book in the weaker sense, that is, as the inductive effort to derive useful generalizations from the particulars of experience; not in the stronger sense, that is, as the abstractive or meditative effort to grasp eternal truth. This usage corresponds to an understanding of *knowledge,* not as the firm certainty of universals, but as the tireless maintenance (and refinement) of generalities. See Bogel, *Acts of Knowledge,* 90, on the devotion of Pope's Epistles to the problem of knowledge.

2. Actually Emily falls and bumps her head in one of her confrontations with Montoni. And she is forcibly hugged a time or two.

3. *The Popular Novel in England* (London: Constable, 1932), esp. 256–62.

4. "Had Elizabeth been able to encounter [Darcy's] eye," Austen reports in describing an especially intense moment in *Pride and Prejudice,* "she might have seen how well the expression of heart-felt delight, diffused over his face, became him."

5. This whole passage recalls Hume's essay, "Of the Delicacy of Taste and Passion," although I have not located a positive echo. See *The Philosophical Works*, III, eds. Thomas Hill Green and Thomas Hodge Grose (Darmstadt: Scientia Verlag Aalen, 1964), 91–94.

6. David Fairer, *Pope's Imagination* (Manchester: Manchester, 1984), 89–110, points out a common tendency of the eighteenth century to describe wit as feminine—the "fanciful" sex—and judgment as masculine—a tendency that Tristram Shandy satirized in his witty attacks on "gravity."

7. This advocacy of masculine activity and the distinction between masculine business and feminine responsiveness run all through the *Spectator*. See, for example, No. 108, which deplores Will Wimble's lack of "Application to Affairs," and, especially, "The Occupations of Trade and Commerce"; and, contrariwise, No. 81 on patches, which urges women "to distinguish themselves as tender Mothers and faithful Wives." See also Alison Sulloway, *Jane Austen and the Province of Womanhood* (Philadelphia: Pennsylvania, 1989) for a modern exposition of the feminine condition that Radcliffe and Austen encountered, one aspect of which Sulloway characterizes, 160, as "a restrictive verbal purdah." See also Valerie Rumbold, *Women's Place in Pope's World* (Cambridge: Cambridge, 1989); and Ruth Bernard Yeazell, *Fictions of Modesty* (Chicago: Chicago, 1991), who suggests (xi) that female modesty affords the opportunity "for observation and questioning." This is in literary fact the situation of the "omniscient narrator" in the English novel as Radcliffe and Austen develop it.

8. In the *Dialogues* Philonous explains that he is "altogether passive" in the recipiency of natural impressions.

9. In the Introduction to the *Treatise*, for example, Hume insists that in studying moral philosophy, that is, human nature, one cannot make experiments "purposely, with premeditation," but that one must take evidence "from a cautious observation," as chance allows, "in the common course of the world, by men's behavior in company, in affairs, and in their pleasures." A patient, unobtrusive attentiveness, that is to say, is the appropriate attitude—in philosophers as in women.

10. In *The Italian*, which Radcliffe wrote after the *Mysteries*, she withdraws from this dedication to experience, and provides merely another exercise in the Gothic.

11. Sterne has usually a more rigorously inductive understanding than this— as one would expect considering his dedication to the living details of things: "I think it wrong," he insists in volume VII of *Tristram*, "merely because a man's hat has been blown off his head by chance the first night he comes to *Avignon*— that he should therefore say, '*Avignon* is more subject to high winds than any town in all *France*.'"

Chapter 6. Austen's Acknowledgments

1. I am, admittedly, neglecting Radcliffe's *Gaston de Blondeville* which is, in the first place, an exercise in historic nostalgia and which, in the second place, Radcliffe did not intend for publication.

2. Emmeline's true love does not show up until well into the novel; but she is always rightfully dubious of Delamere, her romantic opposite in the first part of it; and she easily recognizes Mr. Right once he appears.

3. Maggie Lane, *Jane Austen's England* (London: Robert Hale, 1986), has given a beautiful account of the Austen environment. She describes what she represents, 62, as a "landscape in which nature and civilization are perfectly balanced."

4. Alistair M. Duckworth, "The Improvement of the Estate," *Jane Austen's Mansfield Park*, ed. Harold Bloom (New York: Chelsea House, 1987), 23–35, has described Sotherton and its improvements—actual and proposed—in compelling detail; indicating, moreover, the symbolic resonances of the whole process.

5. A number of scholars have described a gradual change, which I must neglect for the time being, in Austen's attitude to the natural out-of-doors: Lane, 79, for example; and Pam Walker in a paper presented a few years ago at an SCMLA convention.

6. See Lane, esp. 30 and 99–103, on the "picturesque."

7. Several critics have recognized the centrality of epistemology to Austen's fiction: Richard F. Patteson, "Truth, Certitude and Stability in Jane Austen's Fiction," *PQ*, 60 (1981), 455–69, asserts, for instance, "the matter of perception and knowledge underlies all else"; and Susan Morgan, *In the Meantime* (Chicago: Chicago, 1980) insists, 3, that Austen's subject is the problem of perception. Morgan describes Austen as rejecting "the inheritance of Locke," however, and reads the novels "through Shelley's epistemological interests." This may explain the considerable difference between her description of the novels and my own.

8. Jocelyn Harris, *Jane Austen's Art of Memory* (Cambridge: Cambridge, 1989), 7, argues that Catherine is fooled by a "wrong supposition of analogy"—that is, between Udolpho and Northanger—and thus accepts Henry's judgment. Although I seriously question the adequacy of this judgment, finally, I strongly endorse her account of Austen's awareness of English culture and, particularly, of Locke. For another valuable indication of Austen's extensive grasp on the best understanding of her time see Claudia L. Johnson, "Jane Austen and Dr. Johnson Again," *MLQ*, 44 (1983), 23–38.

9. See Patteson, "Truth, Certitude, and Stability," 462 on the "instability of character" in Austen's fiction; also Max Byrd, "Pope and Metamorphosis," *MP*, 85 (1988), 448–52, on "the fluid uncertain experience of individual consciousness" that all the Augustans recognized.

10. See Marylea Meyersohn, "What Fanny Knew," *Jane Austen*, ed. Janet Todd (New York: Holmes and Meier, 1983), 224–30, for an exposition of Fanny's reticence and passivity, which suggests—according to my argument—the intellectual stance that I have earlier described in Radcliffe's Emily.

11. Claudia L. Johnson, "The 'Twilight of Probability,'" *PQ*, 62 (1983), 171–86, gives a nice account of the "epistemological problems" of *Sense and Sensibility*, noting the prevalence of uncertainty in the characters' opinions.

12. See Margaret Satz, "An Epistemological Understanding of *Pride and Prejudice*," in Todd, 171–83, esp. 172, on the "paucity of evidence," from which Elizabeth must compose such substances as "Darcy."

13. See J. M. Q. Davies, "*Emma* as Charade," *PQ*, 65 (1986), 231–42, which notes accurately how clues (or, as I call them, items of evidence) are hidden and revealed; and shows that they are generally sifted through the mind of Emma.

Chapter 7. Conclusion

1. Karen Newman, "Can this Marriage be Saved?" *ELH*, 50 (1983), 697–99, notes the balanced interest between personal and material concerns in *Pride and Prejudice*.

2. John Dashwood and Peachum, to whom every criminal in the account book is strictly equal to forty pounds and thus to every other, are indeed brothers.

3. The emergence of Richardson's fiction as a collection of letters that refer to external reality—letters of which Richardson is only the editor—seriously modifies any resemblance between *Pamela* and *Pride and Prejudice*, giving the prevailingly materialistic expression of *Pamela* an emphatically materialistic form. Defoe's presentation of *Moll Flanders* as secret history has a similar effect.

4. Morris Brownell, *Alexander Pope and the Arts of Georgian England* (Oxford: Clarendon, 1978), 5, makes a broad observation, to which this book offers confirmation, illustration, and, I hope, added depth: "Georgian England . . . was the period when taste was discovered in England, the beginning of a Renaissance in appreciation and connoisseurship if not in the arts themselves—the age of the Spectator."

Bibliography

Atkins, G. Douglas. "Interpretation and Meaning in *A Tale of a Tub.*" *EL* 8 (1981): 233–39.

———. *Quests of Difference: Reading Pope's Poems.* Lexington: Univ. Press of Kentucky, 1986.

Barthes, Roland. *Image, Mosaic, Text.* New York: Hill and Wang, 1977.

Bogel, Frederic V. *Acts of Knowledge: Pope's Later Poems.* Lewisburg: Bucknell Univ. Press, 1981.

Brady, Frank. "Vexations and Diversions: Three Problems in *Gulliver's Travels.*" *MP* 75 (1978): 346–67.

Brown, Wallace Cable. "Gay's Mastery of the Heroic Couplet." *PMLA* 56 (1946): 114–25.

Brownell, Morris. *Alexander Pope and the Arts of Georgian England.* Oxford: Clarendon, 1978.

Byrd, Max. "Pope and Metamorphosis: Three Notes." *MP* 85 (1988): 447–59.

Cummings, Robert. "*Windsor Forest* as a Silvan Poem." *ELH* 54 (1987): 63–79.

Damrosch, Leopold, Jr. *The Imaginative World of Alexander Pope.* Berkeley: Univ. of California Press, 1987.

Davidson, Donald. *Inquiries into Truth and Interpretation.* Oxford: Clarendon, 1984.

Davies, J. M. Q. "*Emma* as Charade and the Education of the Reader." *PQ* 65 (1986): 231–42.

Downie, J. A. *Jonathan Swift: Political Writer.* London: Routledge and Kegan Paul, 1984.

———. "The Political Significance of *Gulliver's Travels.*" In *Swift and His Contexts,* edited by John Irwin Fischer, Hermann J. Real, and James Woley. New York: AMS, 1989.

Duckworth, Alistair. "The Improvement of the Estate." In *Jane Austen's "Mansfield Park,"* edited by Harold Bloom. New York: Chelsea House, 1987.

Ehrenpreis, Irvin. *Swift: The Man, His Works, and the Age.* Vol. 3. Cambridge: Harvard Univ. Press, 1983.

Empson William. *Some Versions of Pastoral.* London: Chatto and Windus, 1935.

Erskine-Hill, Howard. "The Significance of Gay's Drama." In *English Drama: Forms and Development: Essays in Honour of Muriel Clara Bradbrook,* edited by Marie Axton and Raymond Williams. Cambridge: Cambridge Univ. Press, 1977.

Fairer, David. *Pope's Imagination.* Manchester: Manchester Univ. Press, 1984.

Fox, Christopher. "Locke and the Scriblerians: The Discussion of Identity in Early Eighteenth-Century Literature." *E-CS* 16 (1982): 1–25.

Gilson, Étienne. *History of Christian Philosophy in the Middle Ages.* New York: Random House, 1955.

Grandy, Richard E. "The Physical Reality of Colors." In *Mind, Value, and Culture: Essays in Honor of E. M. Adams,* edited by David Weissbord. Atascadero, Calif.: Ridgeview, 1989.

Harris, Jocelyn. *Jane Austen's Art of Memory.* Cambridge: Cambridge Univ. Press, 1989.

Harth, Phillip. *Swift and Anglican Rationalism: The Religious Background of "A Tale of a Tub."* Chicago: Univ. of Chicago Press, 1961.

Jackson, Gabriele Barnhard. "From Essence to Accident: Locke and the Language of Poetry in the Eighteenth Century." *Crit* 29 (1987): 27–66.

Johnson, Claudia L. "The 'Operations of Time and the Changes of the Human Mind': Jane Austen and Dr. Johnson Again." *MLQ* 44 (1983): 23–38.

———. "The 'Twilight of Probability': Uncertainty and Hope in *Sense and Sensibility.*" *PQ* 62 (1983): 171–86.

Keesey, Donald. "The Distorted Image: Swift's Yahoos and the Critics." *PLL* 15 (1979): 320–32.

Kelling, Harold. "Reason in Madness." *PMLA* 64 (1954): 198–222.

Kelly, Ann Cline. *Swift and the English Language.* Philadelphia: Univ. of Pennsylvania Press, 1988.

Kelly, Veronica. "Following the Stage Itinerant: Perception, Doubt, and Death in Swift's *Tale of a Tub.*" *Studies in Eighteenth-Century Culture* 17 (1987): 239–58.

Kuhn, Thomas. *The Structure of Scientific Revolutions.* Rev. ed. Chicago: Univ. of Chicago Press, 1970.

Lane, Maggie. *Jane Austen's England.* London: Robert Hale, 1986.

Leavis, F. R. *The Common Pursuit.* New York: New York Univ. Press, 1952.

Lund, Roger D. "Martinus Scriblerus and the Search for the Soul." *PLL* 25 (1989): 135–50.

Mack, Maynard. *The Augustans.* 2d. ed. English Masterpieces series, vol. 5. Englewood Cliffs: Prentice Hall, 1961.

Manlove, C. N. "Swift's Structures: 'A Description of the Morning' and Some Others." *SEL* 29 (1989): 463–72.

Meyersohn, Marylea. "What Fanny Knew." In *Jane Austen: New Perspectives,* edited by Janet Todd. New York: Holmes and Meier, 1983.

Morgan, Susan. *In the Meantime: Character and Perception in Jane Austen's Fiction.* Chicago: Univ. of Chicago Press, 1980.

Newman, Karen. "Can This Marriage Be Saved?: Jane Austen Makes Sense of an Ending." *ELH* 50 (1983): 693–710.

Nuttal, A. D. *Pope's Essay on Man.* London: Allen and Unwin, 1984.

Patey, Douglas Lane. "Art and Integrity: Concepts of Self in Alexander Pope and Edward Young." *MP* 83 (1986): 364–78.

Patteson, Richard F. "Truth, Certitude, and Stability in Jane Austen's Fiction." *PQ* 60 (1981): 455–69.

Paulson, Ronald. *Breaking and Remaking: Aesthetic Practice in England, 1700–1820.* New Brunswick: Rutgers Univ. Press, 1989.

———. "The Parody of Eccentricity." In Bloom, *Jonathan Swift.*

Piper, William B. "Common Sense as a Basis of Literary Style." *TSLL* 19 (1977): 624–41.

Pohli, Carol Virginia. "'The Point Where Sense and Dullness Meet': What Pope Knows about Knowing and about Women." *E-CS* 19 (1985–86): 206–34.

Pollak, Ellen. *The Poetics of Sexual Myth: Gender and Ideology in the Verse of Swift and Pope.* Chicago: Univ. of Chicago Press, 1985.

Price, H. H. *Hume's Theory of the External World.* Oxford: Oxford University Press, 1940.

Probyn, Clive. *The Art of Jonathan Swift.* New York: Barnes and Noble, 1978.

———. "Haranguing upon Texts." In *Proceedings of the First Munster Symposium on Jonathan Swift,* edited by Hermann Real and Heinz J. Vienken. Munich: W. Fink, 1985.

Reilly, Patrick. *The Literature of Guilt: From Gulliver to Golding.* Iowa City: Univ. of Iowa Press, 1988.

Richetti, John. *Philosophical Writing: Locke, Berkeley, Hume.* Cambridge: Harvard Univ. Press, 1983.

Rogers, Pat. *An Introduction to Pope.* London: Methuen, 1975.

———. *Johnson.* Oxford: Oxford Univ. Press, 1993.

Rothstein, Eric. *Systems of Order and Inquiry in Later Eighteenth-Century Fiction.* Berkeley: Univ. of California Press, 1975.

Rumbold, Valerie. *Women's Place in Pope's World.* Cambridge: Cambridge Univ. Press, 1989.

Satz, Margaret. "An Epistemological Understanding of *Pride and Prejudice.*" In Todd, *Jane Austen.*

Smith, Frederik. *Language and Reality in Swift's "A Tale of a Tub."* Columbus: Ohio State Univ. Press, 1979.

———. "Swift's Descriptions." In *Teaching Eighteenth-Century Poetry,* edited by Christopher Fox. New York: AMS, 1990.

Smith, Raymond. "The 'Character' of Lemuel Gulliver." *Tennessee Studies in Literature* 10 (1965): 133–40.

Spacks, Patricia Meyer. *John Gay.* New York: Twayne, 1965.

Spence, Joseph. *Observations, Anecdotes, and Characters of Books and Men, Collected from Conversation,* edited by James M. Osborn. Vol. 1. Oxford: Clarendon, 1966.

Steele, Peter. "Terminal Days among the Houyhnhnms." In Bloom, *Jonathan Swift.*

Sulloway, Alison. *Jane Austen and the Province of Womanhood.* Philadelphia: Univ. of Pennsylvania Press, 1989.

Tompkins, J. M. S. *The Popular Novel in England.* London: Constable, 1932.

Trowbridge, Hoyt. "Scattered Atoms of Probability." *E-CS* 5 (1971): 1–38.

Varey, Simon. "Exemplary History and the Political Satire of *Gulliver's Travels.*" In *The Genres of "Gulliver's Travels,"* edited by Frederik Smith. Newark: Univ. of Delaware Press, 1990.

Walsh, Marcus. "Text, 'Text,' and Swift's *A Tale of a Tub.*" *MLR* 85 (1990): 290–303.

Watt, Ian. *The Rise of the Novel: Studies in Defoe, Richardson, and Fielding.* Berkeley: Univ. of California Press, 1957.

Weinbrot, Howard D. *Alexander Pope and the Traditions of Formal Verse Satire.* Princeton: Princeton Univ. Press, 1982.

Williamson, George. "The Rhetorical Pattern of Neo-classical Wit." *MP* 33 (1935): 55–81.

Yeazell, Ruth Bernard. *Fictions of Modesty: Women and Courtship in the English Novel.* Chicago: Univ. of Chicago Press, 1991.

Zimmerman, Everett. *Swift's Narrative Satires: Author and Authority.* Ithaca: Cornell Univ. Press, 1983.

Index